CINCINNATI BOXING

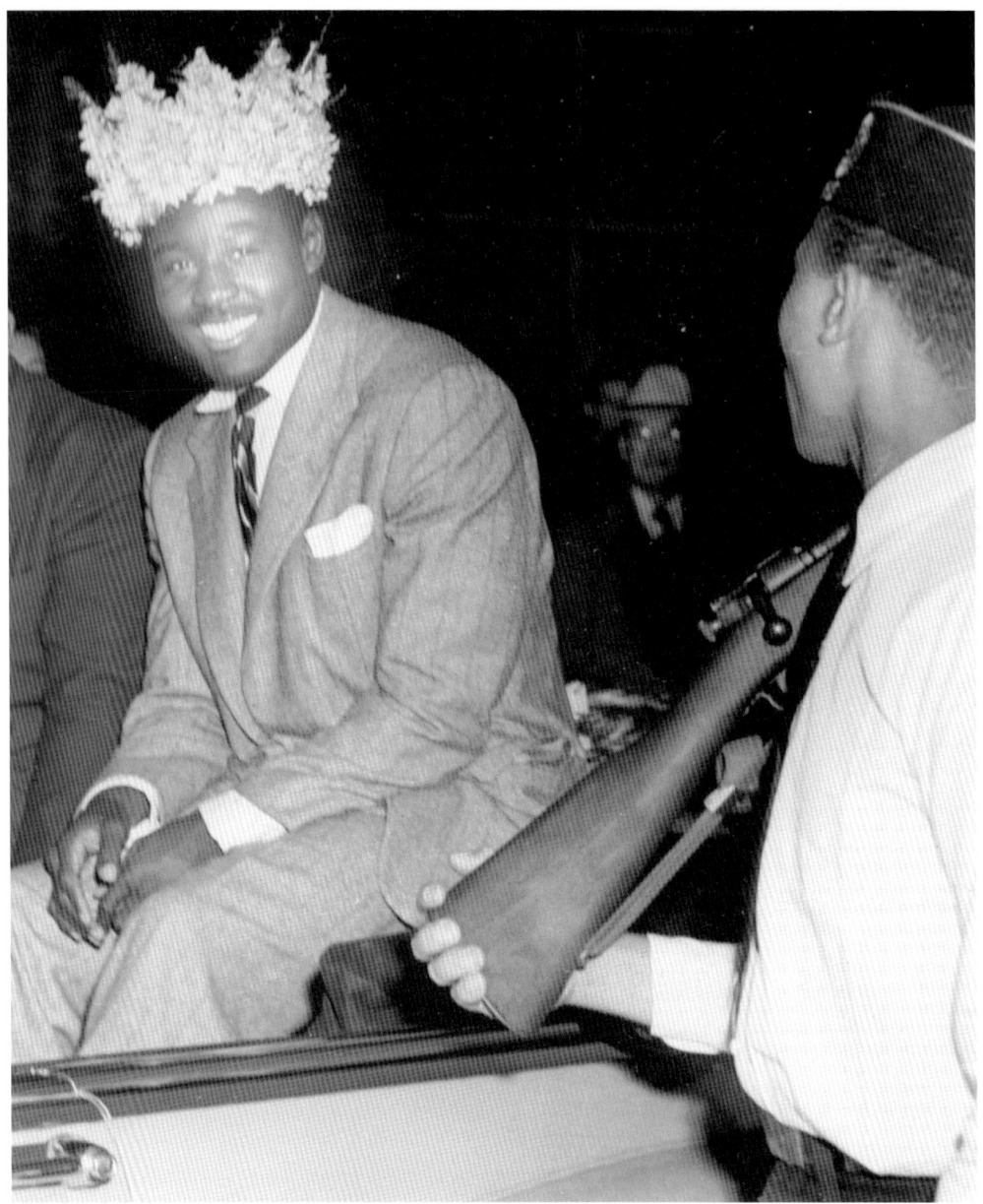

Ezzard Charles was the king of Cincinnati after he won the undisputed heavyweight boxing title in 1950 with a victory over Joe Louis. His earlier 1949 title win over Jersey Joe Walcott in Chicago was not recognized by the New York State Boxing Commission, but beating Louis in the ring led to a crown of chrysanthemums and a victory parade from Union Terminal through his Cincinnati neighborhood of the West End. (Photograph by Jack Klumpe.)

On the front cover: Please see page 55. (Photograph courtesy of Buddy LaRosa.)
On the back cover: Please see page 102. (Authors' collection.)
Cover background: Please see page 61. (Photograph courtesy of Buddy LaRosa.)

CINCINNATI BOXING

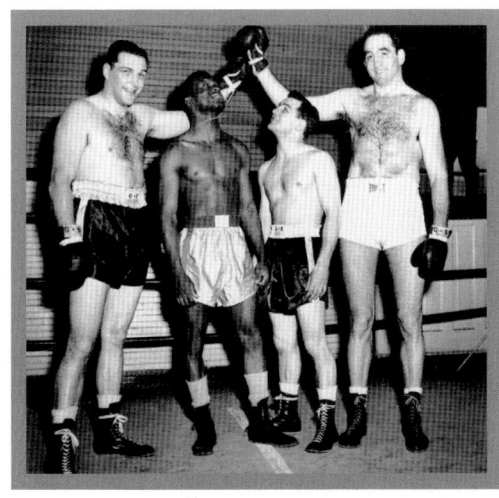

Kevin Grace and Joshua Grace
Foreword by Buddy LaRosa

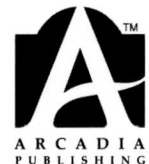

Copyright © 2006 by Kevin Grace and Joshua Grace
ISBN 0-7385-4112-5

Published by Arcadia Publishing
Charleston SC, Chicago IL, Portsmouth NH, San Francisco CA

Printed in the United States of America

Library of Congress Catalog Card Number: 2006932235

For all general information contact Arcadia Publishing at:
Telephone 843-853-2070
Fax 843-853-0044
E-mail sales@arcadiapublishing.com
For customer service and orders:
Toll-Free 1-888-313-2665

Visit us on the Internet at www.arcadiapublishing.com

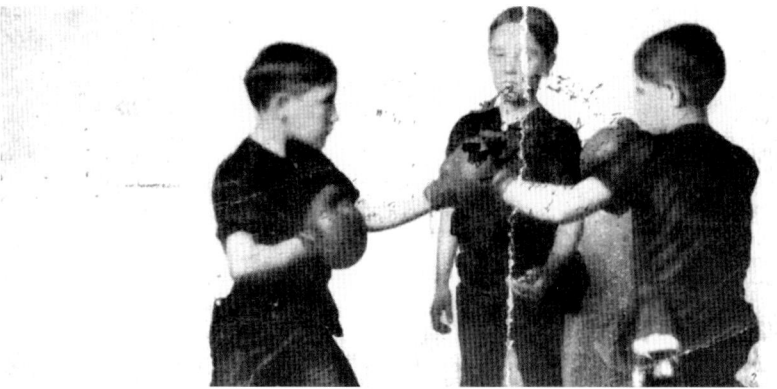

Evolving out of the county fair boxing booths of England and America, pugilistic exhibitions had become a circus sideshow by the 20th century. In 1911, the Barnum and Bailey Circus hit town, setting up camp at the Cumminsville show grounds. One of its sideshows was the boxing Taylor brothers, William, Jennings, and Bryan, cleverly named for the noted orator and common-man presidential candidate.

CONTENTS

Acknowledgments 6

Foreword 7

Introduction 9

1. Fight Town: The 19th Century 11

2. Pugilism Becomes a Key Cincinnati Sport: 1900–1918 25

3. From Local Clubs to a World Champion: 1919–1933 35

4. The Golden Age: 1934–1960 45

5. Contending for a Dream: 1961–1990 105

6. Building on a Heritage: 1991–2006 115

Selected Bibliography 127

ACKNOWLEDGMENTS

For assistance in a wonderful variety of ways, we thank Harry Andreadis; Paul "Scrappy" Andreadis; Dave Bergin and Pugilistica.com; Russell Brazzle for the great boxing conversation at work over the years; Debbie Katzler Burns; Larry Burton; Danny "DC" Calhoun; Patty Castor; Christina Cooper; Mae Corrion of the Jesup Memorial Library of Bar Harbor, Maine; Charlie Curro; Sean Grace; Susan Harris of Lawrenceville, Georgia; Dan Hayes, Martin Horwitz, and Kay Taylor of the Cincinnati Athletic Club; Stuart Hodesh for his extraordinary memories and generous help; Rev. Thomas Kennealy, S.J.; Jack Klumpe; Maria Kreppel; Donald "Buddy" LaRosa; Tim McCabe of the Xavier University Library; Stephanie McGowan; Reggie Marshall of Mars Jazz Booking Agency; Nanci Mays; George and Alice Russell; Glenn Sample; Bill Schutte; the inestimable Harry Shaffer; Jerome Shochet; and Marsha Wirtz. Unless otherwise noted, all images are from the collections of the authors.

As always, thanks to my wife, Joan Fenton, to my son Josh for doing this book with me, and to my other children: Sean, Courtney, Bonnie, and Lily.

—K. G.

To my father, Kevin Grace, for his help guiding me through this project and my family and friends for their support.

—J. G.

FOREWORD

Boxing is more than just conditioning. It is the mind, hands, and feet working all together. It's a ballet. Defense, hit, duck, counter, grace, move around. It takes a lot of character and a lot of courage to get in the boxing ring, maybe going against somebody that you know might be better than you.

I got involved in boxing because of my dad, Tony LaRosa. The LaRosas were from the Bottoms in Cincinnati, along the Ohio River down on Pearl and Sycamore Streets. It was where the produce and fish markets were, and the LaRosas were part of that world. Later they had a produce store on Freeman Avenue. It was a rich culture there when I was a boy. The LaRosas were Sicilian, and my mother's family was Napolitano. I lived in South Fairmount with my mother's family because my parents were divorced, but it seems like it was the Bottoms where I grew up, so that neighborhood was a very colorful part of my life, very alive and vibrant. Down there on Pearl Street, a lot of the people were Lebanese, but no matter what ethnic group we were, we were all "cousins" or "cuz" to each other. My dad was a boxer, and everyone there knew him. He had over 200 fights, starting out as a featherweight, but ending up a middleweight. He was a big-boned man, and did he have war clubs on him! Sometimes he would take me to the gym with him when he trained, and I would sit there and watch.

I was a little guy in high school and probably didn't weigh 135 pounds soaking wet. But because my dad was a boxer, I guess, and you want to be like your dad to a certain extent, I also wanted to box. My mother was against it, and when I went down to the gym, I had to "prefabricate" what I was doing. She finally found out because I had my picture in the paper one time, in the Sunday brown sheets about the boxing program down at the old Fenwick Club. The Fenwick, an athletic club run by the Archdiocese of Cincinnati, had a lot of boxers, pros like Joey Discepoli and Pat Iacobucci, wonderful Cincinnati fighters. When my mother found out I was boxing, I thought I would never hear the end of it! Part of it, I suppose, was that my parents were divorced, and boxing was something connected to my dad. Boxing was sort of the manly thing to do in the inner city, not because you were a tough guy but because it built confidence. And every day when I went in there, I knew I was going to get my butt kicked because I was working out with pros and older guys. In those days, they didn't take it easy on you.

Back then, there were fight clubs everywhere, across the river in Kentucky, in Fort Thomas and Covington. And on the Cincinnati side of the Ohio, there was one at Music Hall and several more around the neighborhoods of Over-the-Rhine and the West End, like Parkway Arena. Fighters would fight every month. My dad would fight twice a month sometimes in a Cincinnati club and then go up to Dayton and fight. All of the fighters did that. In the old days, those fighters might have had a couple hundred fights. Contenders sometimes had dozens of fights before they would get a title shot. I met a lot of good old fighters through my dad, like K. O. Mars, Billy Jungles, Nate Bartell, and, of course, the great featherweight champ, Freddie

Miller. I remember when I was younger I used to go into Ezzard Charles's gym over on Central Avenue. I can still see it today—Jimmy Brown, Ezzard's trainer in there, and Ezzard driving up in his convertible, giving silver dollars to the little kids.

I got into the boxing game because of my dad. My own career was very limited, in part because of my mother. I was in the program for a few years, but I was never on any real team. I was in the ring just getting knocked around. To be honest, I wasn't very good, but I did have a few amateur fights. I was tough, I could take it, but I had no punch! I might have won two and lost eight, but it did give me confidence. When I went to Roger Bacon High School in Cincinnati, I was a much better football player because of that confidence, and it paid off later in the business world as well.

After I got out in the business world and started the LaRosa's pizza chain, I remained interested in boxing because I know what it did for me, along with other sports I had been involved in. Years later, after my own sons got older and took more of a part in the LaRosa's company, I had all this energy I had to use. So I got involved with Rollie Schwartz, the Golden Gloves and Olympics coach, to revive amateur boxing in Cincinnati. Another Gloves official, Phil Smith, was also involved. Back in the 1970s and 1980s, we needed some young blood in local boxing because there was no Golden Gloves franchise anymore. We had to get a franchise back, so we got some coaches to come in. Then we had a few shows and built up a team, sending them to tournaments, and I helped raise money to handle that. I set up a gym for them, down on Plum Street, and called it the Queen City Gym. A place like that, you leave the doors open during training hours, and the next thing you know the kids who live in the neighborhood will look in; they'll come in because it's kind of magnetic. I guess it's the smacking of the leather that draws them in. And boxing is an extended family, appealing to kids who lack a family experience.

So we had this gym, and later we set up another one several blocks over on Findlay Avenue. We trained and guided the careers of two pro champions, Aaron Pryor and Tim Austin. Well, in amateur boxing and the early years of pro careers, after the Aaron Pryors move on, then the Timmy Austins come in the gym, and then the Larry Donalds and the Ravea Springs come in. Then the Ricardo Williams Jrs. and the Rau'Shee Warrens come in. Any number of great talents has come through Cincinnati during its rich heritage in boxing, both pro and amateur. We have a tradition here of talented fighters, and this remains one of the best areas of the country for amateur boxing. We try to help these young men realize their dreams.

Boxing gyms are dingy—they're not well lit. Sometimes there are just old wooden floors, a toilet, a shower, the heavy bags, jump ropes, the speed bag, and the ring. But there is a certain character in there, a certain love. And the boxers know you never really lose that sort of "punch," you keep that power. Maybe part of that love is the smack of the leather. Today I'm doing everything in boxing except making money. But that's okay. I can say I was part of a world champion, and a lot of guys can't. So enjoy this look at the great history of boxing in our city.

—Donald S. "Buddy" LaRosa

INTRODUCTION

On a hot August night in 1929, the Cincinnati Kid climbed into a boxing ring in Bar Harbor, Maine. Hundreds of miles from the banks of the Ohio River, the ocean resort casino in Bar Harbor seemed an unlikely place for a fighter from Cincinnati. But one can imagine how it must have come about. Bar Harbor was a regular venue for Maine boxing, and with navy personnel not far away, many sailors found their way onto the fight cards. The Kid was a 145-pound sailor, matched that August 5 night against a local favorite, Cyclone Violette, one of several Violette family boxers in the region. The sailor probably came to the casino, had his hands taped and gloved, and as he climbed in the ring, the announcer might have said, "Where you from sailor?" "Cincinnati, Ohio." "Okay, then. LADIES AND GENTLEMEN, NOW FIGHTING, THE CINCINNATI KIIIIDD!" Well, the Kid gave Cyclone all he could handle, knocking him down twice, but then he let Violette come back to force a six-round draw. The Cincinnati Kid's real name was never learned, and he was never heard from again.

However, the moment reflected back on the boxer's origins, back where a frontier river port in the 19th century teeming with immigrants and ethnic enclaves grew into a 20th-century metropolis of diverse neighborhoods and industry. Today in the 21st century, the city continues to redefine itself. Throughout its history, however, the love of sport in all its forms has been constant. There have been an untold number of "Kids" in boxing history, and Cincinnati certainly has had its fair share, including a world champion in Tim "the Cincinnati Kid" Austin. And, the city has also had its fair share of wonderful moments in the heritage of the fight game. That is what this book is about.

Boxing in America is derived from prizefighting in England, the popularity of which dramatically increased in the 18th century. Boxing was a curious sport in that it attracted fans of every economic and social stripe. It also attracted controversy and condemnation that varied from era to era according to which political party or group of reformers was in control. By the 19th century, American fighters were crossing the Atlantic to box in England, as British fighters were also seeking their fortunes in America. And the matches were bare-knuckled affairs. Boxers would soak their hands in brine to toughen them. In the bouts, they were careful to slug the face, the neck, the chest, the stomach, or the kidneys, but they avoided the skull. No matter how tough one's hands were, hitting someone's skull would break them. The rounds themselves were considered over when one fighter's knee hit the ground, and sometimes the matches went dozens of rounds. A victor was declared when an opponent could not rise and fight the next round.

With the advent of the Sullivan-McCaffrey heavyweight championship fight in Cincinnati in 1885, the use of gloves gradually became commonplace. The image of boxing changed somewhat as well. Boxing, especially exhibition sparring with gloves, began to be seen as a manly pursuit the middle-class could participate in. By the beginning of the 20th century, in no small part set by the example of Theodore Roosevelt, boxing was considered a means to assert masculinity for boys and to train them for the lessons of life. With the Progressive Era (1880–1920) social betterment ideals of rescuing children from crime-ridden streets, boxing increasingly found its way into community centers and settlement house gyms.

Still, boxing was often more generally viewed as the province of urban ethnic and racial neighborhoods. Boxing was a way out, a way to make a life beyond the urban streets and gain a measure of fame, money, and respect. In Cincinnati, the boxing gyms were filled with the same type of young men in other cities who were pursuing the sport in the decades before World War II—second-generation Jews, Italians, Irish, and Germans. And, of course, there were African Americans who either grew up in the burgeoning industrial centers of the North and Midwest or who migrated there from the South.

Professional boxing was considered a poor man's game, a way for the have-nots to become the haves. The fans—middle-class, working-class, or underclass—loved it all. In Cincinnati, the fans had been witness to the long, bloody, bare-knuckle matches of the late 1800s, often watching them with one eye on the ring and one eye on the door in case the law burst in. By the second decade of the 20th century, the 1920s, and into the Great Depression, Cincinnati fans were cheering for the Italians from the West End, the Germans from Over-the-Rhine, and the Jews from both neighborhoods. Strong amateur boxing thrived. Every neighborhood had a hero. There were fights at local clubs virtually every night of the week.

Following the Great Depression, the golden age of boxing was ushered in with some of the greatest fighters in American sports history. Locally this was the age of Freddie Miller, Ezzard Charles, and Wallace "Bud" Smith, all world champions. Today Cincinnati is still a wonderful place to train amateur boxers for the Golden Gloves and Olympic berths, and many of these have had quite successful professional careers.

The decades pass. One can imagine coming out of a gym in Over-the-Rhine in the winter, hitting the cold air after the steamy indoors and seeing snow on the houses and chimney smoke rising in the air above the city. In the summer, the same exit would be into another humid world of the streets, the sun glaring down. At any season, the click of the jump ropes and the rhythmic smacking of the speed bag would still be part of the boxer's world as he stepped on the sidewalk or back out of a ring in Bar Harbor with Cincinnati on his mind.

Boxing is about the rhythm of days and nights of training and of rounds in the ring. Boxers hear a special music in this rhythm. Because ultimately it is the boxer who must alone account for himself in a bout, the song can end as a mournful sound or a song of quiet accomplishment. It is like Sonny Liston once said, "Some day they're gonna write a blues for fighters. It'll just be for slow guitar, soft trumpet, and a bell."

1

FIGHT TOWN

THE 19TH CENTURY

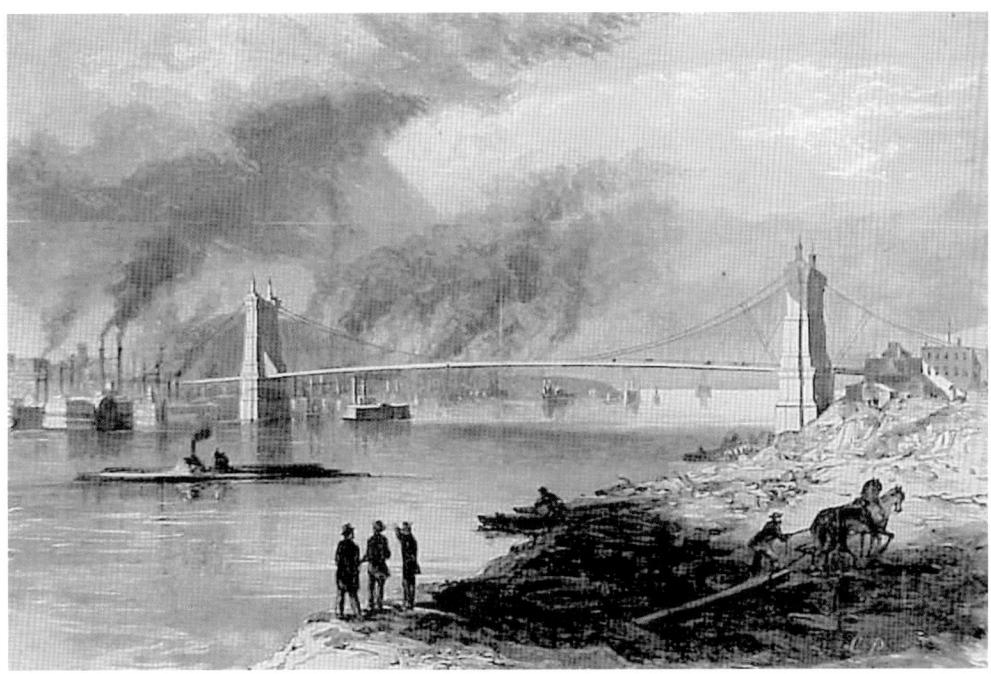

With the completion of the suspension bridge in 1866, Cincinnati continued to grow as an urban center of immigrant settlers, factories, and commercial businesses. In many ways, though, it was still a frontier city. Boxing matches were often fought just beyond the watchful eyes of the law, with sometimes a quick change of venue across the river to the hills and rural areas of northern Kentucky to avoid arrest.

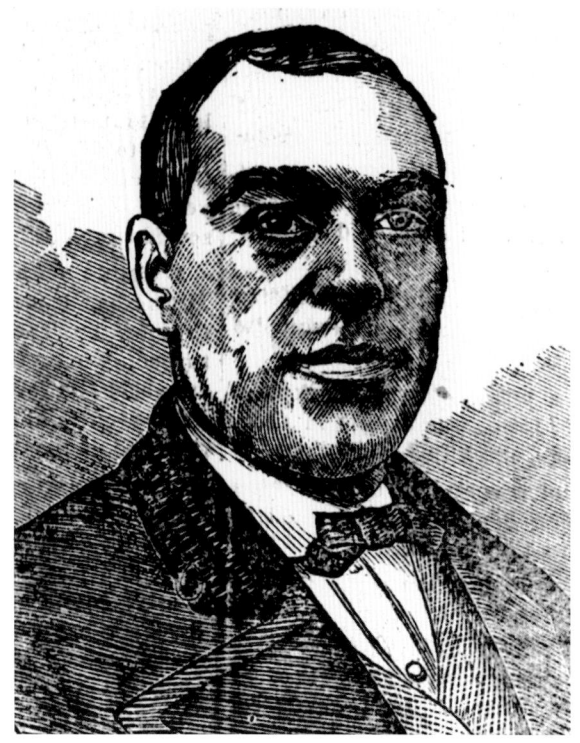

Jem Coyne ventured to Cincinnati in 1869 in search of a prizefight. The English-born Coyne began fighting in 1862, and in Cincinnati, he hoped to land a bout in the match everyone was talking about—an upcoming fight between two notable pugilists, Mike McCoole and Tom Allen. At Mozart Hall on October 30, Coyne fought an exhibition against Young Newell, "drawing blood with a sturdy wipe in the first round." It was reported that master of ceremonies "Butt" Riley did his duty in a "very creditable manner."

Mike McCoole was one tough character. Irish-born, he came to America and worked as a bargeman in Cincinnati on the Ohio River, building up a massive physique along with an irascible nature. His first notable fight was in Louisville in 1858, and since then, he had won the championship belt, 34 inches long and covered with gold and silver plates. After losing the title to Tom Allen in 1868, he was in Cincinnati to challenge Allen and recapture the championship.

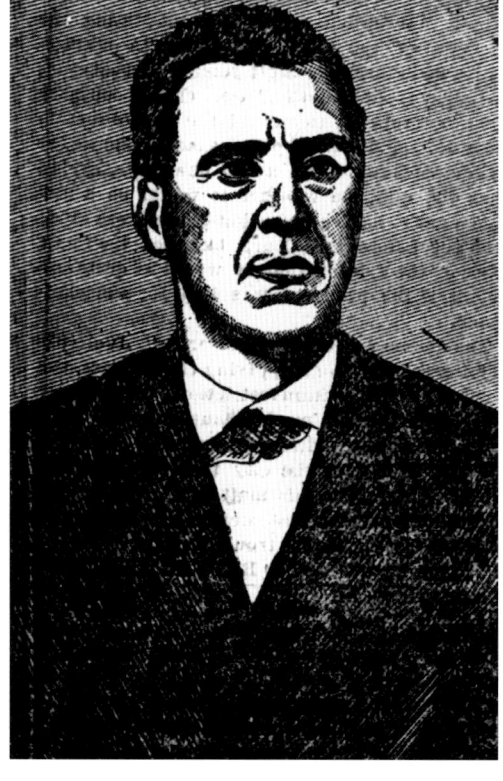

In their eventual rematch in Missouri, Tom Allen (right) stopped McCoole to retain the heavyweight championship and held it for a few years until his fellow Englishman, Joe Goss (below), stepped forward with a challenge. Coming to Cincinnati in 1876, the two fighters had to avoid the local authorities who only permitted "exhibitions" and not out-and-out prizefights. Allen and Goss, with thousands of fans following, headed across the river to Kenton County. On September 1, the match began, but after just 37 minutes and seven rounds, state troops were on the trail and the bout was declared a draw. Six days later, on September 7, they resumed the fight in neighboring Boone County. After 14 rounds, Allen was disqualified when he punched Goss while he was down. Goss was declared the heavyweight champion.

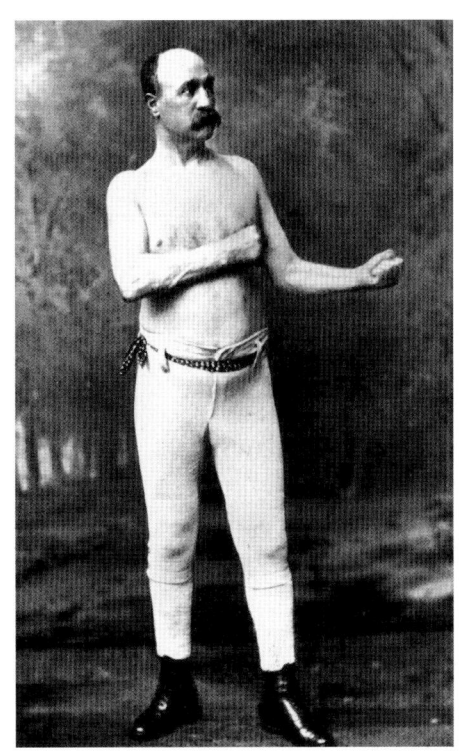

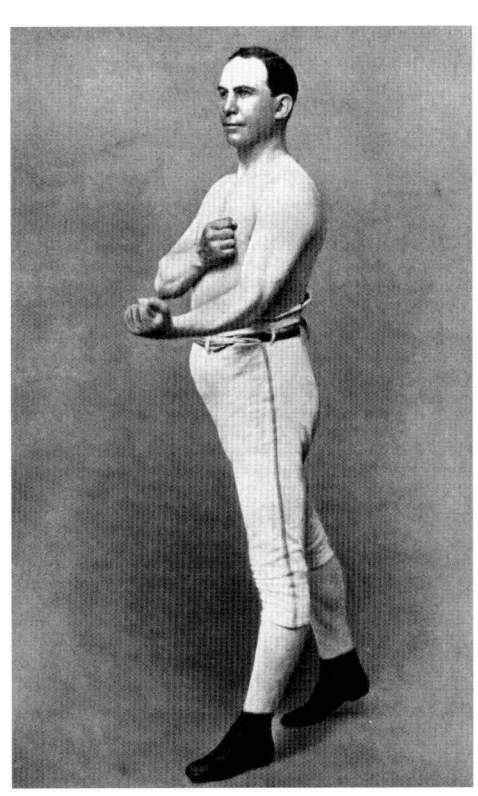

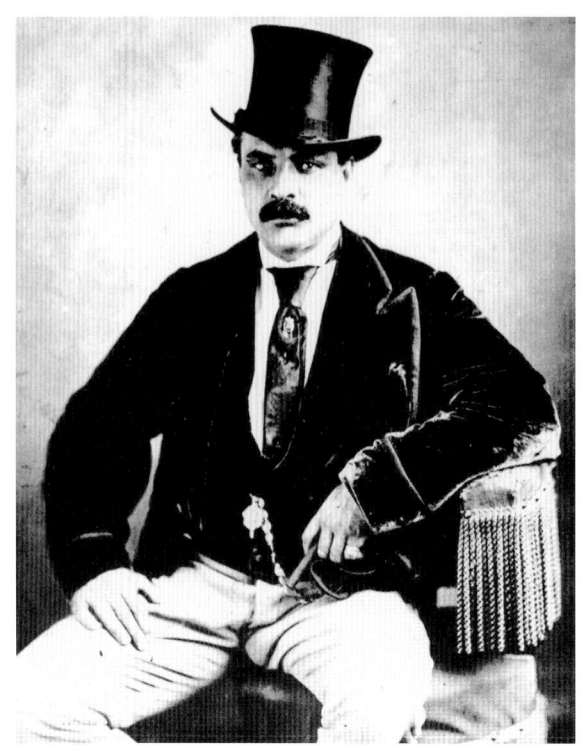

Englishman Jem Mace, "the Swaffham Gypsy," and New Zealander Herbert Slade, "the Maori," were two bare-knuckled boxers who had success in their own countries and then sought their fistic fortunes in America. Mace began his career in the boxing booths of England where he used either gloves or bare fists, depending on the wishes of his opponent. In 1861, he won the British heavyweight championship. Slade and Mace staged exhibition matches together around the country, journeying to Cincinnati in March 1883 for a demonstration in front of local fight mavens. Mace (left), particularly, was instrumental in promoting the use of boxing gloves and bringing the bare-knuckle era to an end.

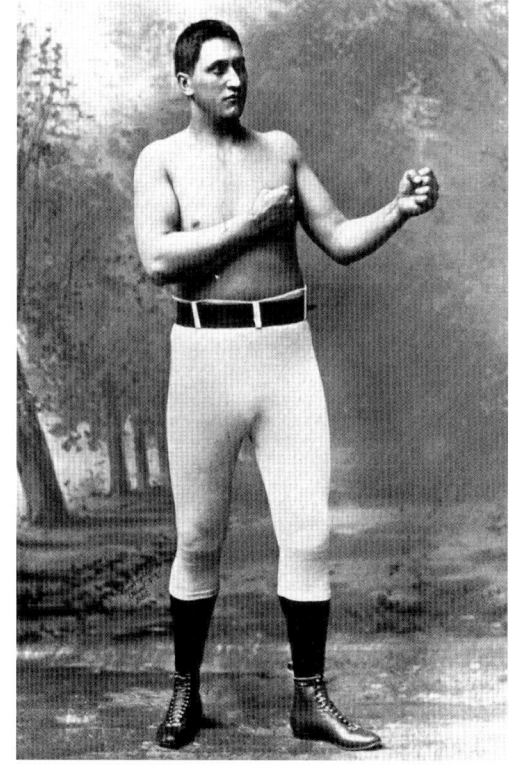

Sam the Scaramouch was a Cincinnati tabloid that lampooned virtually everything in American society—temperance and prohibition, politicians and foreign policy, and ethnic groups and the pursuits of everyday leisure. Published in 1885 and 1886, the weekly newspaper took on the growing infatuation with sparring by the gentlemanly classes of Cincinnati, poking fun at the "academies" of pugilism.

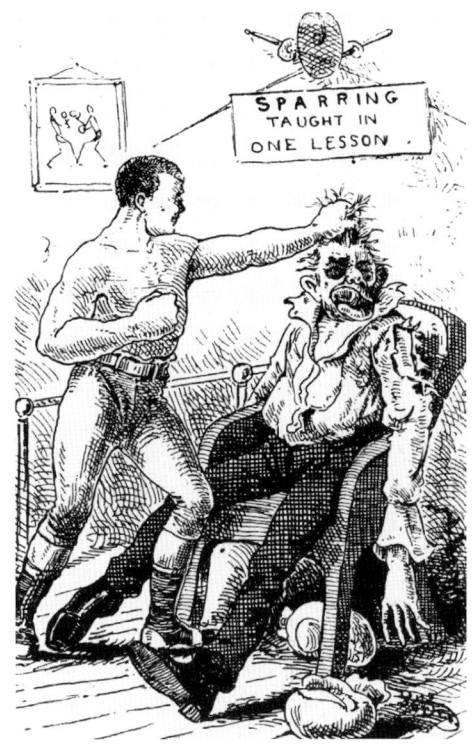

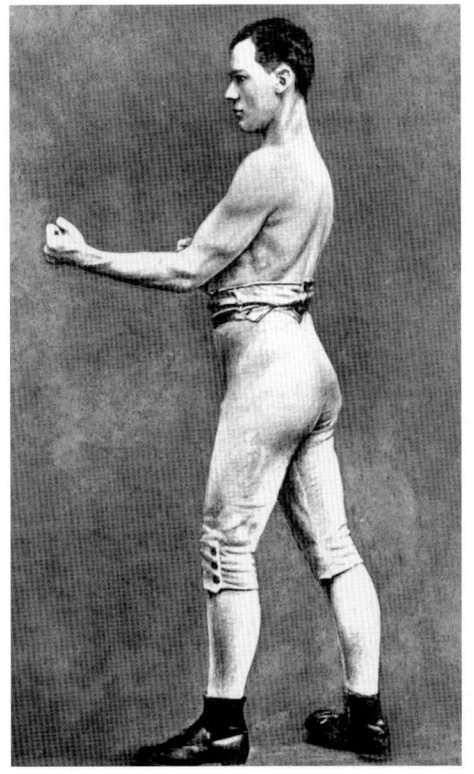

One of the teachers of the sport was "Professor" John Donaldson, who considered himself a scientific boxer. In December 1880, Donaldson and a young John L. Sullivan fought an exhibition in Cincinnati, and Sullivan got the best of him. Dissatisfied with the outcome, Donaldson issued a challenge to fight with gloves for $500. A year later on December 28, the two fought in a small Cincinnati gym, and Sullivan thrashed Donaldson again, winning in 10 rounds.

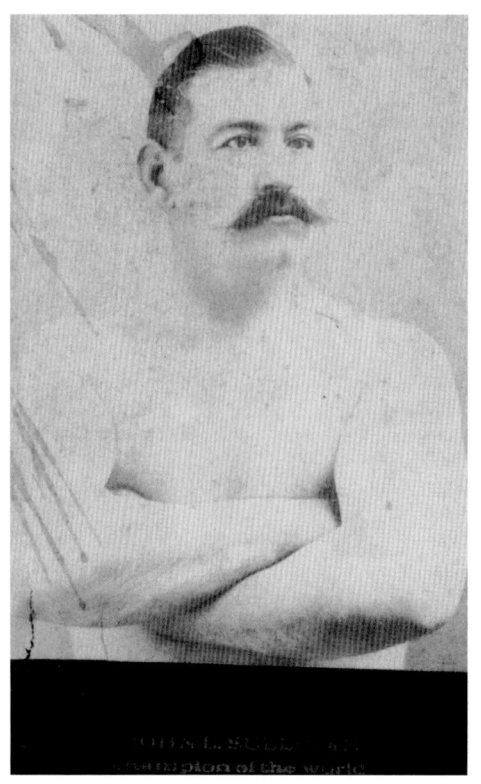

It was indeed the fight of the century. Under Marquis of Queensberry rules, the first heavyweight championship bout in America wearing boxing gloves was fought on August 29, 1885. John L. Sullivan (left), the "Boston Strong Boy," noted pugilist, and man of the never-empty bottle, took on Pittsburgh's Dominick McCaffrey (below) at Chester Park. The boxing ring was 24 feet and the gloves only three ounces, a bit of protection for the slugs against the skull, but not much. The day before, while McCaffrey trained hard, Sullivan was arrested at the behest of the Law and Order League, which opposed prizefighting. He was let out on bond, and the arrest did nothing to forestall the fight on August 29. McCaffrey announced his intention to walk into the ring in a flesh-colored sleeveless shirt, flesh-colored knee breeches, and the colors of the Stars and Stripes. As he said, "I am of Irish descent, but I'm a true son of America." (Below, courtesy of Harry Shaffer/Antiquities of the Prize Ring.)

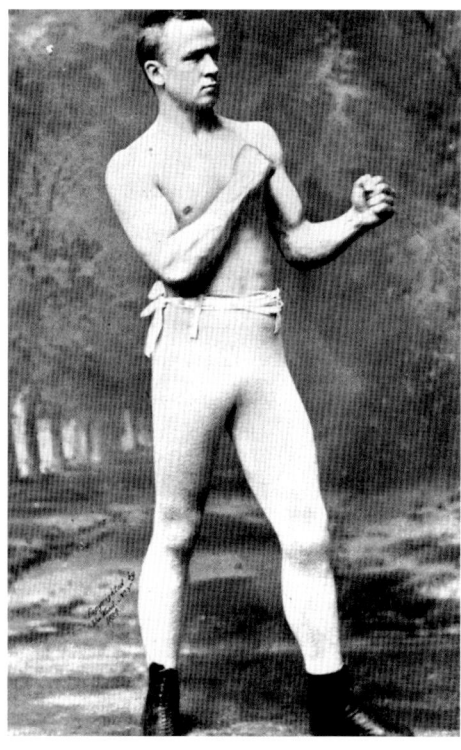

LOVE TAPS.

GREATEST SPORTING EVENT IN 20 YEARS
DOM AND JOHN
Will Exchange Greetings at Chester Park, Saturday Afternoon, August 29th.
The Champions of the World.

The bout that was capturing the attention of the entire city was covered in *Sam the Scaramouch* as well, promising the fans who attended the fight that they would be witness to the pugilistic "love taps" as the boxers "exchanged greetings." However, it was not overstated when it was claimed the set-to would be the biggest event in two decades. Tickets sold for the extraordinary rate of $3 and $5.

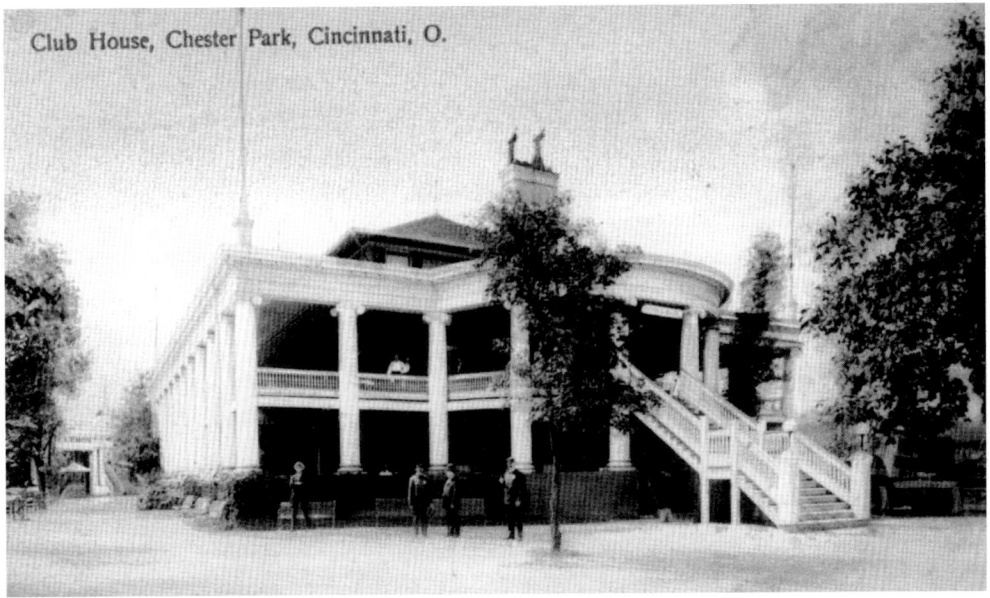

Chester Park was the perfect spot for such a huge match. Located just north of the Clifton neighborhood along Spring Grove Avenue, Chester Park was built in 1875 by a group of racehorse enthusiasts. Over the years, it featured not only racing but also swimming, dancing, concerts, and even some football games. The park was easily accessible by streetcar and railroad, leading more than 15,000 fans to make their way there to witness the match.

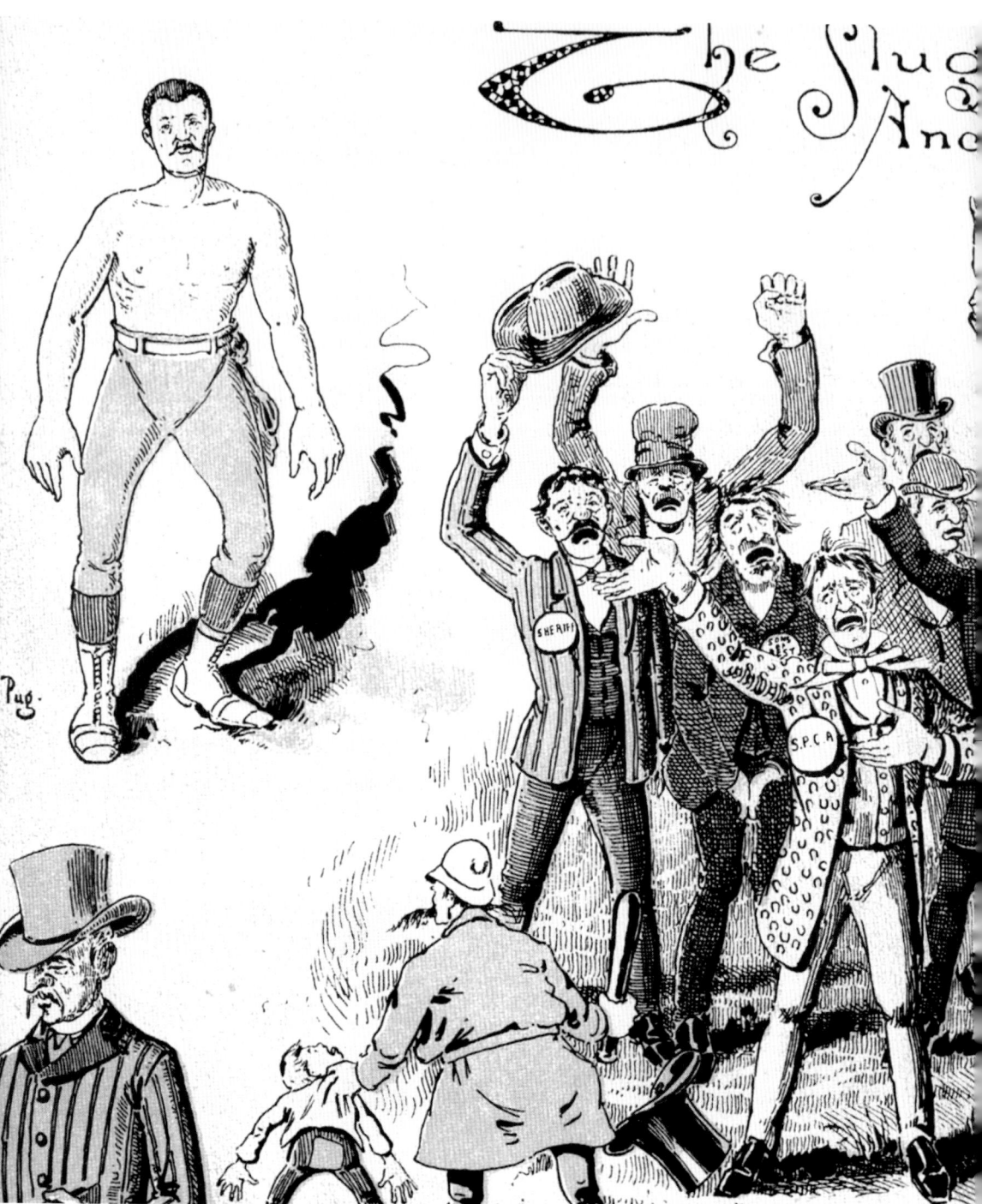

John L. Sullivan prevailed in a disputed seven-round decision and spent the next day getting drunk. The following week, *Sam* captured the excitement of the match with a cartoon showing the victor, Sullivan (upper left), and the vanquished, the quite beaten Dominick McCaffrey (lower right). Included in the cartoon is the range of witnesses to the match, from the police,

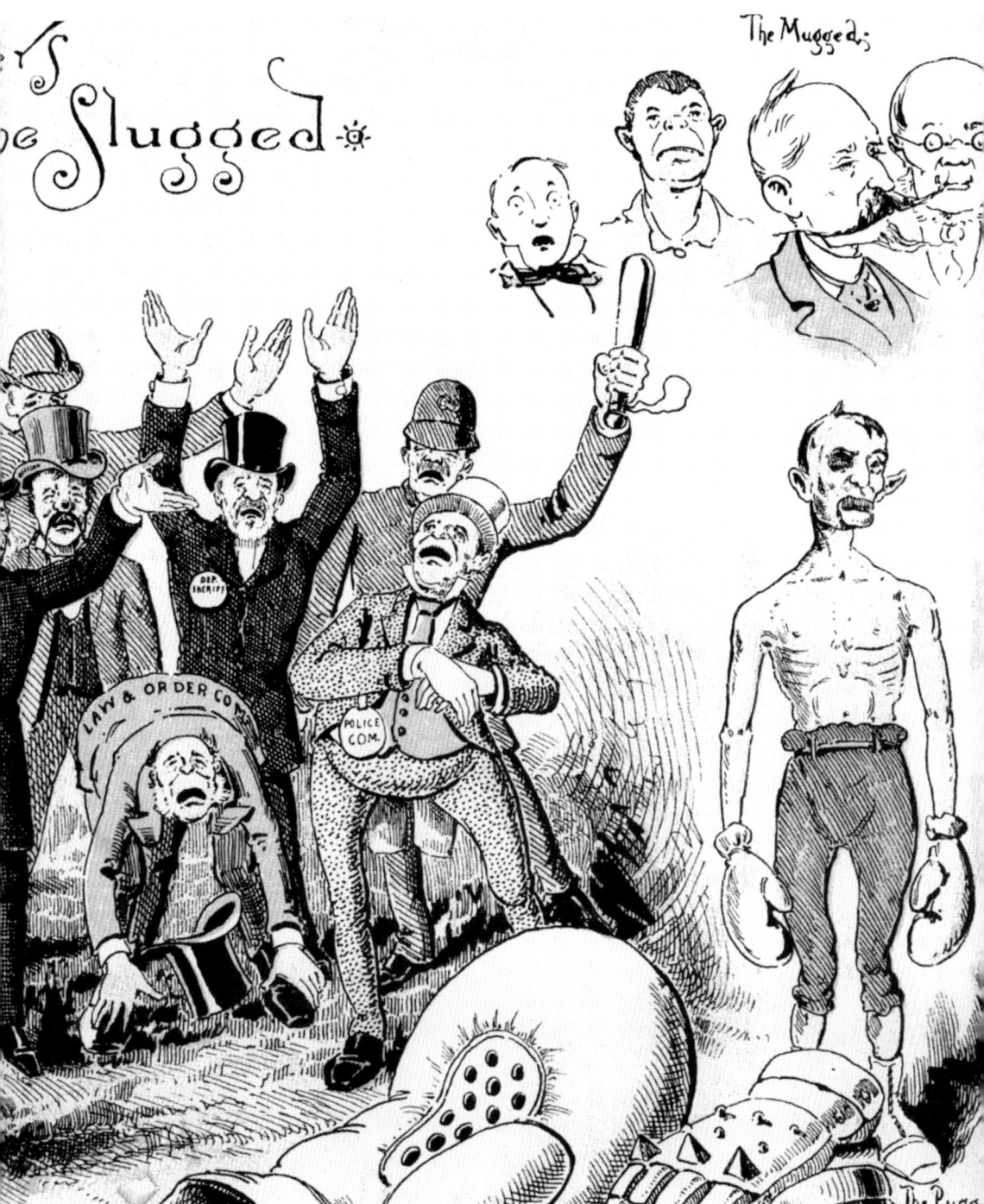

civic officials, and various do-gooders who sought to halt the fight to the gamblers who won and the gamblers who, sadly, lost. It was a monumental event in the history of American boxing and one that Cincinnatians would remember for decades.

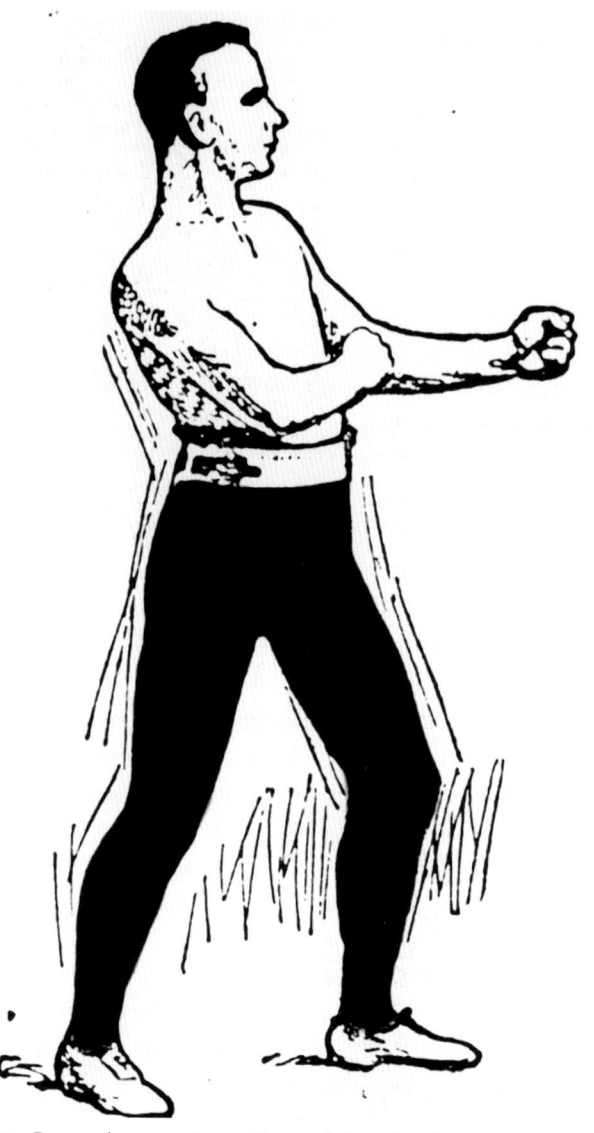

Bantamweight Louis Bezenah was the oldest of five brothers and one sister who boxed professionally. Bezenah grew up in Cincinnati and began as a "booth fighter" in county fairs. These bare-knuckle matches were often vicious affairs, and Bezenah did not don gloves until 1889 when he became a lightweight. It is said that he killed three men in the ring. He came to an untimely end himself. In 1896, Bezenah was in a George Street brothel with a woman named May Riley. Riley had recently dumped her boyfriend, a petty thief called Kid Dugan, and Dugan was out for revenge. He stormed into the room where Bezenah and Riley were with another couple, a prostitute named Lizzie Evans and a stranger. Shouting, "If I can't have you, no one else will," Dugan fired a gun four times. The first shot hit Riley in the arm, the second knocked out Evans's false teeth, and the final shots hit Bezenah in the chest and abdomen. He died the next month. At one time, Riley had also been lovers with Dugan's friends "Windy Dick" and "Canada Jack." Perhaps a good nickname would have saved Bezenah.

Charles "Kid" McCoy, from Kokomo, Indiana, was one of the sterling fighters at the beginning of the 20th century. He was also known as the "Corkscrew Kid" for his technique of twisting his glove as he connected with a punch in order to inflict more damage on his opponent. Between 1894 and 1897, McCoy made five visits to Cincinnati, taking on the luckless Al Roberts in the first three. Roberts and McCoy tangled twice in October 1894, fighting to draws, and then again in January 1895 when Roberts was knocked out in the fifth.

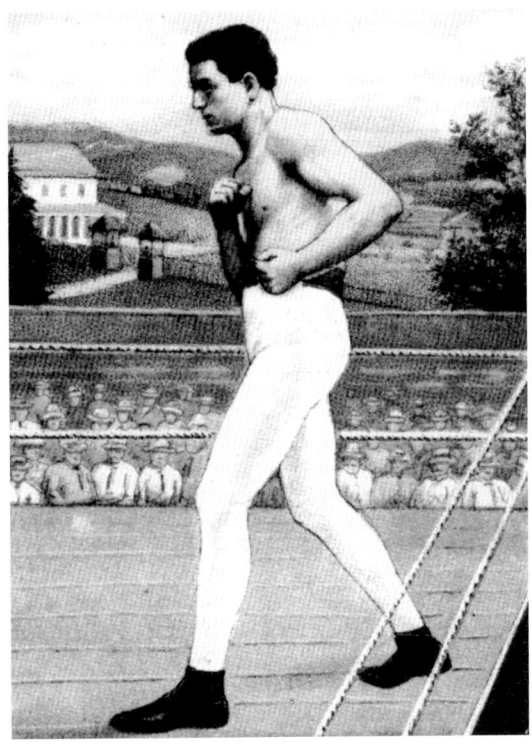

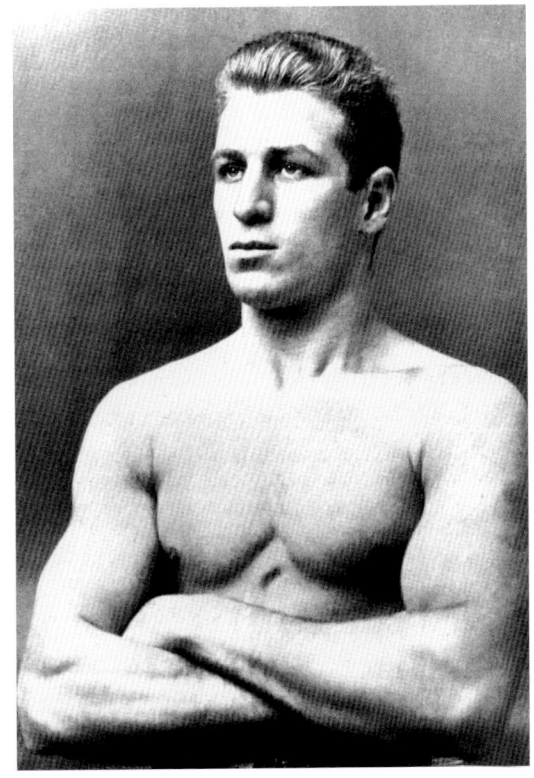

"Chrysanthemum Joe" Choynski hailed from San Francisco and made his way to Cincinnati to box a local by the name of Harry Miller in 1894. Apparently the city made an impression; he married Louise Anderson Miller of Cincinnati the next year. The last time he fought in Cincinnati was in 1899 at the Olympic Athletic Club, where he knocked out Tom Carey in the second round.

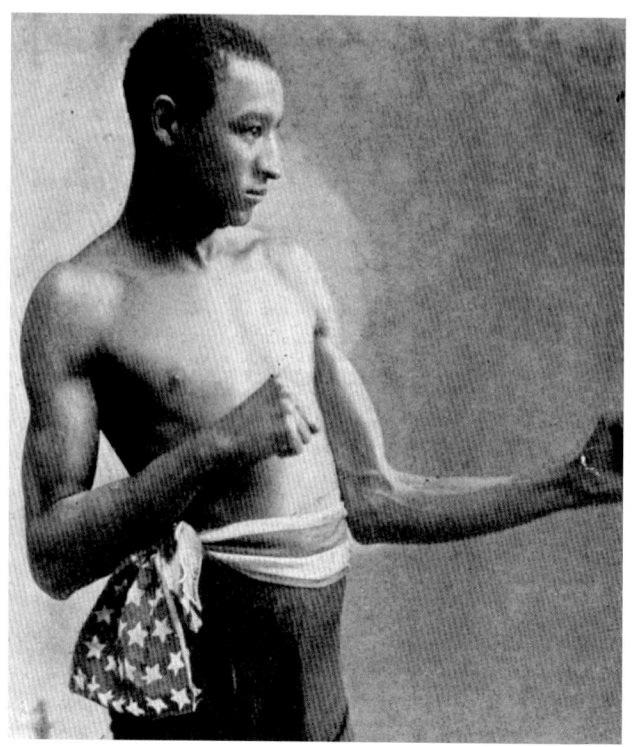

One of the earliest local African American professional fighters was "Kid Blue," a journeyman who fought out of several cities before coming to Cincinnati to live in 1899. While race and racism have always been a matter of contention and discussion in pugilism, it seems the lighter weight classes saw more integrated bouts than the heavyweight class. Kid Blue was a lightweight featured in the *Police Gazette*, a lurid tabloid on America's underbelly whose editor, Richard K. Fox, regularly wrote about the boxing world. It was Fox who provided the best written and graphic chronicling of the sport in the 19th century.

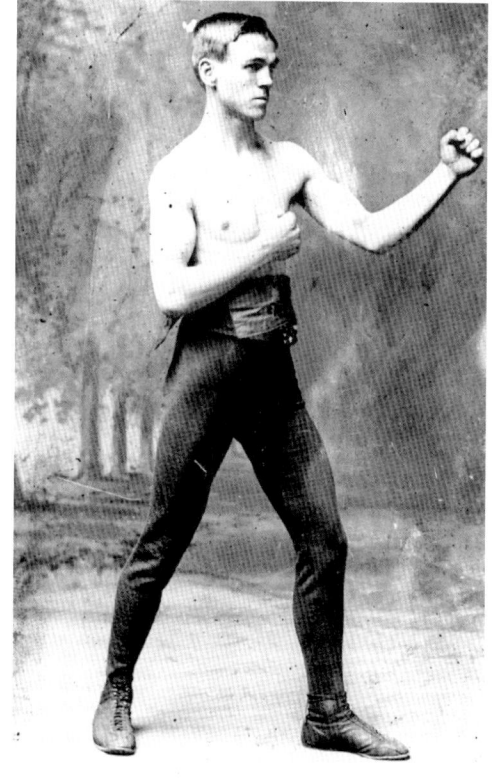

"Terrible Terry" McGovern, one of the great boxers in American history, got his start in the clubs of Brooklyn. After winning the world bantamweight title on September 12, 1899, he came west to Cincinnati, where on December 18, he took on two fighters the same day at the Peoples Theatre. He knocked out Charlie Mason in the second round of their match and then took on "Freckles" O'Brien, scoring a knockout in the first. The next year, Terrible Terry added the featherweight crown to his achievements.

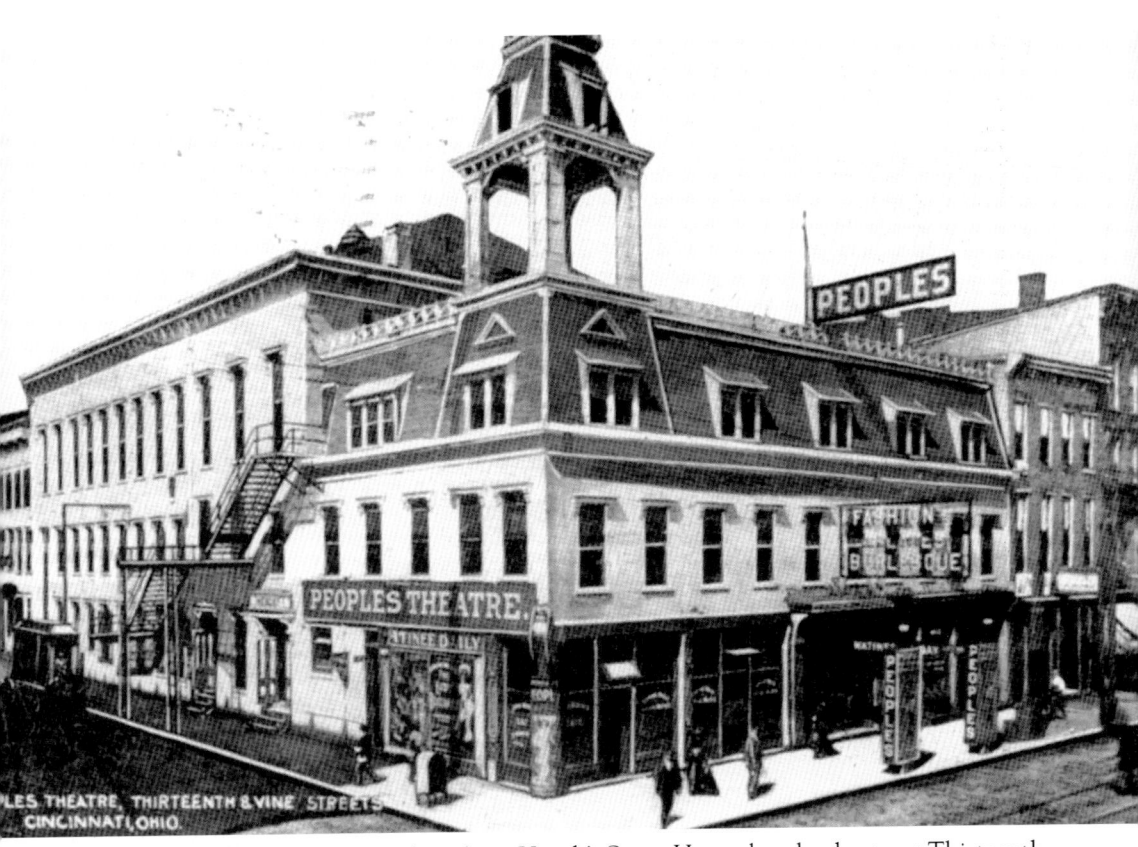

Its formal, and original, name may have been Heuck's Opera House, but the theater at Thirteenth and Vine Streets in Over-the-Rhine was more popularly known as Peoples Theatre. It was constructed by impresario Hubert Heuck and became a vital part of life in the neighborhood. The bill was alternately high art and low entertainment, a German drama often being followed the next week by a burlesque show. Like other theaters on the streets around it, such places as Rappold's, Cosmopolitan Hall, and the Pacific Garden, the Peoples Theatre was also the spot to see some of the best boxers in the city, even if the view of the boxers was not the best. The theater was built for stage shows, and in the long, narrow hall, it was often difficult to see the action of a bout up on the stage. That did not seem to damper the enthusiasm of the fight fans, however.

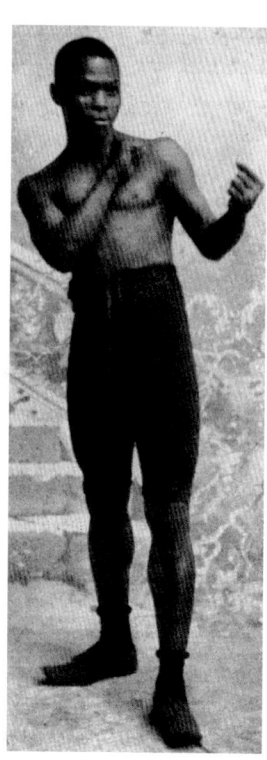

Kid "the Pork Chops King" Ash was a featherweight boxer who fought out of Cincinnati from 1899 to 1915. Although he often traveled to New York, and on one occasion all the way to the West Coast and Seattle, Ash primarily fought in Cincinnati venues like the Peoples Theatre, Robinson's Opera House, and the Phoenix, Ohio, and Stag athletic clubs. (Photograph courtesy of Harry Shaffer/Antiquities of the Prize Ring.)

Joe Gans, the "Old Master," fought over 160 bouts in his career, which extended from 1891 to 1909. Coming out of Baltimore, he got his start in the infamous battles royal in which several African American fighters were put in the ring at the same time to see who would be the last one standing. Gans was one of the greatest lightweights of all time and the first native-born African American to win a title belt when he captured the championship in 1902. He fought in Cincinnati on December 11, 1899, taking on Kid Ash at the Peoples Theatre and giving him a grueling pounding for a 15-round decision.

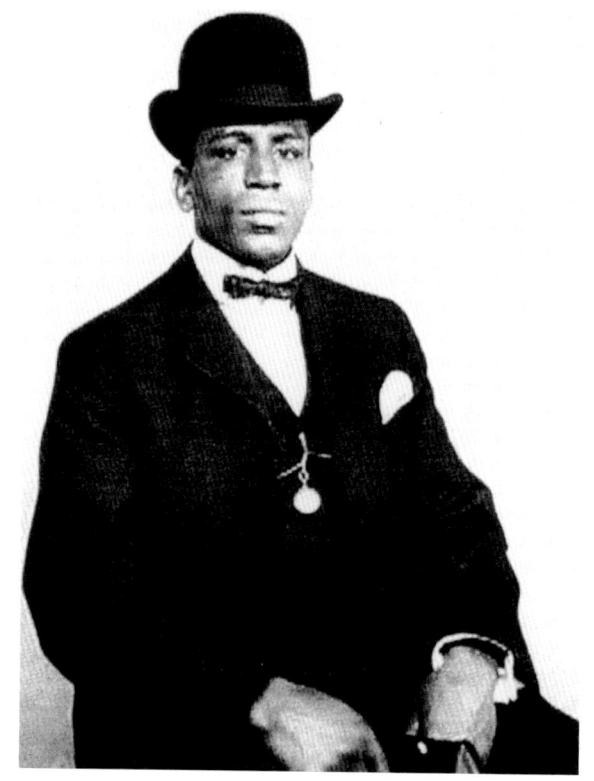

2

Pugilism Becomes a Key Cincinnati Sport

1900–1918

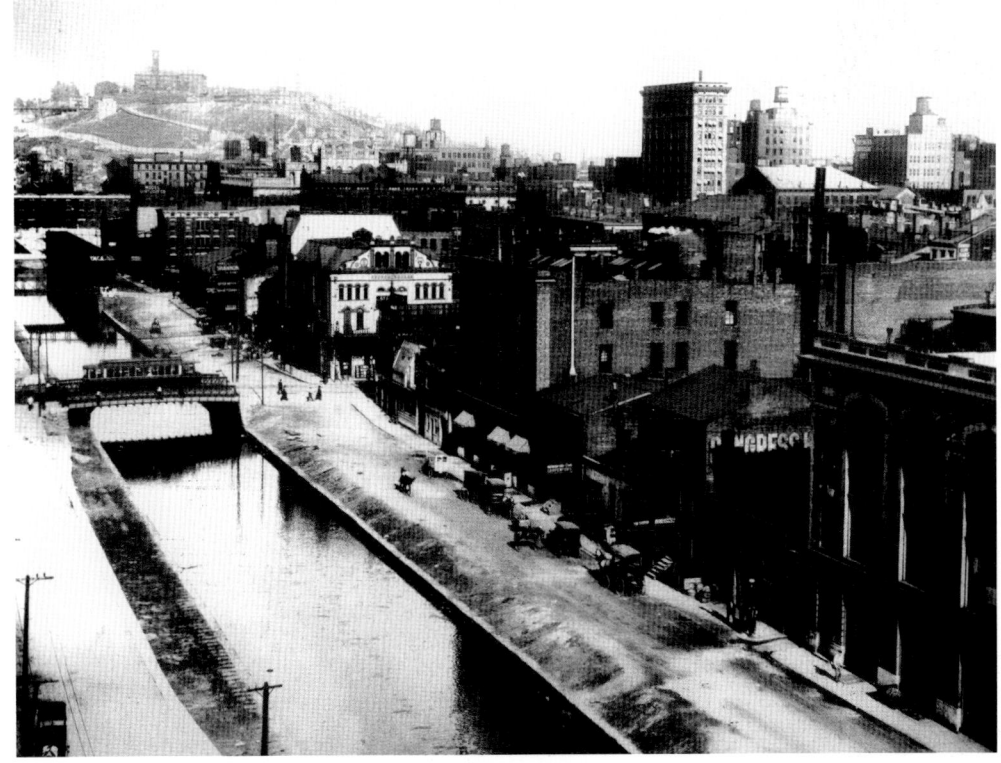

In the early years of the 20th century, Over-the-Rhine (so-called because of the Miami-Erie Canal that bisected the German neighborhood) was home to many boxing gyms and clubs—the Yokum Club, Batche's on Pleasant Street, Altman off Liberty Street, and the Harrison gym on Mound Street—along with professional clubs at Canal Street and Race Street, or near Redland Field and Music Hall.

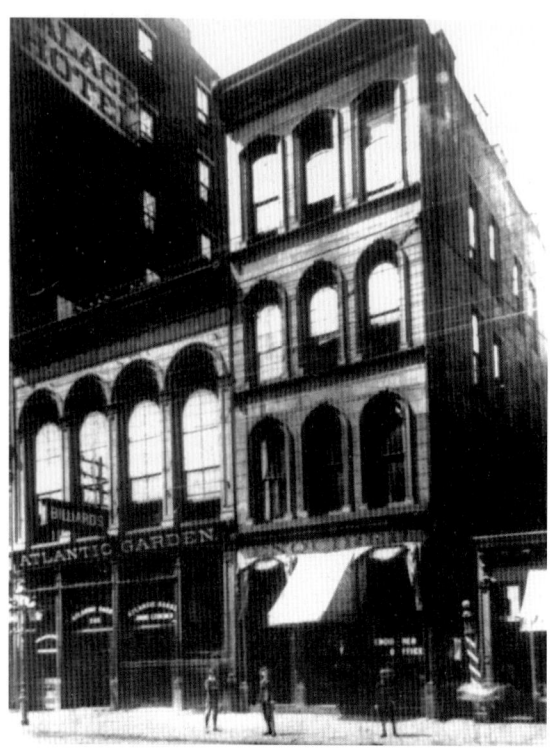

The Atlantic Garden was located just north of Sixth Street and was a rowdy, raucous place that attracted performers from the surrounding vaudeville houses, as well as a fair share of gamblers and boxers. Dispensing only rivers of beer to its clientele, it often featured a line of chorus girls on its small stage, performing along with boxing matches.

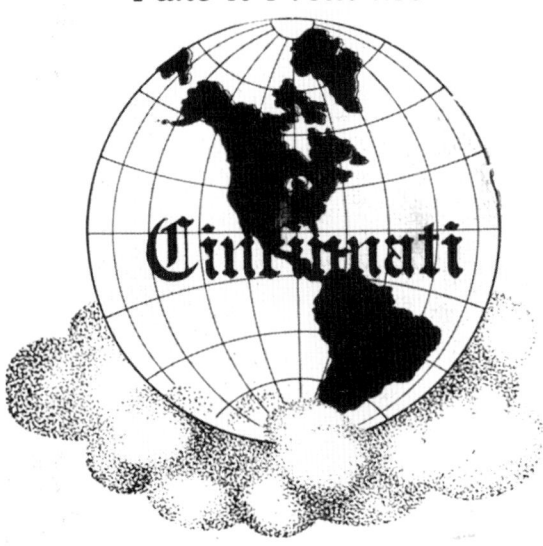

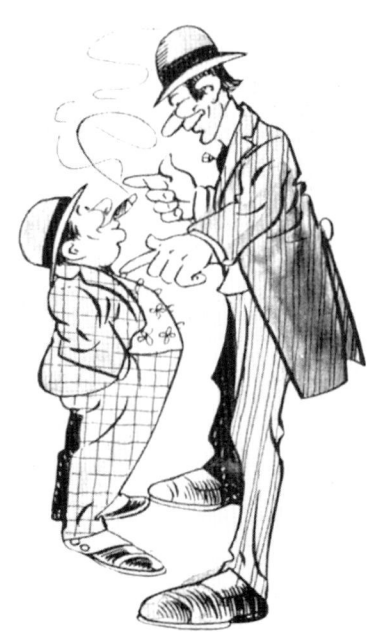

Such places as the Atlantic Garden attracted many journeyman boxers hoping to pick up a few extra dollars on the saloon circuit. On the back of this postcard, a fighter named "Slim" wrote to his pal in Columbus that he had won his match when "Johnny Donnelly dropped his gloves" in surrender.

The late lightweight Louis Bezenah was one of a family of boxers in Cincinnati. His brothers, Eugene, Andy, Al, and Gus, were also fighters, along with a sister, Violette. Later Al's sons, Elmer "Buddy" and Joe also became boxers. Brother Eugene (pictured to the right) was a credible welterweight who fought from the early 1890s to 1906 and, like brother Louis, started as a bare-knuckler, sometimes in fights lasting more than 30 rounds. And brother Gus also boxed as a lightweight. The flyer advertising his 1910 match against a Toledo fighter at the Chester Park clubhouse on Spring Grove Avenue made a point of stating that it was a "glove contest," indicating, perhaps, that bouts were occasionally still fought without them.

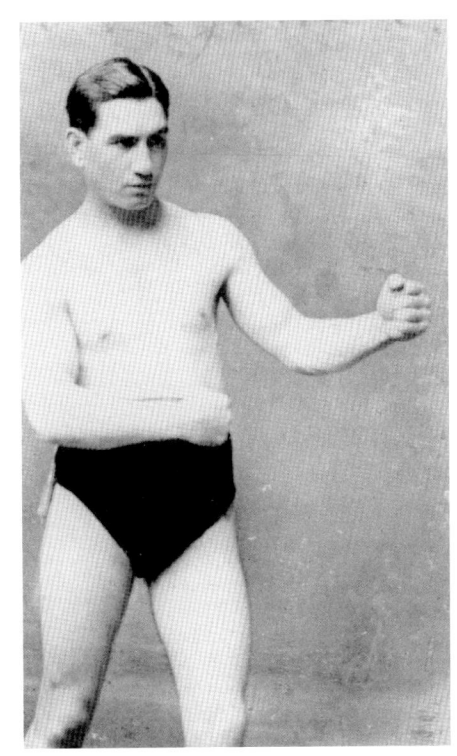

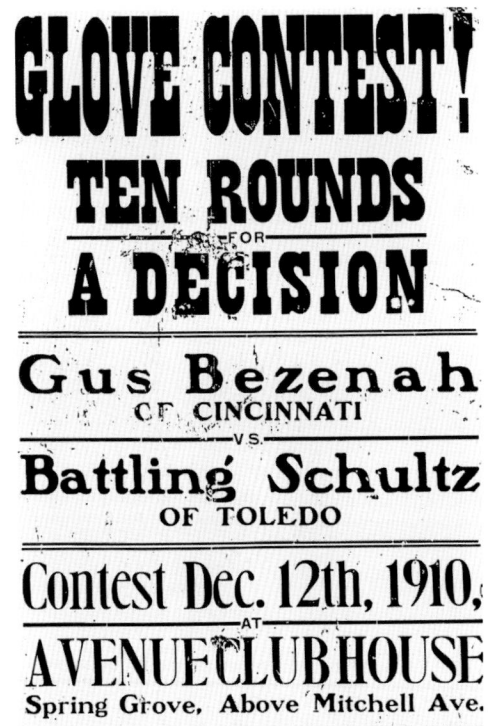

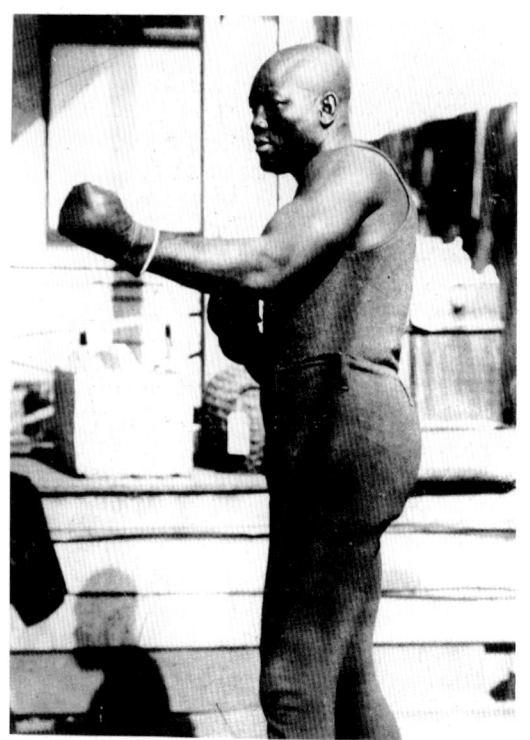

One of the greatest heavyweights in boxing history never fought in Cincinnati but had a dramatic effect on the city nevertheless. When Jack Johnson fought the "Great White Hope" Jim Jeffries in Reno, Nevada, on July 4, 1910, the African American's victory had nationwide repercussions as whites rioted against black citizens. In the Cincinnati area, a riot broke out across the river in Covington when dozens of whites and African Americans fought at Pike and Madison Streets.

Sam Langford was an accomplished African American heavyweight who, because of his race, was denied opportunities to fight the best white boxers in the country. Langford's home base was Boston, and from 1902 to 1926, he fought in over 300 bouts. Toward the final years of his illustrious career, he made a few trips to the Cincinnati area, knocking out George Godfrey in Covington in August 1921, then fighting to a draw with Brad Simmons in Cincinnati in October and losing to Bill Tate in Covington in December.

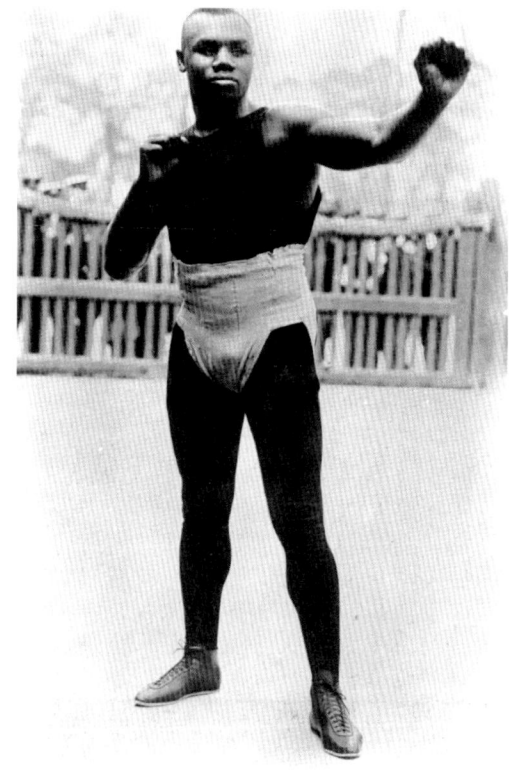

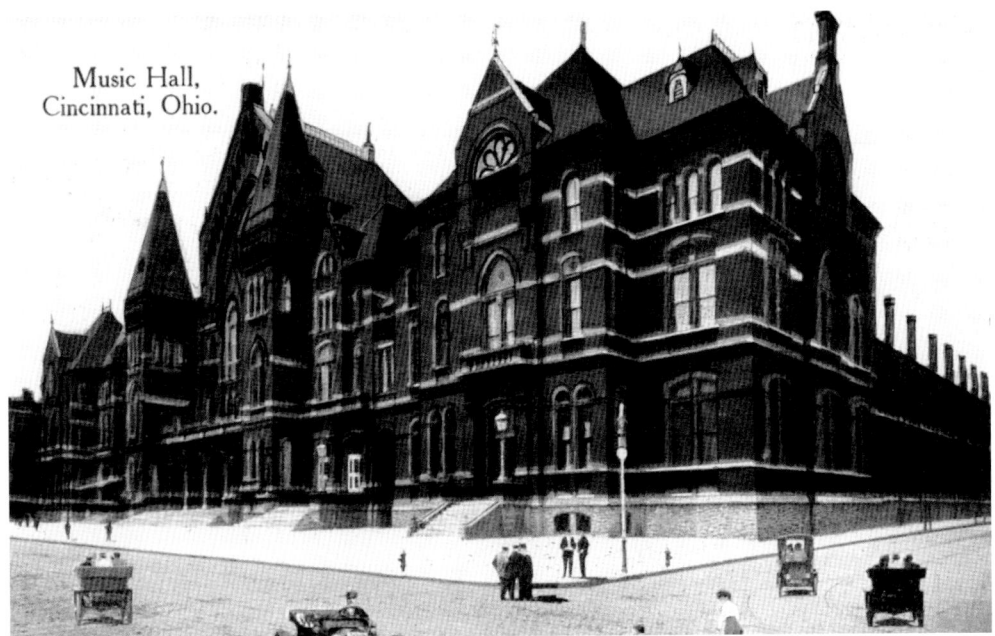

Music Hall, Cincinnati, Ohio.

Music Hall was constructed in 1878 and immediately became a venue not only for the city's rich music festivals but also for political conventions, plays, concerts, and recreation. It was an elaborate continuation of the mid-19th-century concert halls and opera houses that served multiple entertainment purposes. By World War I, boxing matches were favored attractions. Two years prior to the building of Music Hall, the Bellevue Incline was built, part of several inclines that carried Cincinnatians from the basin to the surrounding hillsides. In this view of the incline, the working-class redbrick neighborhood of Over-the-Rhine can be seen, the center of Cincinnati's boxing universe.

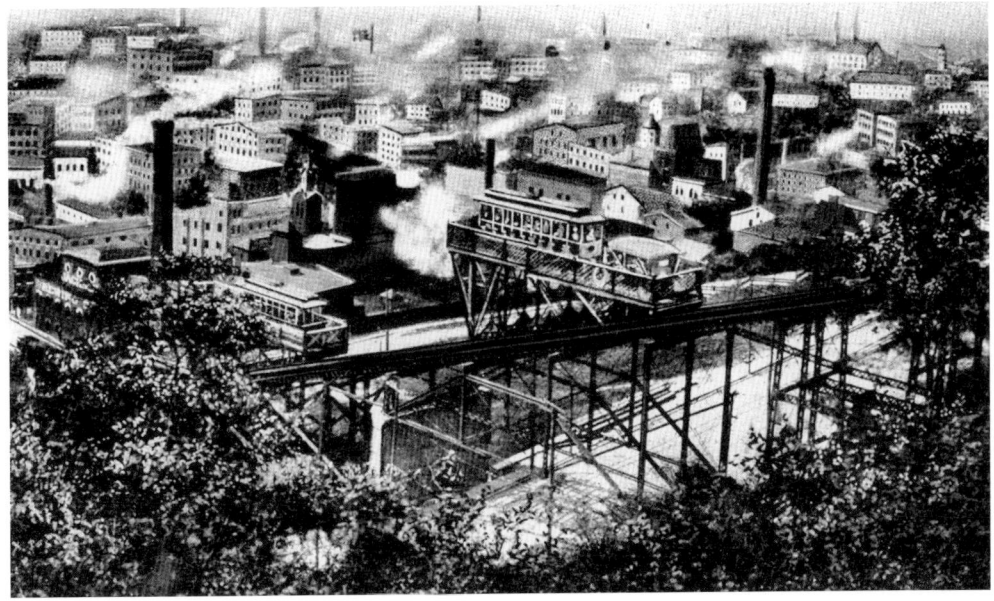

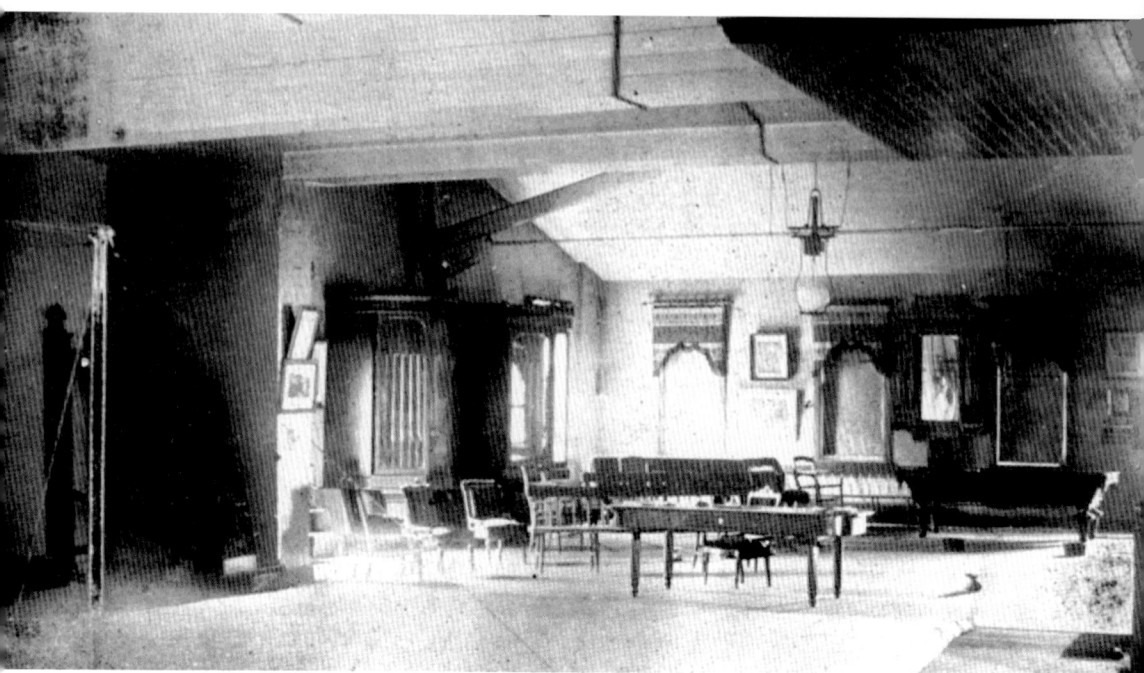

By the late 1880s, it was believed that Cincinnati policemen were becoming soft, "sauntering" on the beat rather than walking it. Most of the crime fighting was done on foot, and the local force was out of shape to deal with the various criminals, blackguards, and general ne'er-do-wells. As one report stated, "Except for the swinging of his club by his side, his arms get no exercise, save in an infrequent battle with a muscular and recalcitrant law breaker." A gym was created at the Hammond Street station house, part of which included a punching bag, seen in the right side of this photograph. A. C. Brendamour became the first instructor, followed a few months later by Charles Folger, who had been a contortionist in the John Robinson Circus.

August Gulow, a local German American who was a physical fitness instructor, became the superintendent of the police gymnasium in 1894 and continued in that position for over 20 years. According to a biographical sketch published in 1901, Gulow was an expert "sparrer" and "under his guidance the local blue coats have picked up many valuable points . . . in self-defense" along with strengthening their wind.

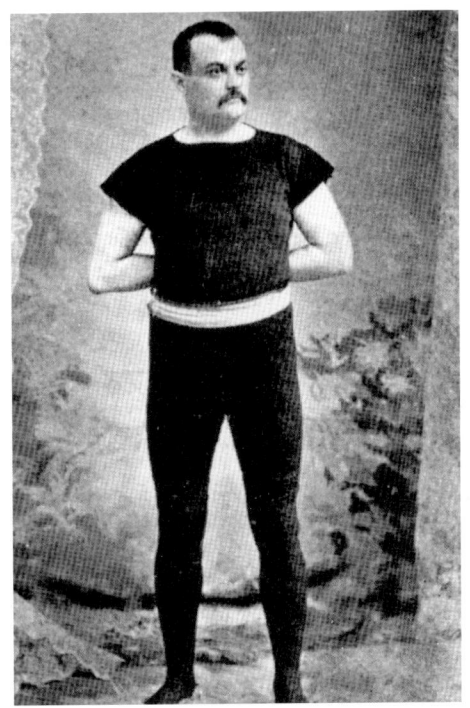

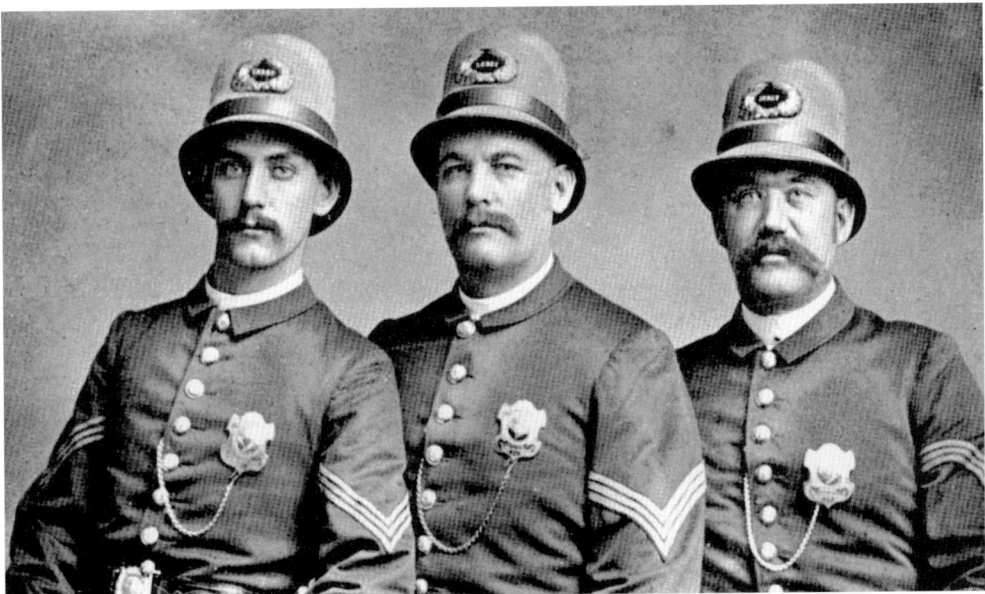

Sgt. Samuel T. Corbin of the 2nd District (pictured in the middle of this photograph with his comrades F. B. Newman [left] and Luke Drout) was a pugilistic pupil of Gulow's and one of the best boxers on the force. His skills came in handy as the 2nd included some of the roughest neighborhoods in the city in Over-the-Rhine, Sausage Row, and Rat Row. Another outstanding boxer was Frank Hall, a patrolman who rose through the ranks to detective and then became the first African American elected to city council.

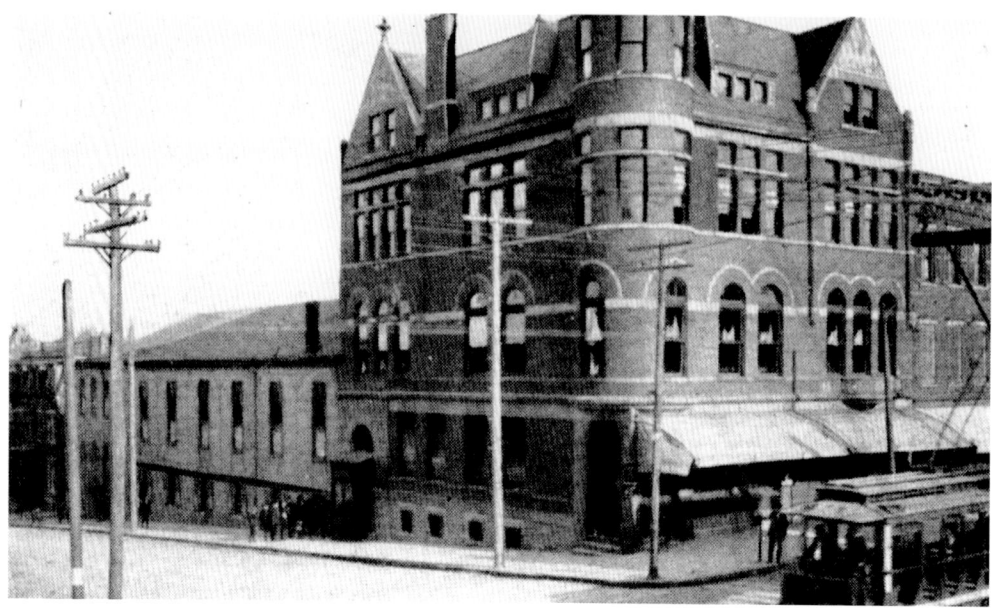

The city's German Americans often belonged to Turner organizations, a movement that began in Germany in the 18th century and was established in this country in 1848 in Cincinnati. The Turners emphasized the development of a strong mind and strong body, along with a commitment to civic duty. Physical fitness programs were paramount, and, in fact, German American Turners were instrumental in establishing physical education programs in public schools. Boxing, though, attracted mixed feelings among some turnverein organizations, viewing it as something for the lower classes. In 1915, one of the elite Turner halls, the North Cincinnati Turn-Verein in Corryville, decided to stage amateur matches as a way to "elevate boxing as a legitimate sport." Attendance was small, leading one report to lament that in the case of professional versus amateur boxing, "habitual patrons while enjoying to see the taming of the shrew do not care to see the tamed shrew."

Amateur Boxing Tournament

to be held in the Gymnasium of N. C. T. V. Hall

Saturday, January 2, 1915, at 8:30 p. m. sharp

The Program will consist of several lively bouts between some of the best local amateur boxers of Cincinnati

FOR MEMBERS ONLY!

ADMISSION, 50c, 75c and $1.00

THE COMMITEE ON PHYSICAL CULTURE

R. FINKELMEIER, Chairman
N. C. SEUSS
HENRY HOEFLE
GEO. RHEIN
MICHAEL KUHN
JACOB WIEBELL

CARL MEYER
JOHN LIPPS
WM. BROKATE
GEO. ANGERT
WM. PETRI
ED. LINDEMANN

Benny Becker was representative of a strong Jewish presence in Cincinnati boxing before World War I. In addition to literacy classes and job skills training, boxing programs, along with other athletics, were usually part of an ethnic settlement house or community center whose purpose was to provide a healthful respite away from the streets. In many American cities like Cincinnati, second-generation Jewish citizens embraced boxing. After his boxing career was finished, Becker became a manager and promoter.

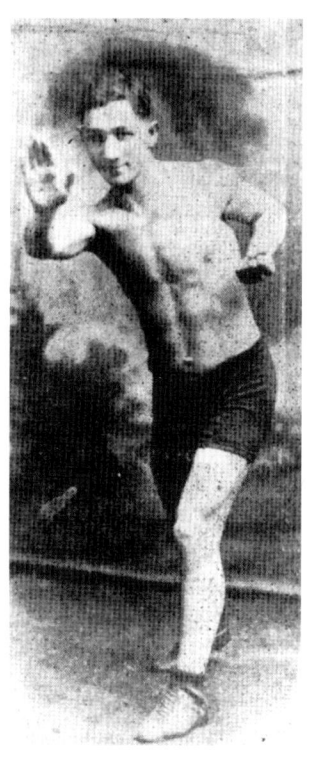

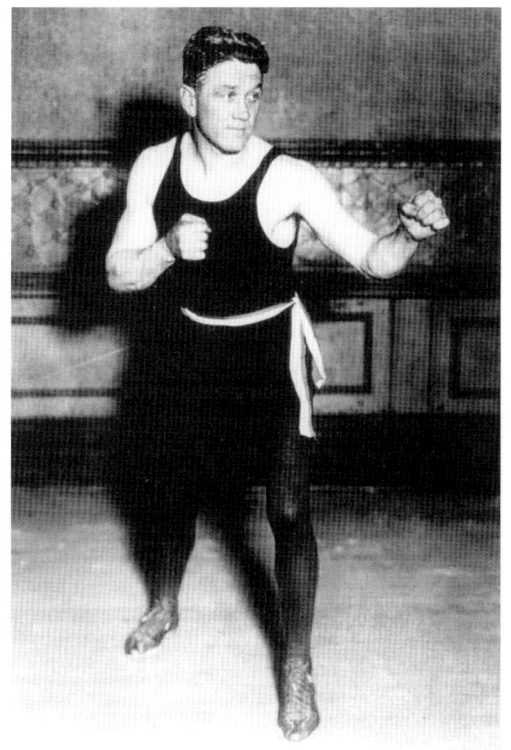

Cleveland native Johnny Kilbane (pictured here) was a colorful and popular prizefighter who held the featherweight belt from 1912 to 1923. In 1913, he came to Cincinnati to defend his title against local fighter K. O. Mars. Mars, born Louis Margolis, was 18 at the time and thought to be the youngest boxer ever to contend for a championship. The more experienced Kilbane knocked him out in the seventh round. But Mars remained a Cincinnati favorite his entire life, even after his more-than-300-bout career was over.

JACK SHEPPARD

Contender for the Welterweight Championship

A Whirlwind of Action

Always in Condition

Some of the Boys he has met and defeated

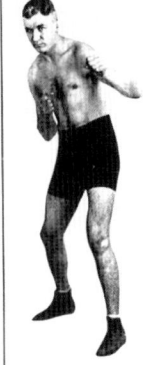

Open to Meet Anyone

Any Place

Any Where

Any Time

DEFEATED:	K. O'D:		
Benny Becker	Tommy Fitzsimmons	Just Match	SHEPPARD is the
Frankie Nessler	Sam LaVeague		welterweight that the
Jack Lawler	Buddy Wallace	**SHEPPARD**	
Johnny Martin	Sammy Nagel		Cincinnati welters
Frankie Burns	Young Lawrence	and the Fight	
Don Curley	Nifty Nash		and middleweights
Young Webb	Bobby Ward	Fans will want	
Jean Watson	Russell Montague		absolutely will not
Roy Hurts	Spider Kelly	him back	
Jimmy Shevelin	Bob Ross		fight . . . . .
Billy Voss	Mike Kearney		
Frank Sturm	Terry Nelson		
Almer Hogan			
Micky Forkins			
Mike Kearney			
Red Herring			
Ever Hammer			
And Other Good Boys	And great many others		

Cincinnati, Ohio
Rand Hotel

UNDER THE MANAGEMENT OF
BOB URICHO, JR.

Phone
Main
2340

Local fight manager Bob Uricho assembled a stable of boxers in the years following World War I, including Cincinnatians Joe Carson and Jack Sheppard, seen here in one of Uricho's flyers. Sheppard was a welterweight of some talent, getting most of his wins in local clubs on both sides of the river. Operating out of a local hotel, Uricho's task in getting matches for his fighters was, of course, to promote them as exciting pugilists who would draw a lot of fans and thus make a lot of money for rival promoters and venues. It was typical of the best in boxing hyperbole of that age. Some of Sheppard's opponents were legitimate fighters; others were just the bums of the night.

3

FROM LOCAL CLUBS TO A WORLD CHAMPION

1919–1933

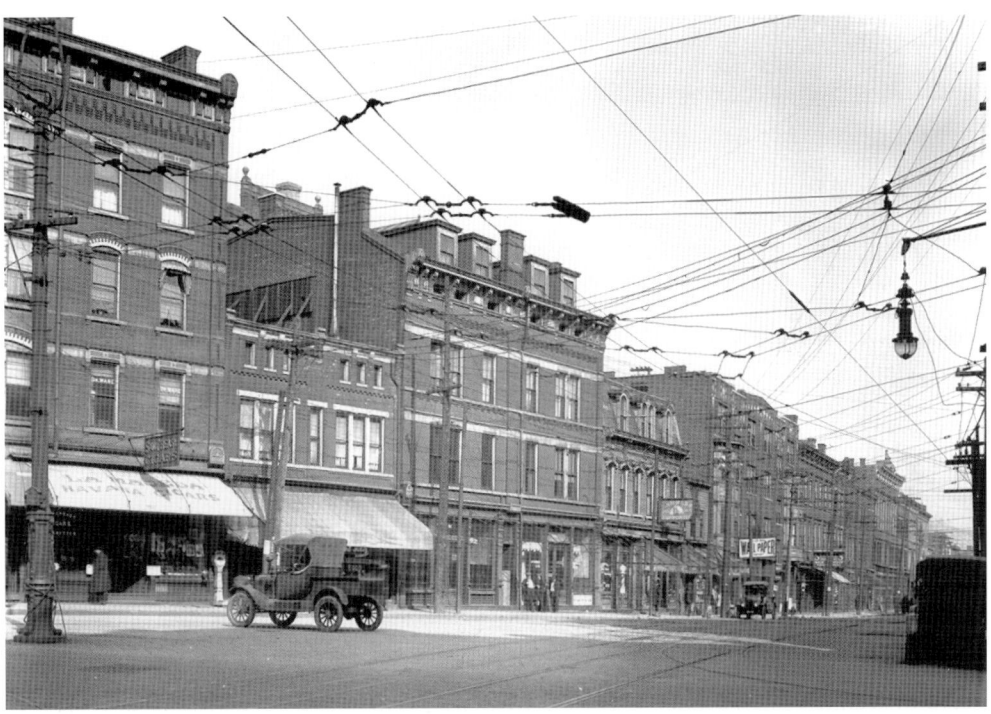

A melting-pot neighborhood before the Great Depression, the city's West End gave rise to a number of fine boxers, Italian, Jewish, and German. Over the years, names like Tony LaRosa, Vincent Hambright, Danny Millilo, Jimmy and Frankie Zanzoni, K. O. Mars, Maxey Koshover, Frank "Kidd Kotzie" Katzler, Kid Leaders, and Joey and Frankie Palmo all fought in the gyms there, along with those in Over-the-Rhine.

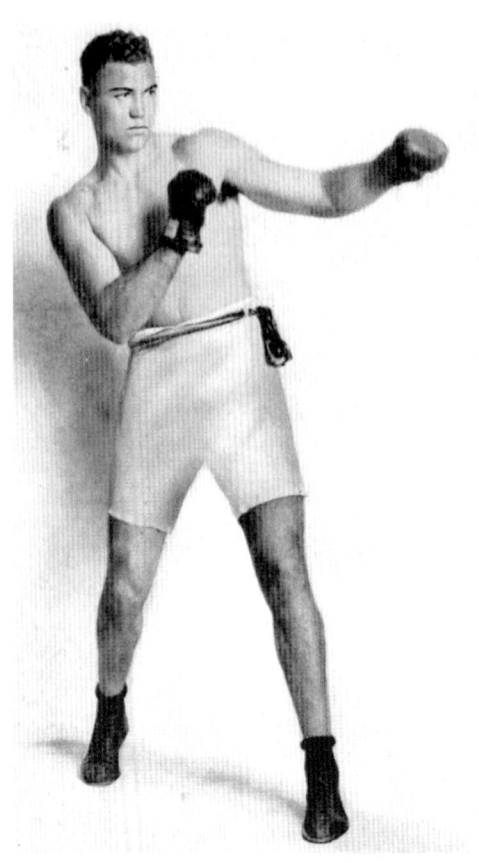

On July 4, 1919, Jack Dempsey, the "Manassa Mauler," beat Jess Willard unmercifully, winning the heavyweight championship on a technical knockout in the third round. Like many other sports figures of his day who wanted to capitalize on a big moment, Dempsey hit the vaudeville circuit. His first stop after winning the belt was Cincinnati, where he earned $5,000 for a week's engagement at Chester Park. The park was still a popular summertime place for Cincinnatians, with a lake, vaudeville shows, an amusement park, bicycle races, and fine dining. Admission fees for the Dempsey act ranged from 50¢ to $1, with the promise of sparring exhibitions as well. Dempsey stood on stage and told how he avoided Willard's tremendous right uppercut until he could pummel him into submission. He performed two shows daily, and the crowds loved him.

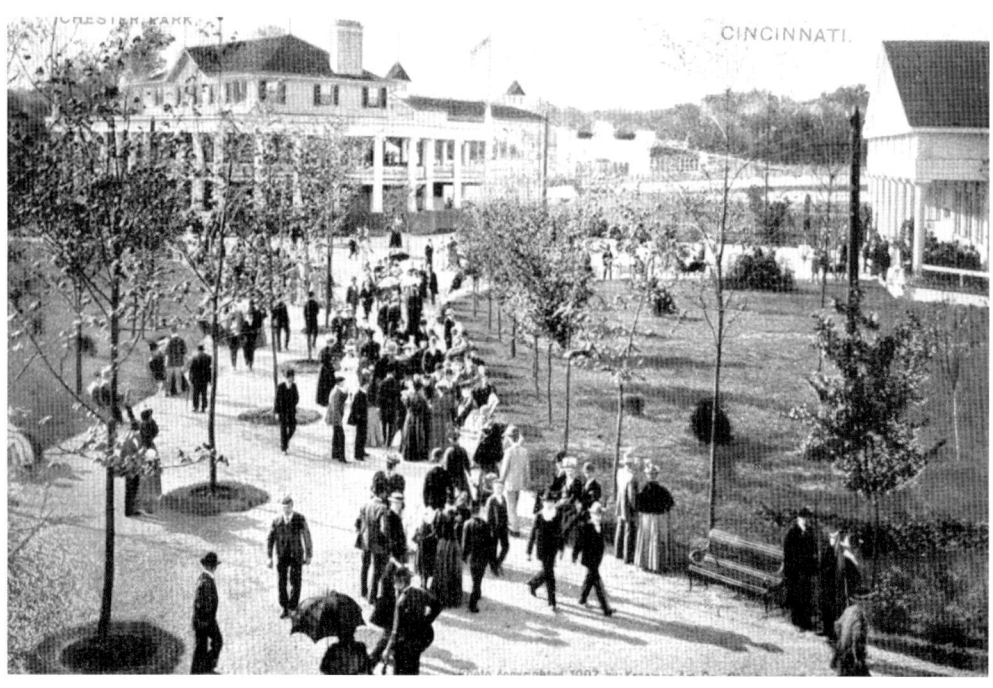

Struggling to get control of professional boxing, the city established a commission in 1919 that would regulate the sport by registering boxers, trainers, promoters, and managers and governing the finances from taxes to purses. A policy book was printed, setting forth the rules for everything from the bouts themselves along with judging them to overseeing the payouts. In 1983, the local boxing commission was dissolved when Ohio created a state boxing commission.

RULES and REGULATIONS

of the

Cincinnati Boxing Commission

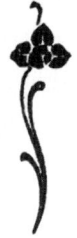

ADOPTED: OCTOBER 1st, 1919

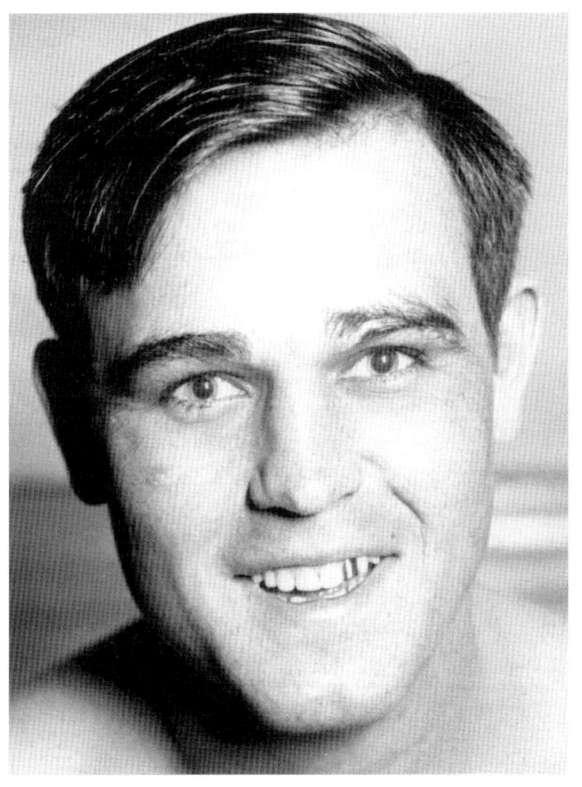

One of the best fighters to come out of the northern Kentucky ranks was Kenton County native Joe Anderson. Anderson's first four professional fights were across the river in Cincinnati, beginning with Rapid Waters in 1922. A top middleweight contender who often fought on both sides of the Ohio River, his last fight came in 1936 against Dandy Harry Smith, when he broke his arm in the second round and it became a compound fracture in the fifth. Anderson finished his career with a record of 56-20-22 and later operated the Bluegrass Gym in Covington, Kentucky.

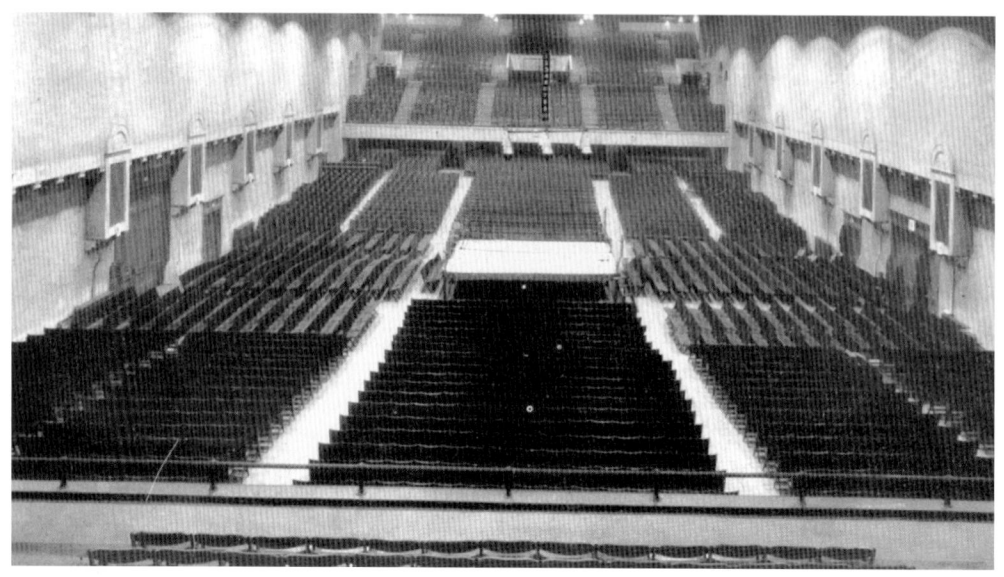

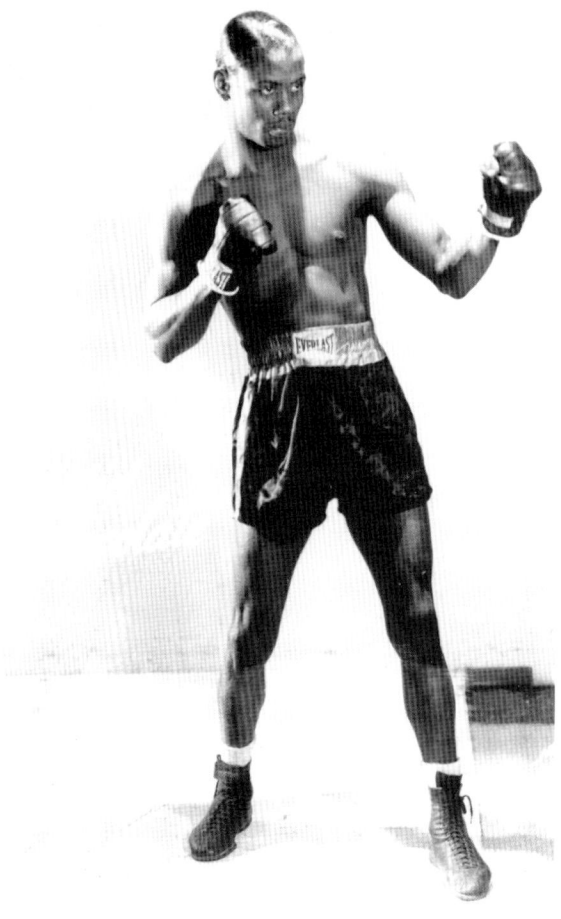

When Kid Chocolate, the Cuban featherweight, came to town in 1932, his effect on local boxing went well beyond the Music Hall matchup against Johnny Farr. Kid Chocolate's real name was Eligio Sardinius Montalvo, and he was as stylish as his name, driving through the West End in an open car and waving to the neighborhood kids. One child in particular noted the boxer's smooth manner and elegant suits. This is what he wanted to be when he grew up. So eleven-year-old Ezzard Charles jumped at the promoter's offer to set up chairs in Music Hall in exchange for a ticket to the fight. Along with other boys, Charles set up the chairs but then the promoter—and the ticket—were mysteriously unavailable. Charles and his friends had to listen to the fight on the radio. The action captured his imagination, and from then on, Ezzard Charles considered boxing his future career.

Born in Messina, Sicily, in 1916, Charles Francis Curro came with his family to America a few years later. Pictured here in 1928 at his first communion with his godfather, Sabastiano LaRosa, another Sicilian immigrant, Curro took up amateur boxing the next year at the age of 13. Curro boxed out of the Friars' Club on Liberty Street but gave up the sport several years later when his front teeth were knocked out and he promised his mother he would not lose any more. (Photograph courtesy of the Curro family.)

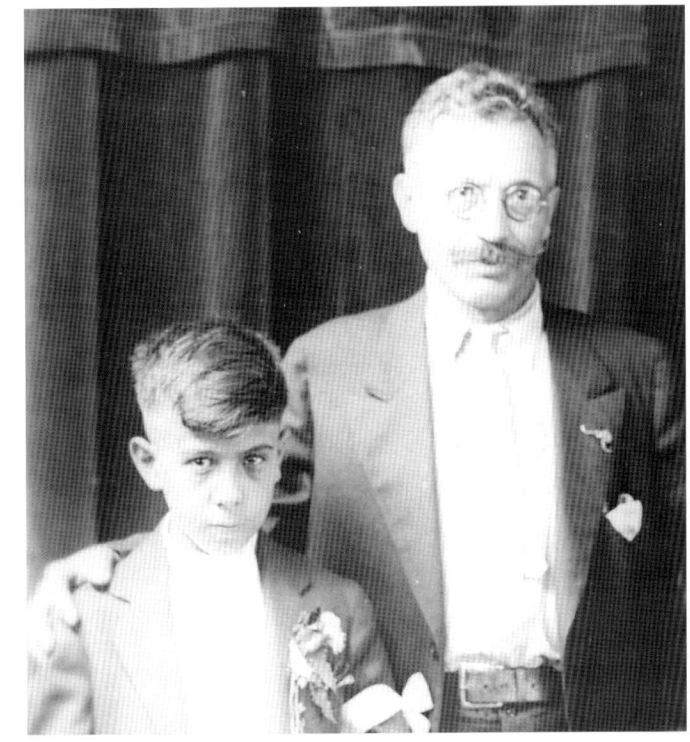

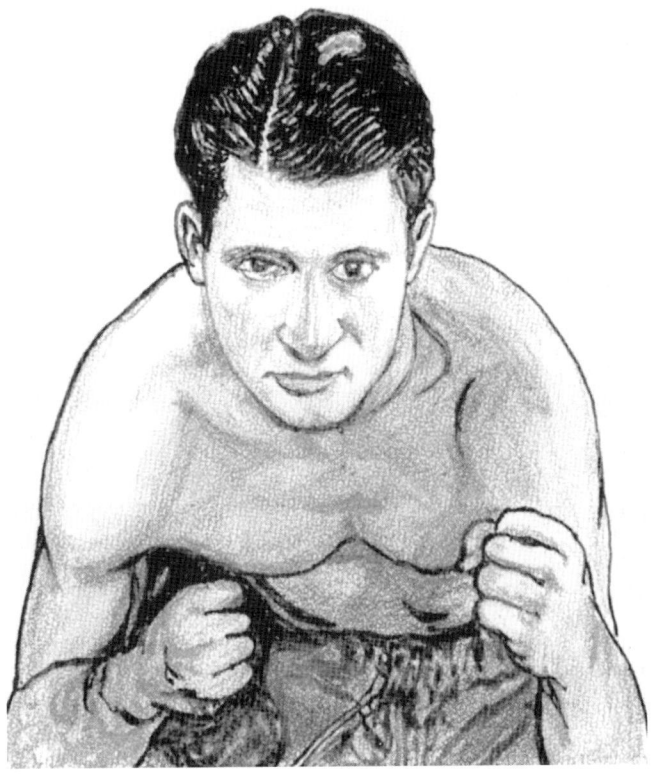

Sabastiano's son, Tony LaRosa, became a notable local pro. Several years older than Curro, LaRosa fought as a lightweight and was a huge draw in Cincinnati, particularly when he boxed other local Italian favorites in monthly club fights. Curro remembers sitting on an empty spaghetti box as a boy and watching LaRosa train: "He was just a beautiful southpaw boxer, and always said a left hand sets up a good right hand." (Image courtesy of Buddy LaRosa.)

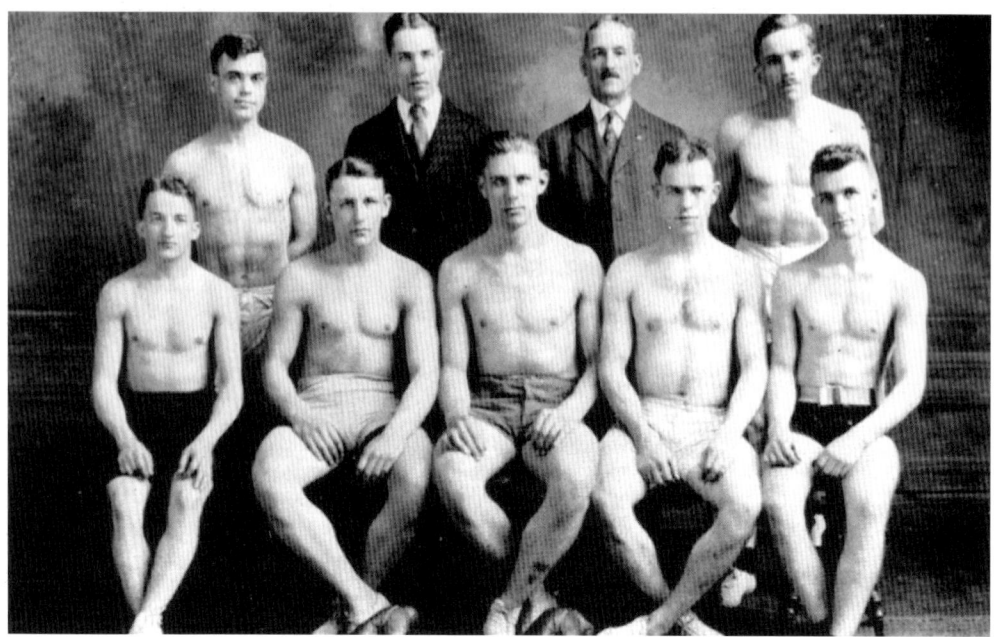

The University of Cincinnati formed a boxing team in 1921, having only one match with Miami University. The result was a draw, with each team winning four bouts. The boxing team grew out of the College of Engineering's "Hobby Hour," in which Dean Herman Schneider decreed that students should spend a part of every day doing anything except engineering. The aim was to make students well-rounded individuals.

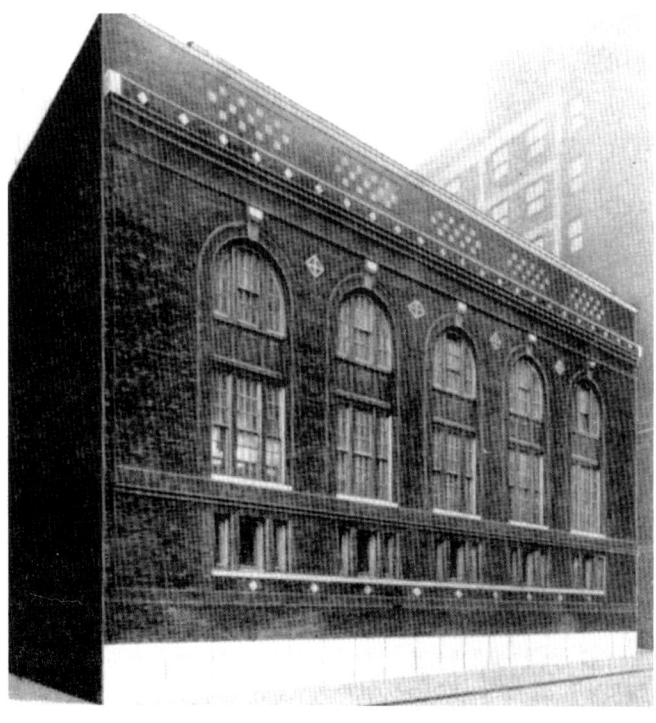

Founded in 1915 by the Archdiocese of Cincinnati, the Fenwick Club provided a place where both Catholic and non-Catholic boys could come for learning, athletics, and civil and spiritual improvement—rather closely following the ideals of the Progressive Era. A gymnasium was opened in 1922 on Fifth Street, and the Fenwick Club became a center for teaching boxing to Cincinnati's young men. Over the years, some of the best local amateur fighters came out of the Fenwick.

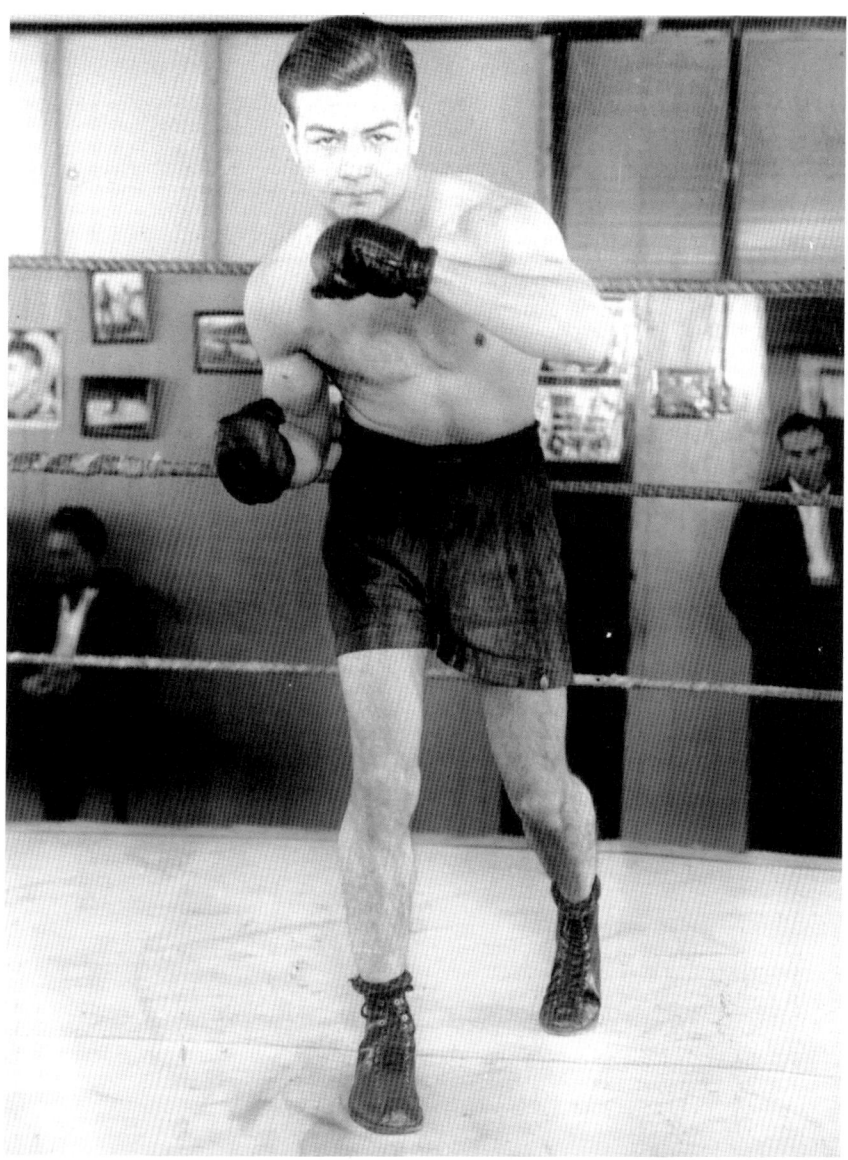

Freddie Miller was Cincinnati's first homegrown world champion. A beautiful southpaw featherweight from Over-the-Rhine, Miller was born Frederick Y. Muller on April 3, 1911. His parents, Wilhelm and Elizabeth, were German immigrants who ran a bakery in the neighborhood. By his early teens, he had dropped out of school and was fighting under the tutelage of local trainer Danny Davis. On April 1, 1927, two days before his 16th birthday, he had his first fight across the river in Fort Thomas, Kentucky, where he knocked out Billy Barnes in the third round. Amateur fighter Charlie Curro, who also grew up in Over-the-Rhine, remembers that Miller was "always in the ring" either training or fighting a bout. "His brother Louis was a friend of mine, but at first I thought Freddie was pigheaded and snotty. He really was the opposite—it's just that he was working so hard on his boxing skills. He always kept his right hand out to set up the left, and his lateral motion was perfect."

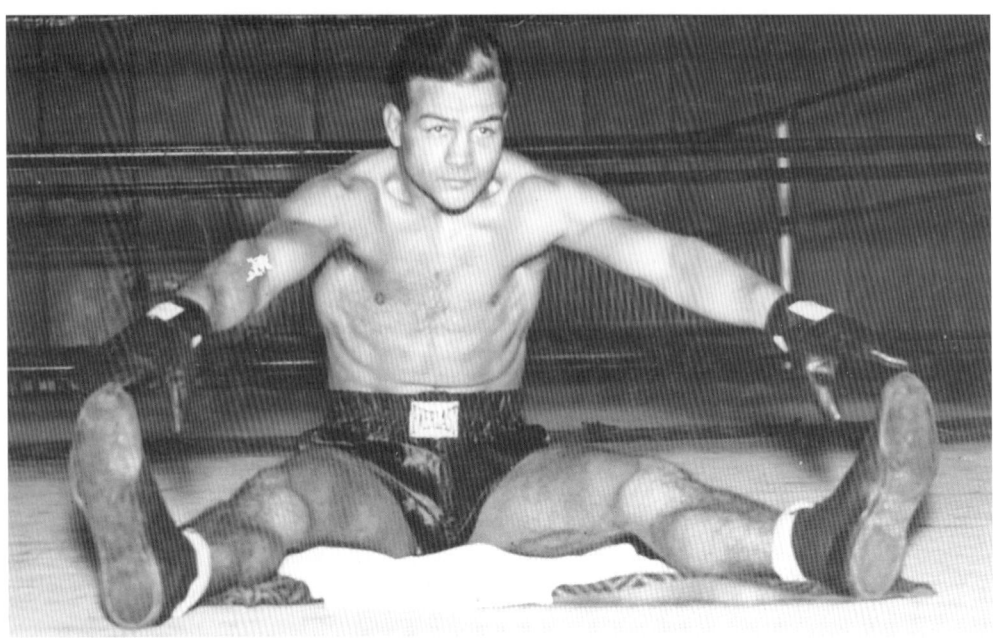

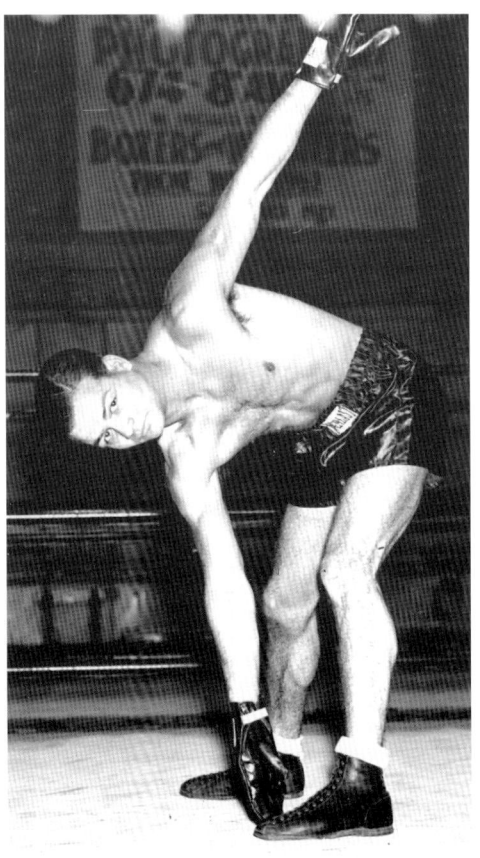

As a southpaw, Freddie Miller began building his record and rising in the estimation of boxing officials and sportswriters, but it was sometimes difficult to find an opponent to give him a fight. Left-handed boxers have a reputation for upsetting the punching and movement rhythms of right-handers. To help get around this stigma in the early stages of Miller's career, his manager sometimes had him pose for publicity shots as a right-hander. The ruse did not last long. Miller's long list of victories made him a familiar name, and a contender for the belt. On January 27, 1932, Freddie took on Battling Battalino at Music Hall to try and take the National Boxing Association (NBA) featherweight championship. More than 2,000 fans roundly booed the fighters when there was little action in the first two rounds. In the third, Miller tapped Battalino twice, sending him to the canvas, but the referee stopped the fight when it was obvious Battalino was unwilling to battle. He was fined $5,000 for his inaction. Miller was paid for three rounds work but denied the belt. The fans were given back their ticket money.

The next year, in 1933, Miller won the NBA featherweight championship for real with a victory over Tommy Paul in Chicago. After several defenses of his title, Miller fought at the Armory in Louisville, Kentucky, against Paul Dazzo on May 4, 1934, the first legal title fight in Kentucky after the general assembly okayed such bouts. He knocked out Dazzo in the eighth. For three years, Miller successfully defended his crown, including notable challenges from Jackie Sharkey, Johnny Pena, Petey Sarron, and the British champion, Nel Tarleton. At the end of his career, Miller would come home to Cincinnati, help train the likes of Ezzard Charles, Joey Discepoli, and Pat Iacobucci, and become a noted ballroom dancer and bridge player.

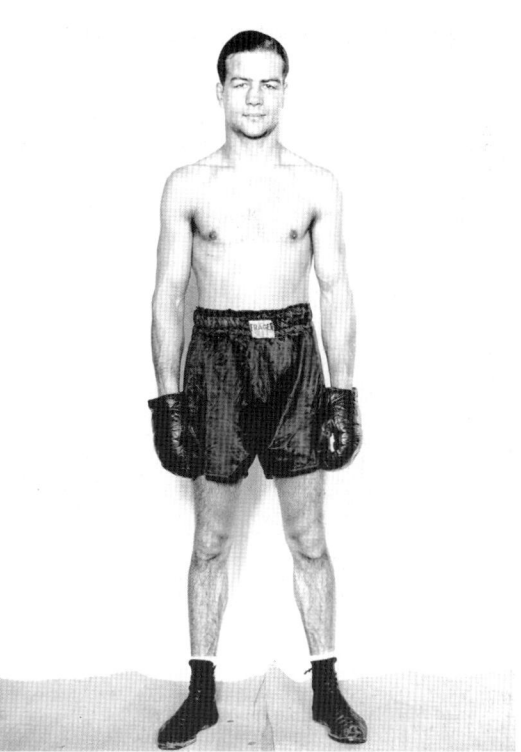

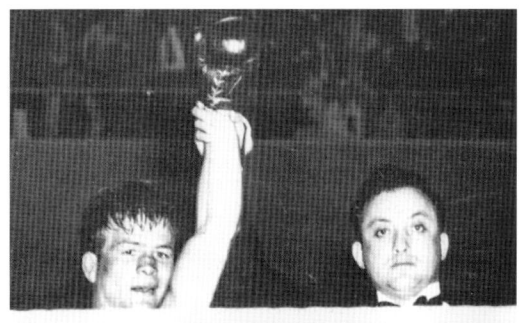

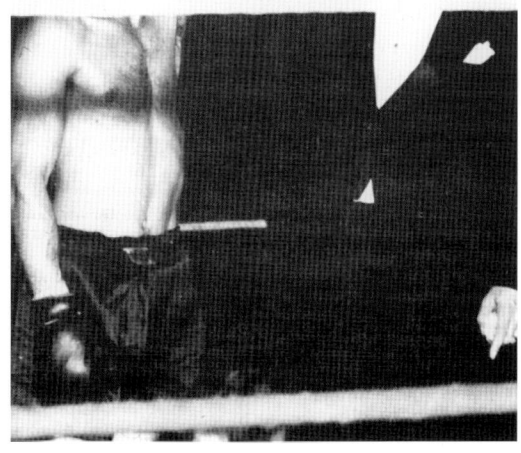

CINCINNATI BOXING

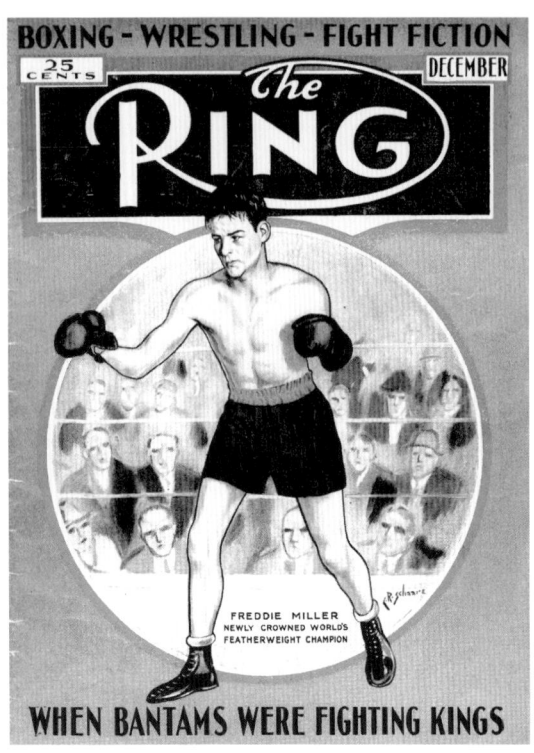

After winning the NBA featherweight crown in 1933, Freddie Miller felt like he was on top of the world. *Ring Magazine,* the "Bible of boxing," featured him on the cover for an article about the excitement the fighters in the lower-weight divisions brought to the sport. A West Coast tabloid called *The Knockout* also featured him, claiming the champion as one of California's own after he started training in Los Angeles. The back cover featured a photograph of the up-and-coming Mexican featherweight Chalky Wright, whose manager stated that "Chalky Wright is the berries, bush and all . . . He wants to fight Freddie Miller for the Featherweight title." Wright did, in 1934, and lost a 10-round decision to the champion.

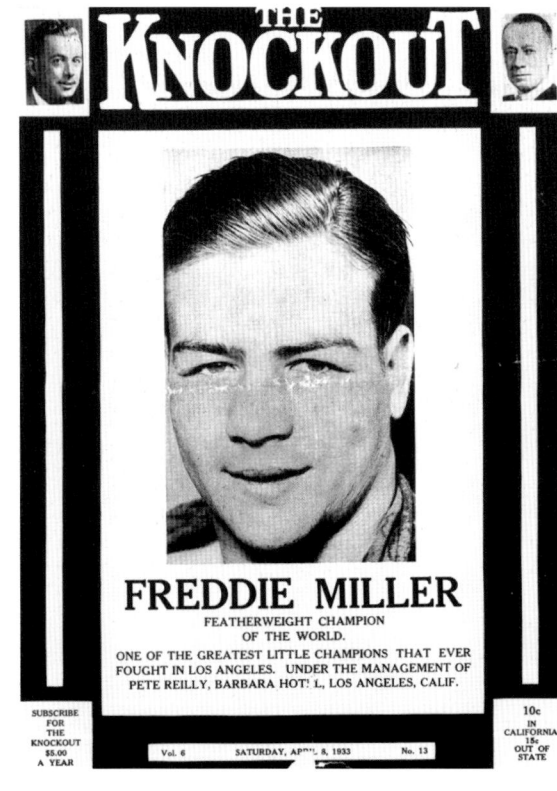

4

THE GOLDEN AGE

1934–1960

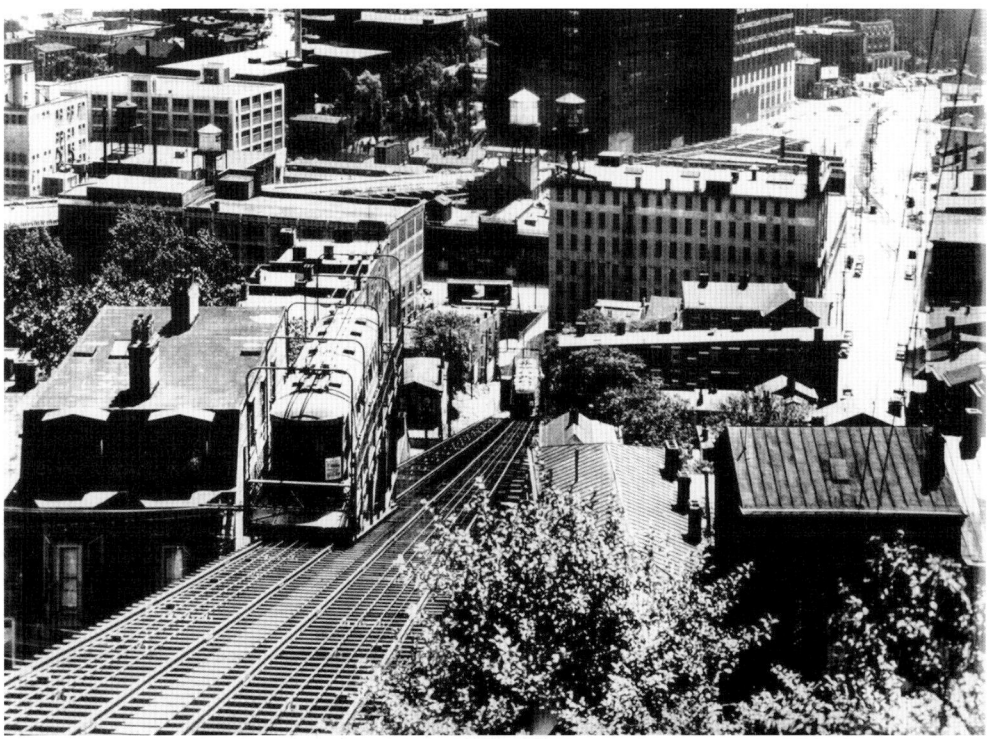

Boxing moved into a golden age in the 1940s and 1950s with the advent of television broadcasts. The fight ring was perfect for the medium at a time when typically only one camera was used to show the action. In the city ringed by hills, the bouts were avidly followed on television at home and in bars and saloons, and, for those who wanted to see live action, there often were matches six nights a week.

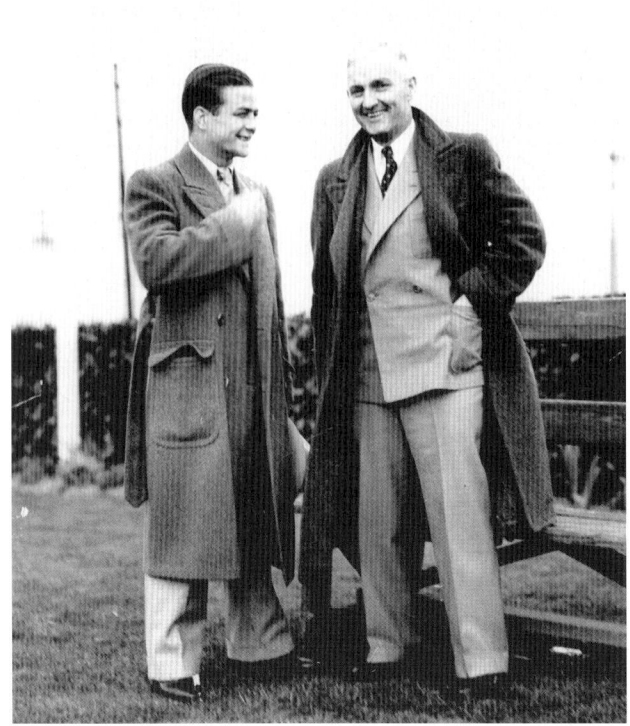

Freddie Miller poses for a photograph with his manager, Pete Reilly. Reilly is the man who brought Miller out to California for training and to line up some fights. In 1933 and 1934, Miller fought 15 times on the West Coast, losing only 3 of them. In his career, Miller had 237 bouts, losing only 22. The only time he was knocked out was in his final fight.

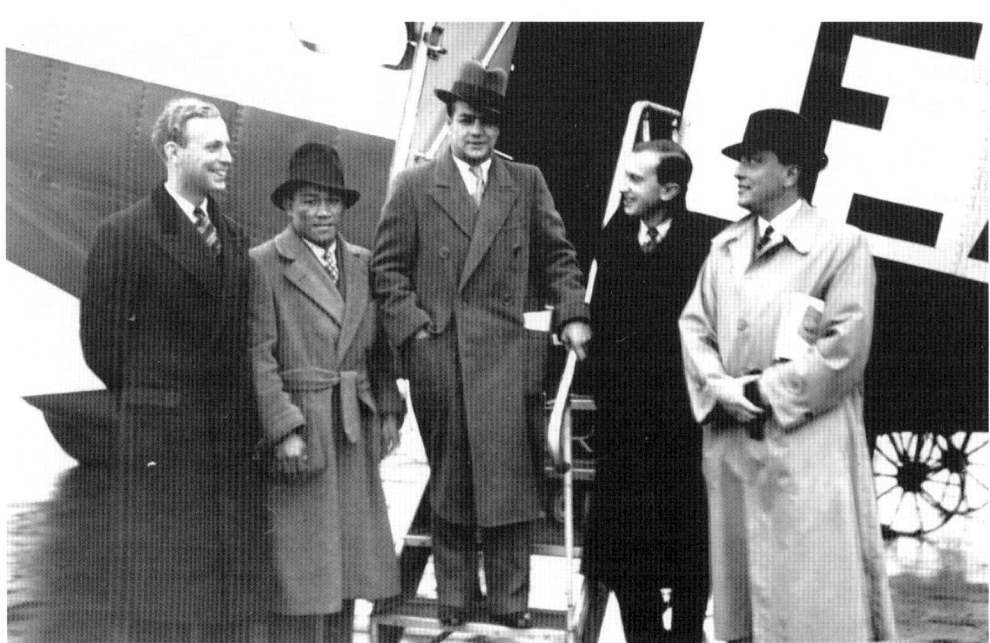

Freddie Miller posing on the steps of an airplane was entirely in keeping with his globe-trotting career. More than any other boxer of his time, Miller traveled the world to fight, and he was immensely popular in Europe, especially in England and Spain. In the last couple of years he fought, he added South Africa and South America to his boxing journeys in 37 countries.

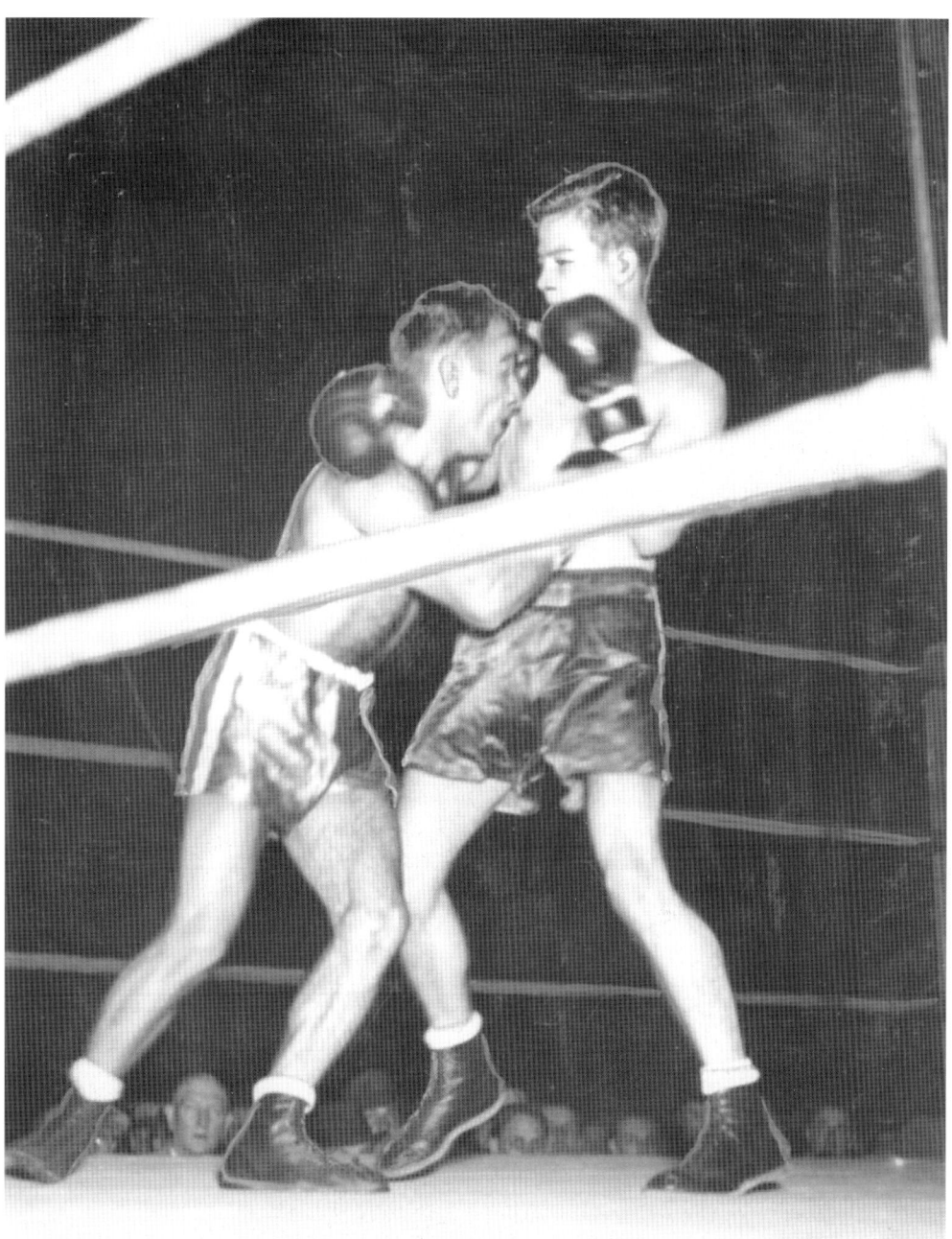

Between 1933 and 1937, Freddie Miller and Petey Sarron fought each other six times, splitting the wins at three apiece. For their fourth fight, on May 11, 1936, the bout was held in Griffith Stadium in Washington, D.C. The match was their typical slugfest, with Sarron coming out on top in 15 rounds and capturing Miller's NBA world featherweight title. It was the same championship that Miller had successfully defended against Sarron's challenge just two months earlier. Two weeks after losing his title, Miller was back home in Cincinnati for another fight.

FOLLOW THE CROWD TO COLUMBIA GYM,

MONDAY, JANUARY 11th
FREDDIE MILLER
10 Rounds   VS.   10 Rounds
JIMMIE VAUGHN

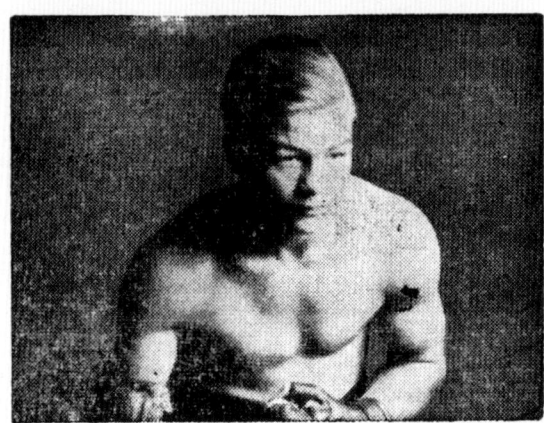

FREDDIE MILLER, former Champ and greatest featherweight since days of Johnny Kilbane—who seeks revenge for loss to Vaughn at Cincinnati last summer.

10- Lloyd PINE	vs	Sammy Angott -10
8 FRED EILER	vs.	HENRY FIRPO 8
6 JOEY LaPELLE	vs.	CECIL POWELL 6

1000 seats at 80c;   Reserved $1.65 and $2.20
Reservations   SHawnee 5040

On May 27, 1936, Freddie Miller lost a fight in Cincinnati to Jimmie Vaughn of Cleveland. At the opening bell, Vaughn came in aggressively, at first trading punches and then covering up before unleashing a counterpunch. He out-pointed Miller in a 10-round decision. For the rematch on January 11, 1937, the promoters sent out flyers touting Miller's greatness in the history of the featherweight division. The 10-rounder was held in Louisville's Columbia Gym, and Miller got his revenge. Miller had won seven straight bouts in the seven months since his defeat at the hands of Vaughn, so the left-hander came back and dominated the fight. He took Vaughn the distance and won the victory on points. Miller's last fight was in 1940. He died May 9, 1962. The hundreds of fights had taken their toll. In his last days, he began having blackouts and was coughing a lot. After his wife found him slumped over the breakfast table, he was rushed to the hospital where he later died of a blood clot in his brain.

Collegiate boxing began at Xavier University in 1927. Behind the coaching of Harold "Buck" Greene and middleweight Eddie Burns (photograph at right), the "Battling Musketeers" squared off against West Point, Washington and Lee, and fellow Catholic institution Notre Dame. After a 10-year hiatus, the Xavier boxing program was resurrected, and under the tutelage of Joseph J. Fillipone, nearly 60 students began their training at the historic Fenwick Club. After teaching calisthenics and the basic fundamentals of the sport, Fillipone put the young boxers through daily workouts and sparring. In 1939, Xavier battled the University of Kentucky in two hotly contested meets, emerging victorious in the latter. (Photographs courtesy of Xavier University.)

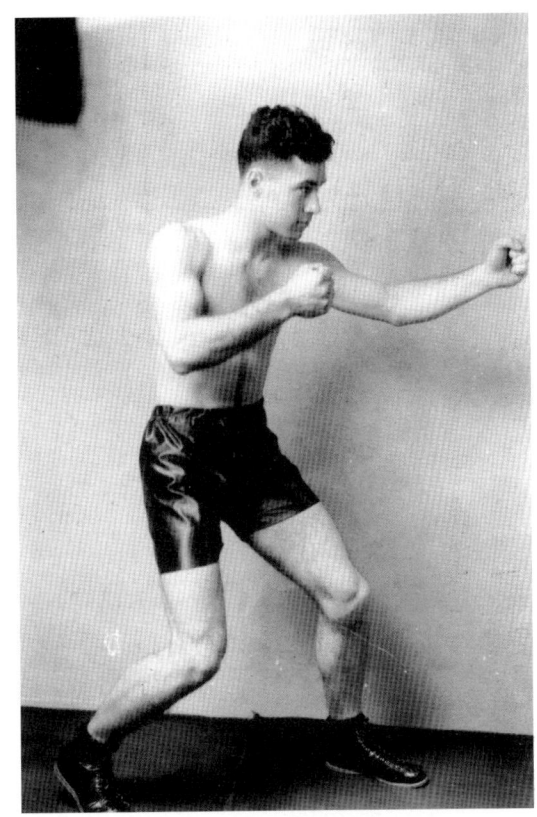

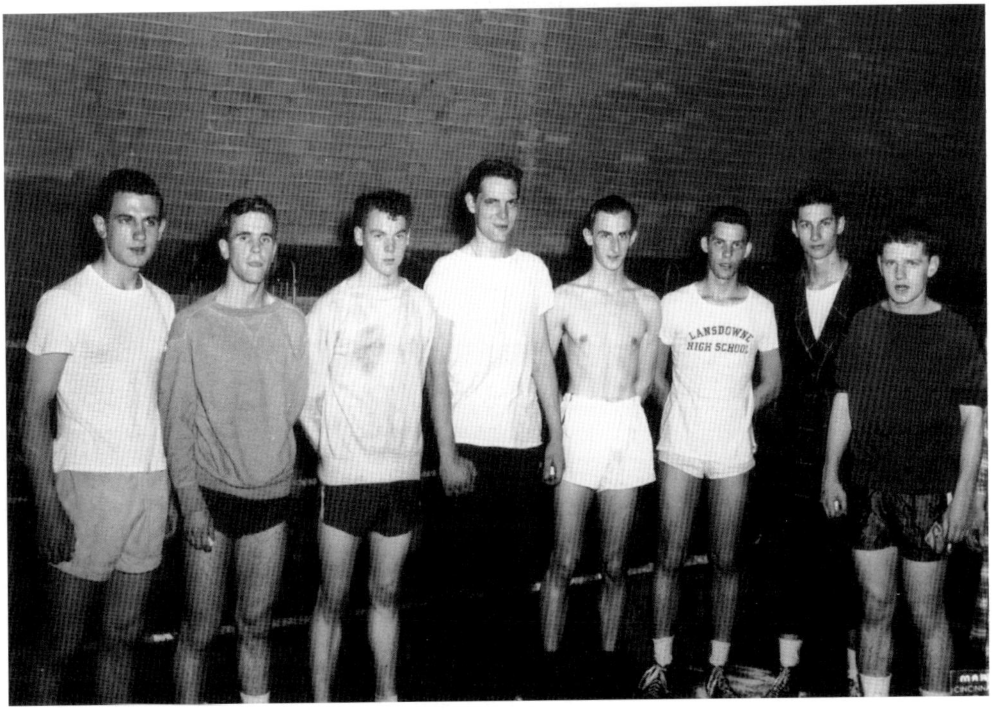

CINCINNATI BOXING

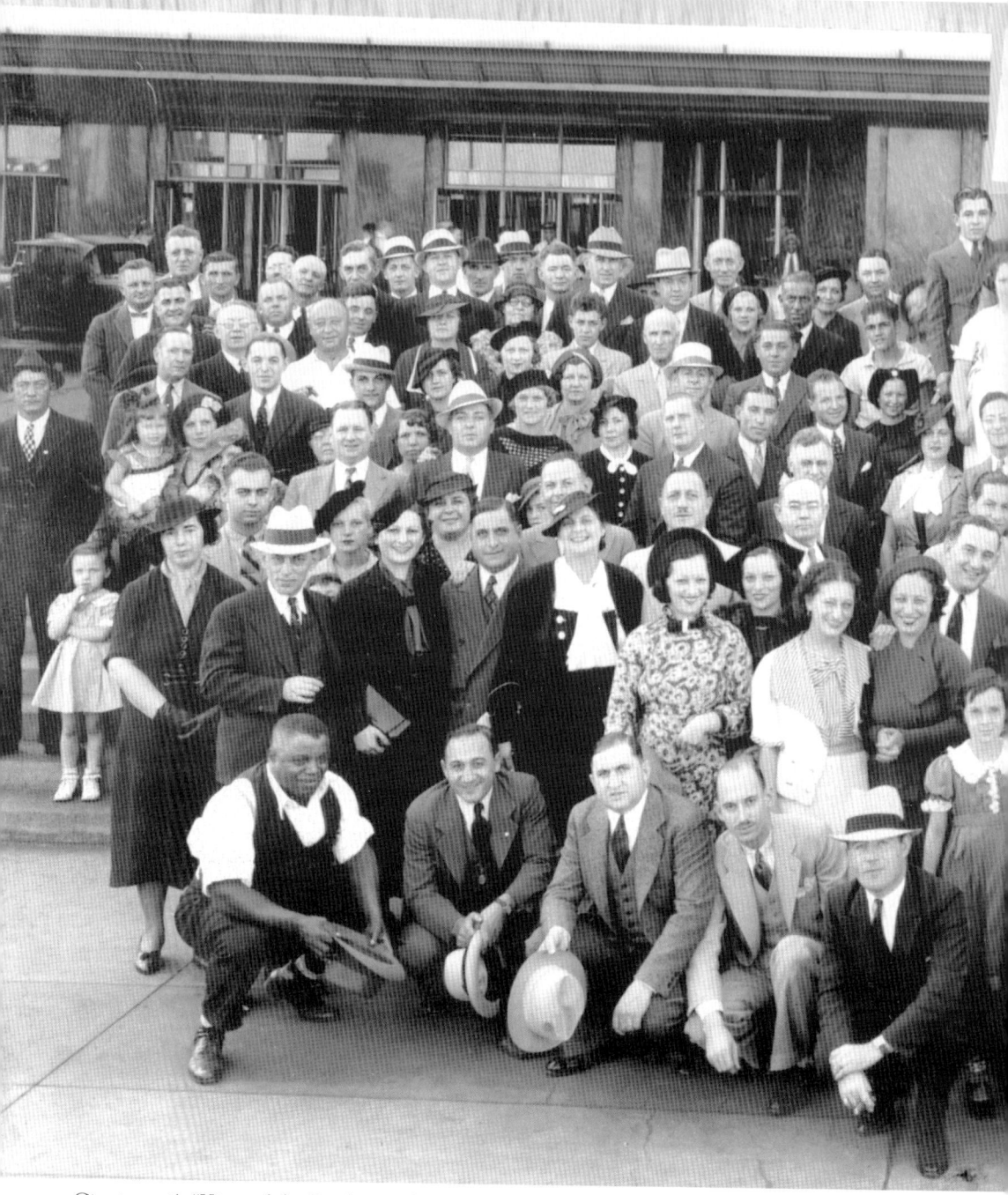

Cincinnati's "King of the Bookies," Ike Hyams was more than just a bookmaker. He was also a supporter of Amateur Athletic Union (AAU) boxing, a local Republican, a businessman, and an entrepreneur who liked to organize excursions to sporting events in Chicago and New York. He particularly enjoyed gathering local fight fans for a train trip that included a championship bout, along with a side trip to whatever racetrack was nearby. For the Joe Louis–Max Baer

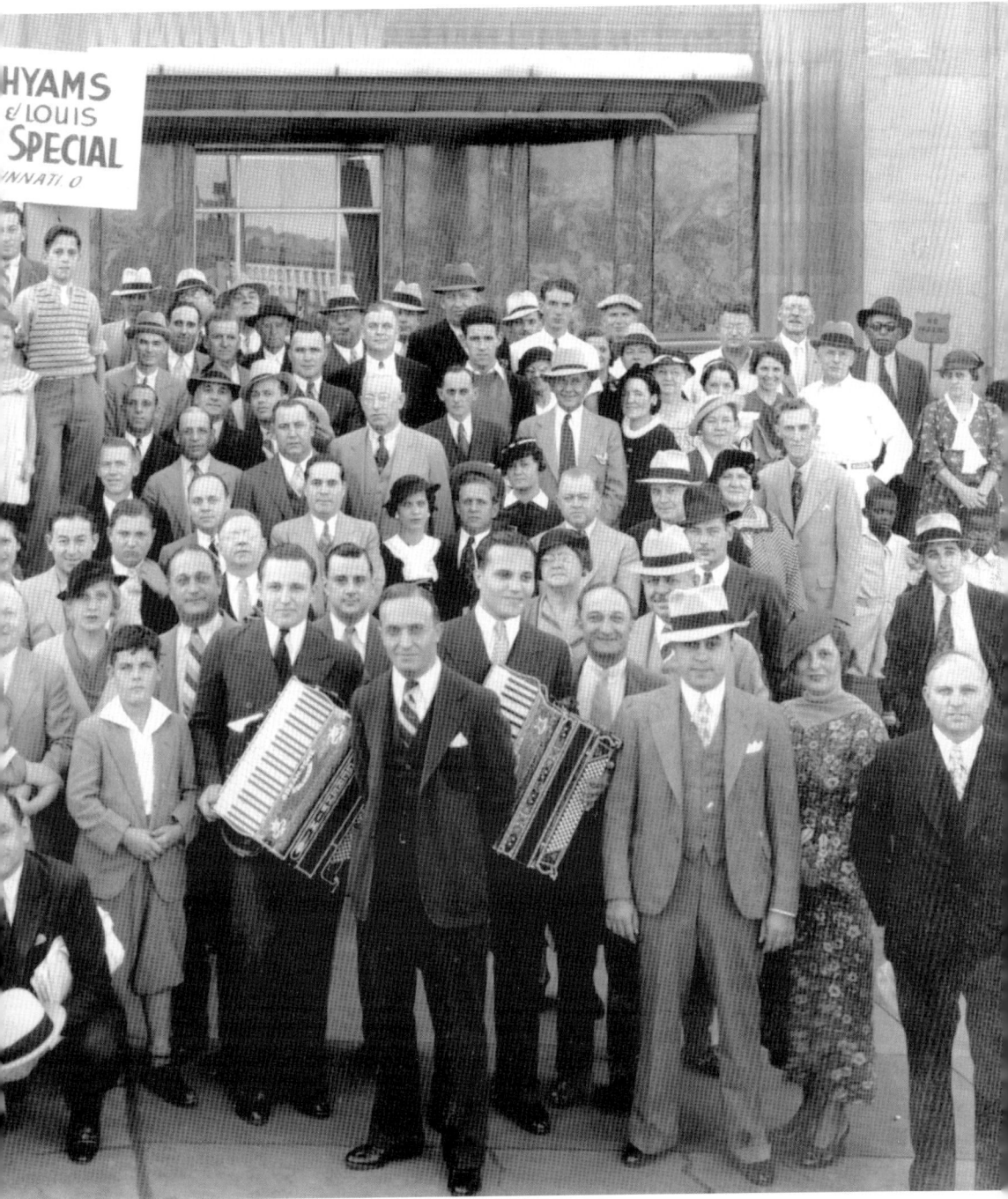

contest in Yankee Stadium in 1934, Hyams poses with his group in front of Union Terminal before boarding the train. It was quite a send-off (note the accordion players), and the diverse crowd included Hyams associates like Red Schneider, owner of the Yorkshire Nightclub, and Ben "Big Porky" Lassoff of Newport. On September 24, the tour group saw Louis knock out Baer in the fourth round. (Photograph courtesy of Stuart Hodesh.)

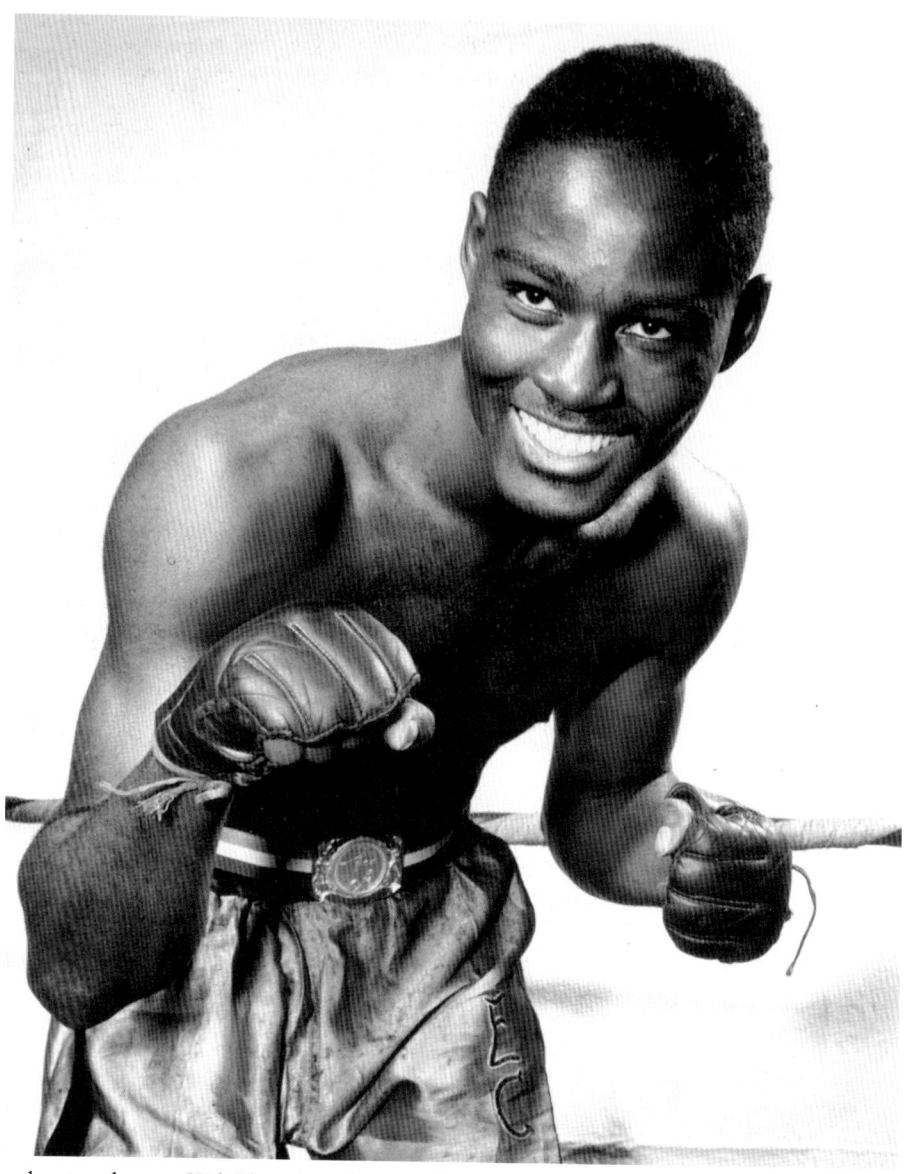

From the time he saw Kid Chocolate driving through his neighborhood, Ezzard Charles wanted to be a boxer. Charles was born May 7, 1921, in Lawrenceville, Georgia, and named after the physician, Webster Ezzard, who delivered him. When he was nine, his parents divorced and young Ezzard was sent to Cincinnati where he was raised by his grandmother, and, for the first time, he attended school. Hanging around the gyms, he began boxing, eventually winning the Golden Gloves title. Charles attended Woodward High School, wearing a coat and tie every day. When the smaller kids wanted to box him, he would just smile, put his hands in his pockets, and bob and weave as they futilely tried to land a punch. He ran up a long list of victories in the Cincinnati arenas and worked part-time at the clothing store of Max Elkus, who also helped manage him. His grandmother gave her permission for him to box professionally as long as his childhood friend Richard Christmas stayed close to keep an eye on him.

Attorney Theodore M. Berry became Charles's legal guardian while Charles was still in high school. Later the first African American mayor in Cincinnati history, Berry saw it as his duty to guide and protect Charles as he rose in his career. His mentorship ranged from the legal matters of contracts to once admonishing him in a letter in 1943, "Make up your mind to be satisfied with one suit. Remember we are at war, there are material shortages, and all citizens are required to make sacrifices."

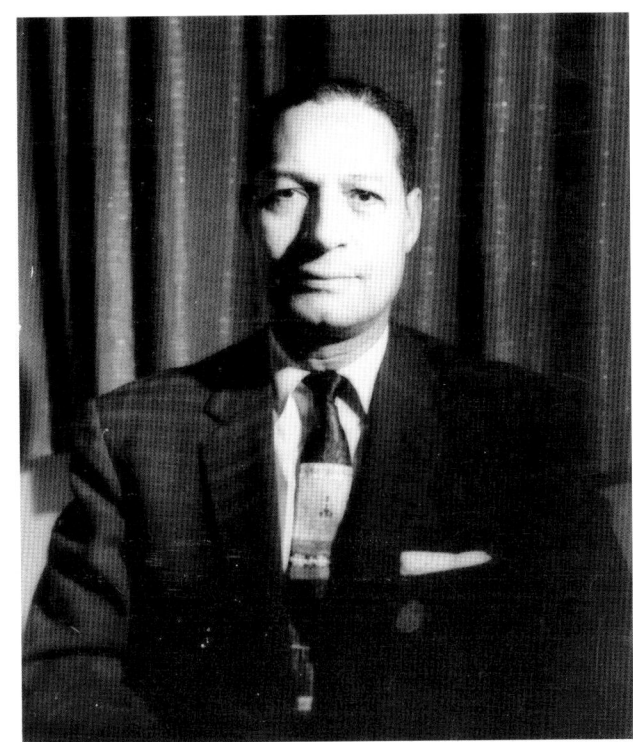

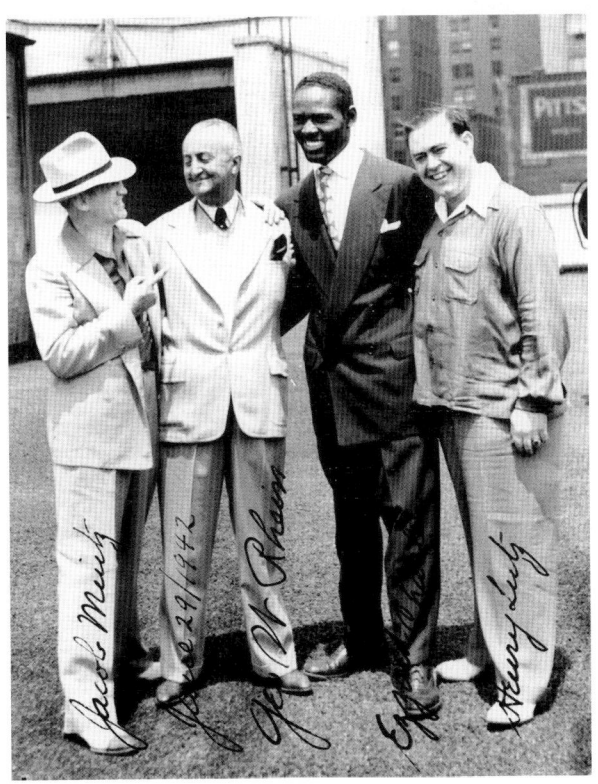

Berry sometimes signed himself in letters to Charles as "Liaison Officer, Group Morale," and he was the one who tempered and counseled everyone else. As Charles's management group grew larger (here in a 1942 photograph are Jake Mintz, George Rhein, and Henry Lutz), Berry felt more obligation than ever to guide Charles into becoming a sober, thoughtful man. (Photograph courtesy of Buddy LaRosa.)

CINCINNATI BOXING

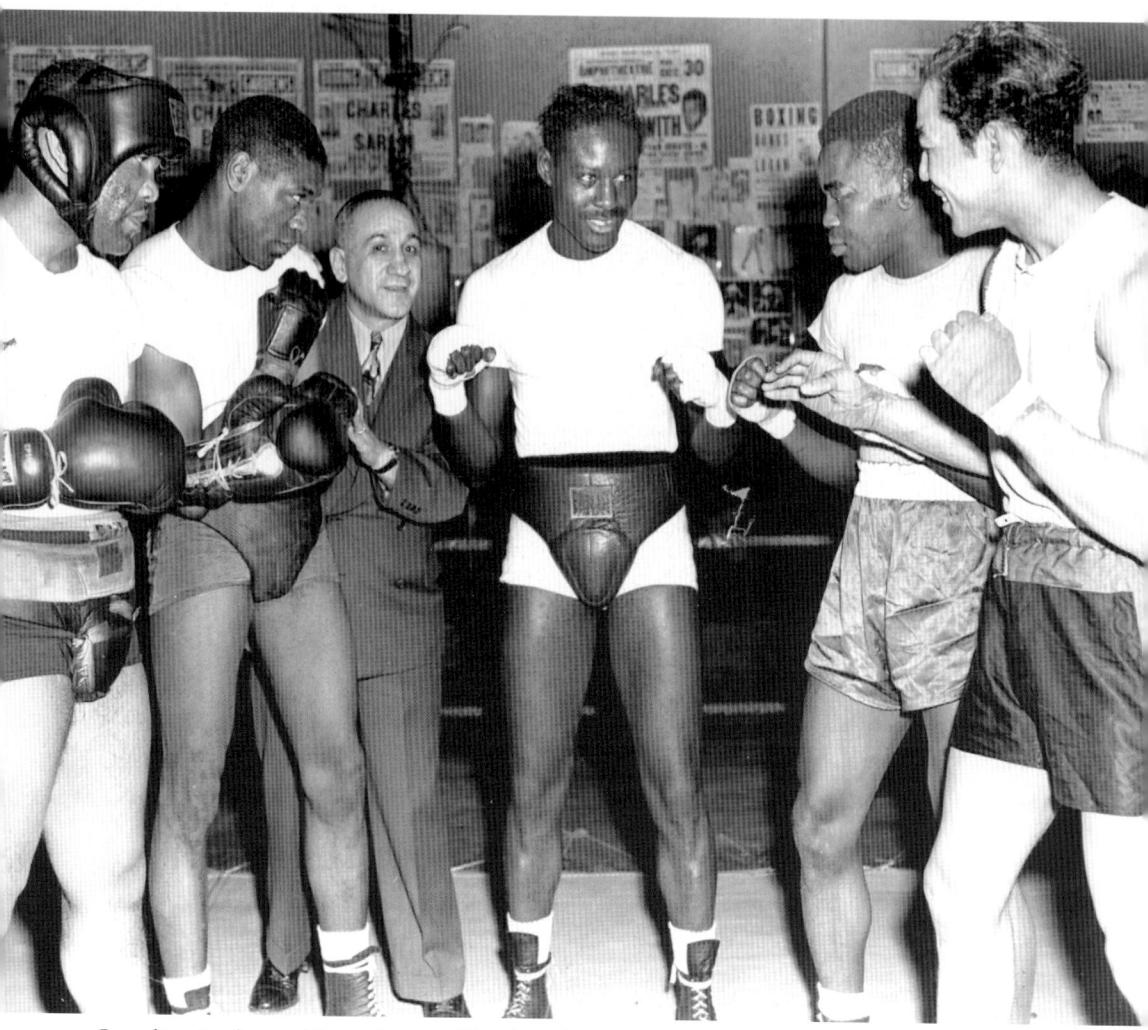

Standing in the middle with one of his handlers, Sam Becker, Ezzard Charles poses with other fighters managed by Becker. On the street, as unassuming and quiet as he was, Charles attracted attention because of his handsome features and fine suits. Very early on, Theodore M. Berry tried to guide him in managing his income wisely, but Charles often listened to the entreaties of others. So Berry would lend his counsel as best he could. One of his early ventures was the "Ezzard Charles Colosseum" on Seventh Street. Charles's notion was to have a building housing a dance floor, swimming pool, poolroom, basketball court, and a boxing gym. Plans were begun, stationary with his high school senior picture was printed, and renovations to the building started, but the investment ultimately failed, a pattern Charles would repeat throughout his career. His boxing management later became muddled when Pittsburgh matchmaker Jake Mintz and businessman Tom Tannas insinuated themselves into Charles's trust and, unfortunately, led the fighter away from Berry, the Elkus family, and George Rhein, the Cincinnatians who cared about him and guided him into his professional career.

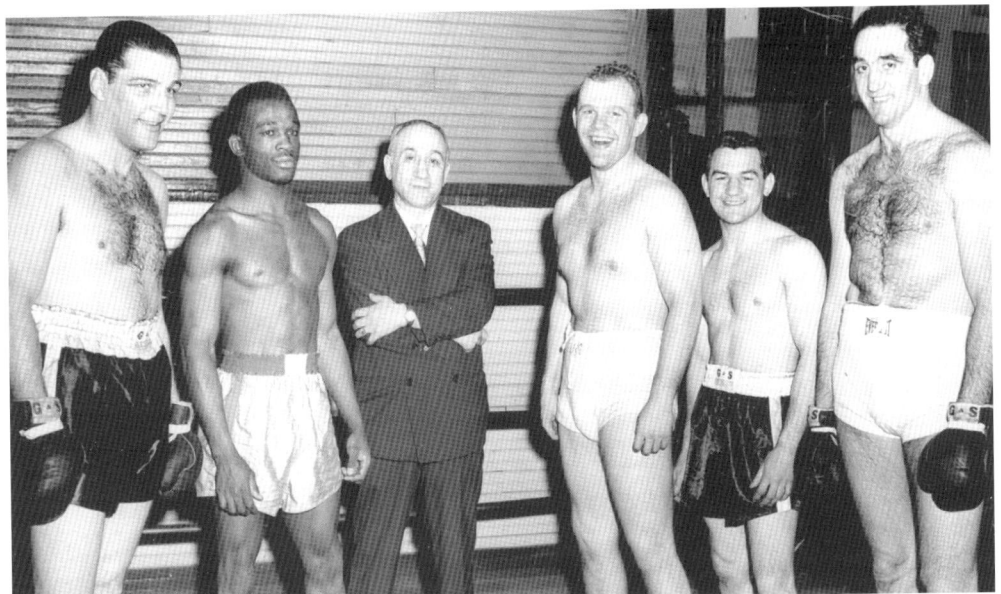

With his brother Sam, former boxer Benny Becker went into the fight game, establishing themselves as local promoters and managers. Earning some success in Cincinnati, they ventured further afield, representing boxers in the Midwest and on the East Coast. In the photograph above, Benny Becker is pictured in the middle of five of his boxers, from left to right, heavyweight Lee Oma, lightweight Wallace "Bud" Smith (who would win a title), heavyweight Ronnie Wulf, featherweight Pat Iacobucci, and heavyweight Bill Weinberg. In the image to the left, the giants Oma and Weinberg clown around over the heads of the little guys. (Photographs courtesy of Buddy LaRosa.)

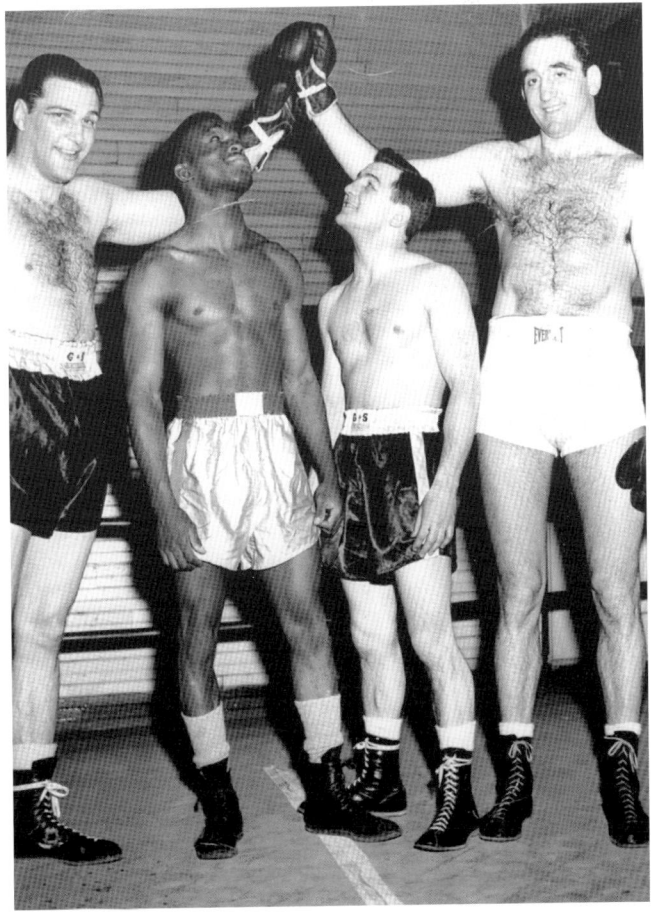

CINCINNATI BOXING

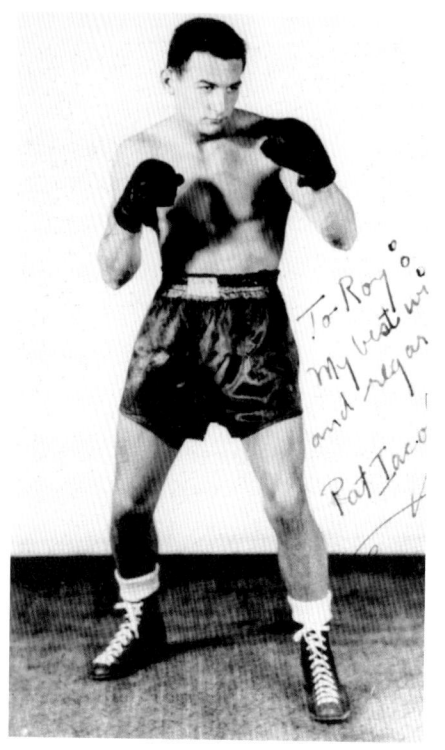

Fighting from 1945 to 1953, Pat Iacobucci was an intense scrapping featherweight in Cincinnati who sometimes trained at the Fenwick Club. He was a favorite of local boxing fans at Music Hall, where he fought many of his early matches. One of his most notable fights was November 10, 1947, in Music Hall when he took on another local fighter, Joe Discepoli. The fight is still remembered as one of the best as the boxers slugged each other to a 10-round draw.

BOXING
PARKWAY ARENA COURTESY PASS
ADMIT ONE
Good Only Night of
WEDNESDAY, AUG. 9
This Pass when Presented at Box Office with Payment of 25 Cents Service Charge will Entitle Bearer to One Ringside Reserved Seat

Signed Parkway Arena

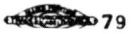

CENTRAL PARKWAY AND FINDLAY STREET

Located at Findlay Street and Central Parkway in Over-the-Rhine, the Parkway Arena was an outdoor summer venue that featured professional boxing and wrestling matches. The arena was built so that the ring was below ground level, with the seats leading down to it. Surrounding it were some trees that the neighborhood kids would climb to get a free view of the boxers, but they had to beware the wrath of Ross Leader, the Parkway's owner and matchmaker. If he saw them, he would rush out, his ever-present cigar lighting the way, to yell at them and pull them from their perches.

For a publicity photograph, promoter Sam Becker hit the streets for some roadwork with his fighter Ronnie Wulf. It looks like it may have been the first exercise Becker had in a while. Except for just an occasional bout out of town, Wulf fought his entire career in the Cincinnati area. (Photograph courtesy of Buddy LaRosa.)

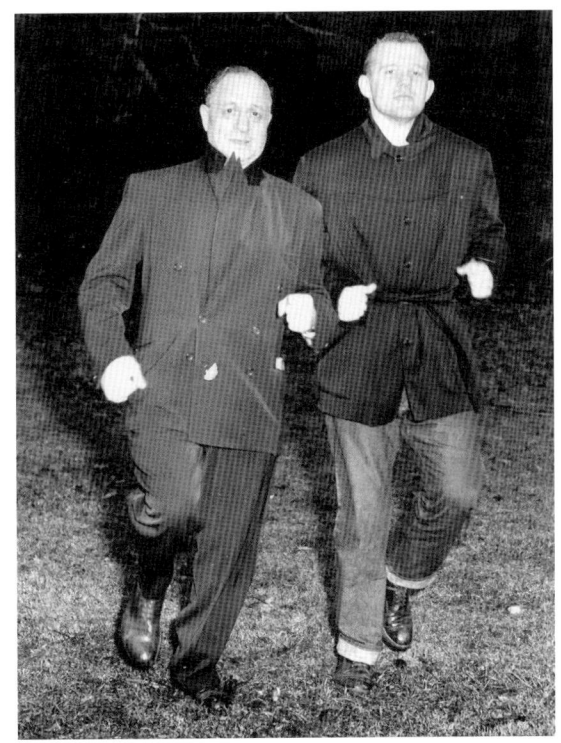

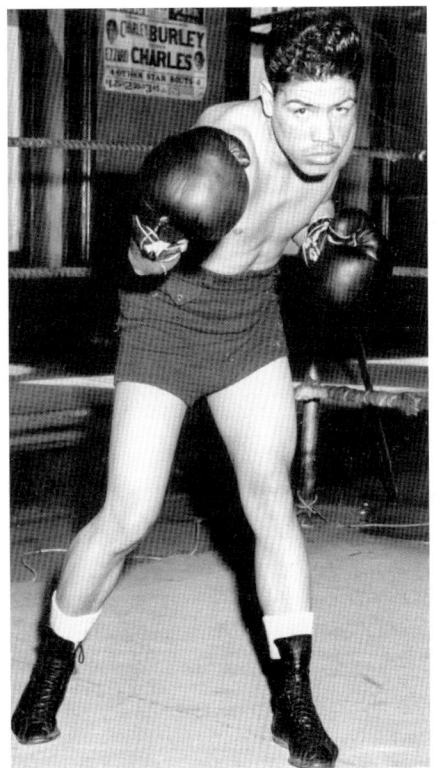

Welterweight Al Diaz was another post–World War II fighter that the Becker brothers managed. Born in Mexico, Diaz moved to Cincinnati to train and box. In his first years here, from 1946 to 1947, Diaz compiled a record of only 4-7, lacking the power he needed to dominate rounds. (Photograph courtesy of Buddy LaRosa.)

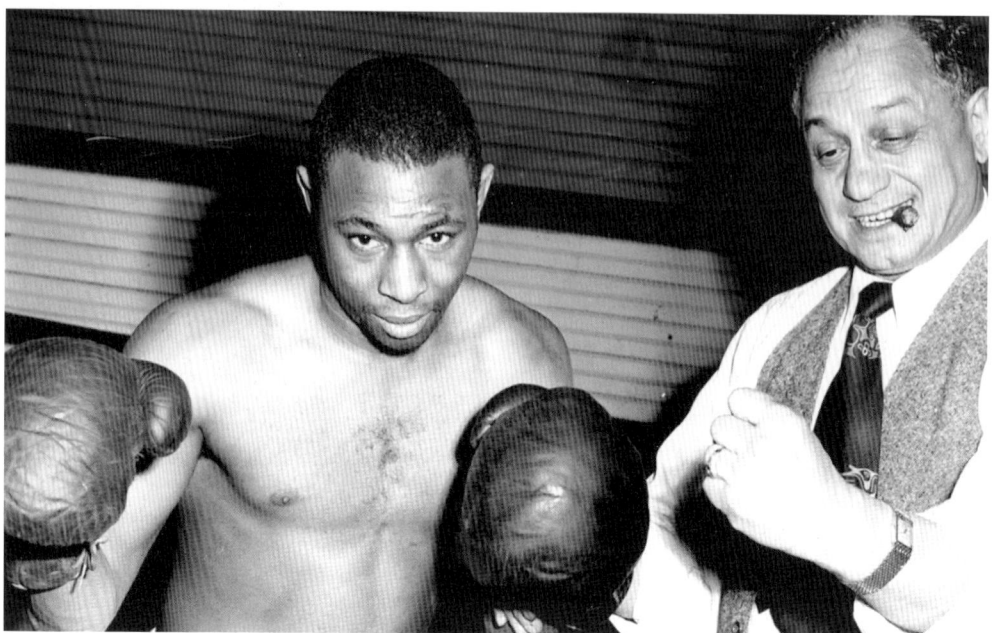

Eddie Burgin was a classy featherweight for the Beckers, with some good knockout power. Although his first match on February 28, 1949, was a loss to Pat Iacobucci's brother Carmen, Burgin reeled off 17 straight wins after that, with 10 knockouts. That string included a win over Carmen in a rematch, and the 17th was a TKO over Frenchman Ray Famechon, an excellent fighter, in a Cincinnati bout. That win was controversial, perhaps because of a language barrier. Famechon was knocked down in the first and second rounds, and when the referee thought he said "No, no quit," he misunderstood and gave Burgin a TKO. Famechon's manager maintained his boxer was saying he wanted to keep going. In these images, Burgin is pictured with Sam Becker and some of his fight posters. (Photographs courtesy of Buddy LaRosa.)

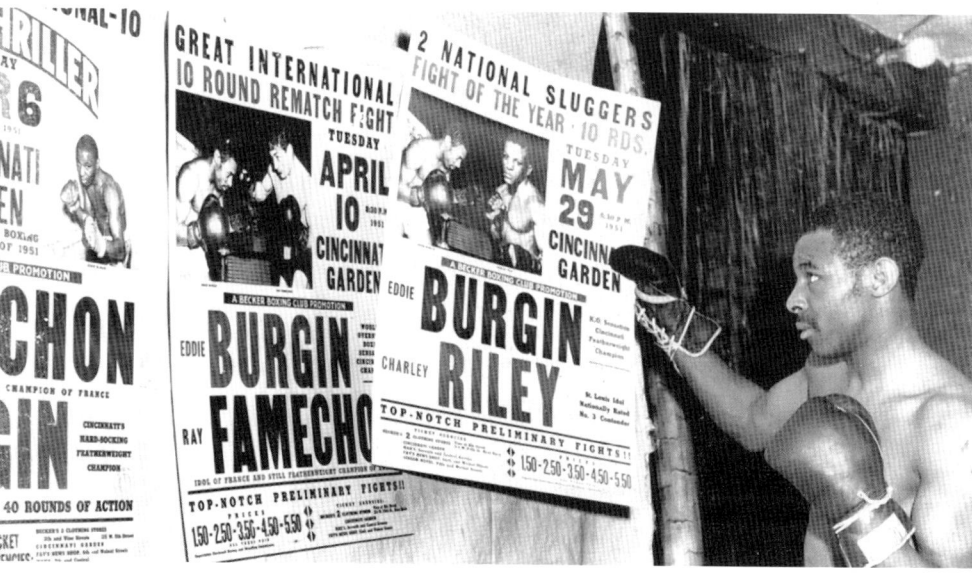

George "Sugar" Costner was a smooth, contending welterweight from Cincinnati during the war years. Growing up in Mount Auburn, Costner went down the hill to the basin gyms to learn the sport, and at the age of 16, he had his first professional fight, knocking out Red Knox in the second round. He then ran off seven more victories before losing to Fast Black the next year, and by 1945, he was fighting the best in his division like Sugar Ray Robinson and Jake LaMotta. Although he was knocked out by both of them, Costner continued to move up in the rankings. Tragedy struck in 1950 when he lost the sight in his right eye in a match. After Robinson knocked him out in the first round of a 1950 bout, he fought three more times, gaining three more victories, and retired. Costner later went to college, graduating at the age of 56 with a degree in labor relations.

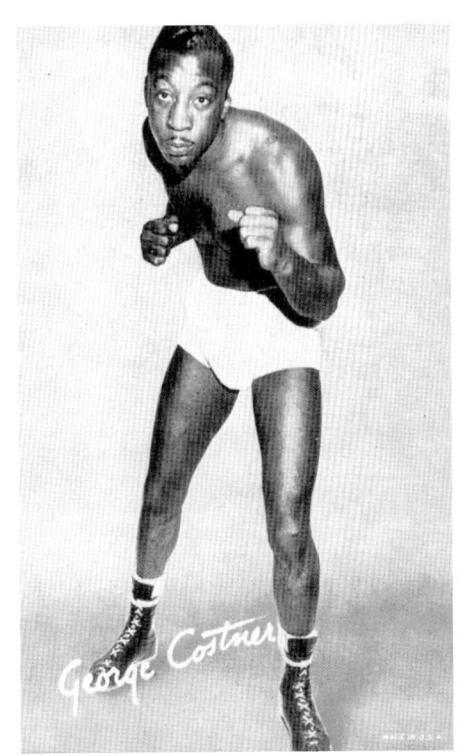

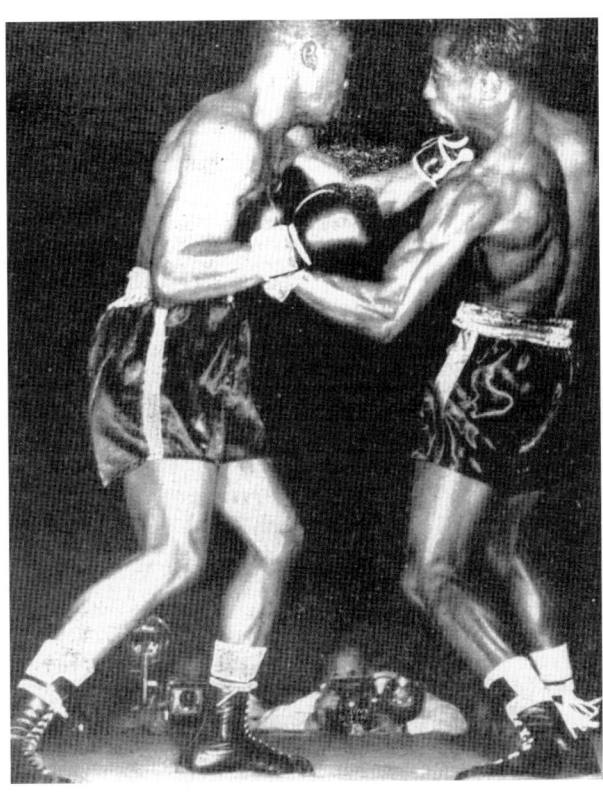

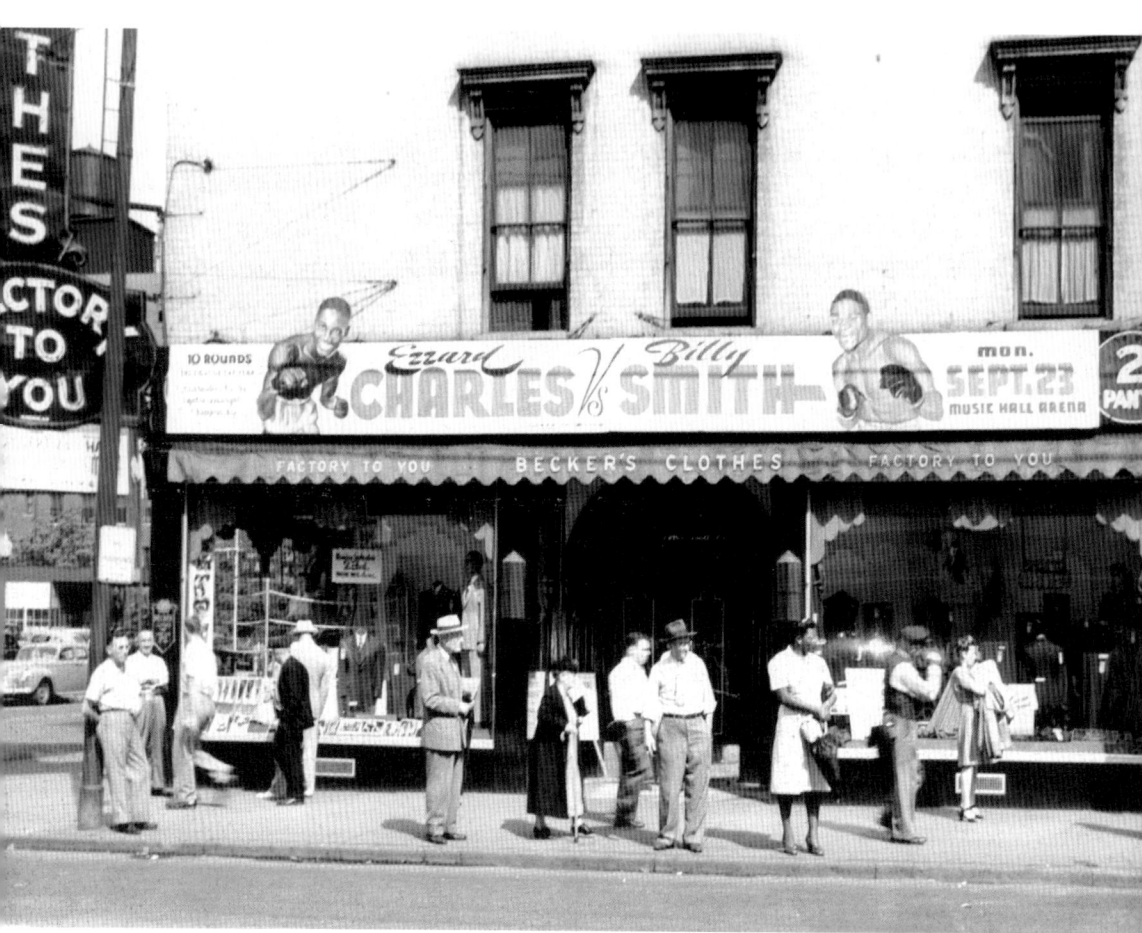

Sam Becker had a clothing store at Eighth Street and Vine Street and loved using his front display windows to advertise the upcoming boxing matches he and his brother were promoting. Sam and Benny got their start as boxing promoters by staging local smokers every weekend, offering the fighters a guarantee of $5 per bout, with $10 going to the winner. They also staged boxing shows at the city's various ethnic picnics. Sometimes it was almost like a cattle drive for the Beckers. They would bus in club fighters from West Virginia, Pennsylvania, Indiana, and throughout Ohio, lace them up, pay them after the fight, and send them on home. The equipment was cheap and utilitarian, the fighters wore gloves with little padding, and mouth guards were little more than alcohol- or juice-soaked cotton packed into their mouths.

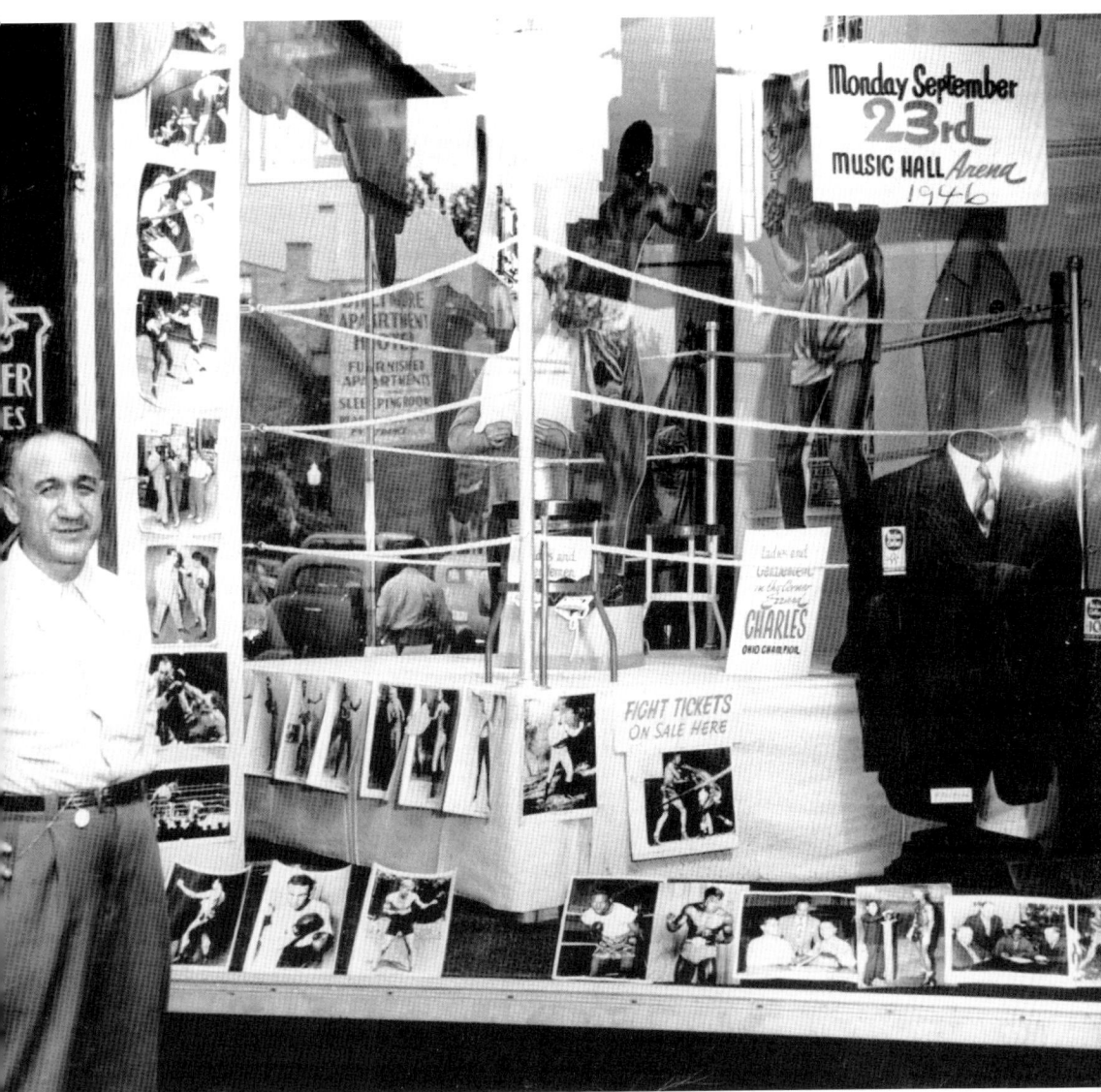

Sam Becker got his big promoting break with Ezzard Charles, though he kept quiet about it. As he finally admitted years later, "I couldn't come out in the open, but when Charles fought Oakland Billy Smith here in 1946, I not only promoted the fight and had a piece of the fighter but I was judging the fight, and I cast the vote that gave him a split decision." (Photographs courtesy of Buddy LaRosa.)

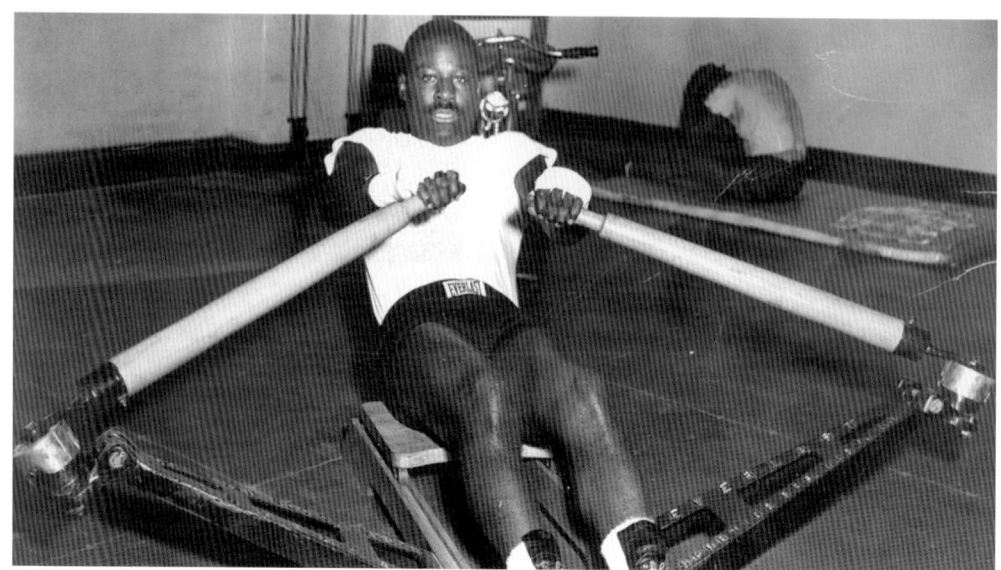

After World War II began, Theodore M. Berry had tried to get Ezzard Charles reclassified, as he was the financial support for his grandmother and great-grandmother. However, Charles entered the army in 1943, stationed mainly in North Africa and Italy with the 115th Trucking Battalion. He continued boxing in exhibitions and longer matches (including losing to Jimmy Bivins). When he was discharged, he was somewhat out of shape but got to work immediately, deciding to fight as a light heavyweight. (Photograph courtesy of Buddy LaRosa.)

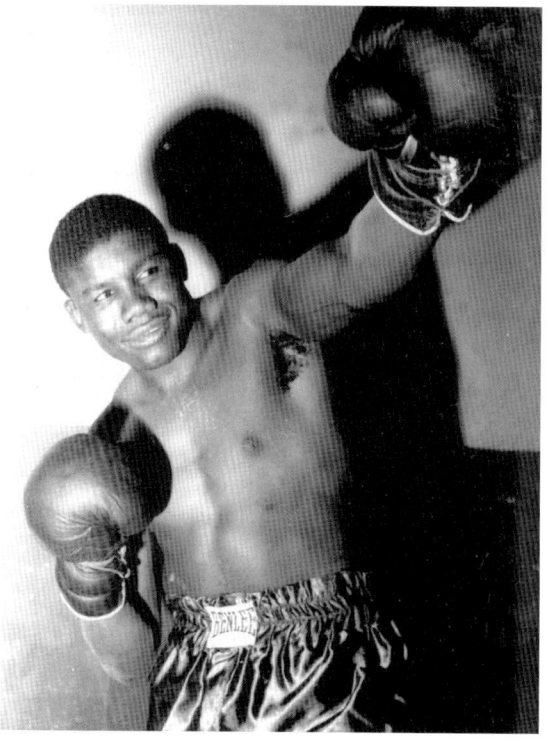

Light heavyweight Jimmy Bivins was given the title of "Duration Champion" in 1943 because Joe Louis had vacated the heavyweight belt to help in the war effort. Bivins beat Charles that year in a 10-round unanimous decision, but Charles came back in 1946 and decisioned Bivins in another bout. In 1947, Charles knocked him out in the fourth round of a fight and then beat him again in 1948 and in 1952.

Perennial title contender Archie Moore had three bouts with Ezzard Charles. The two first matched up in 1946 at Forbes Field in Pittsburgh, and Charles won a unanimous decision. He beat Moore again in 1947 and 1948, the last time coming back from a tremendous Moore left hook in the eighth round to knock out Moore with a right cross.

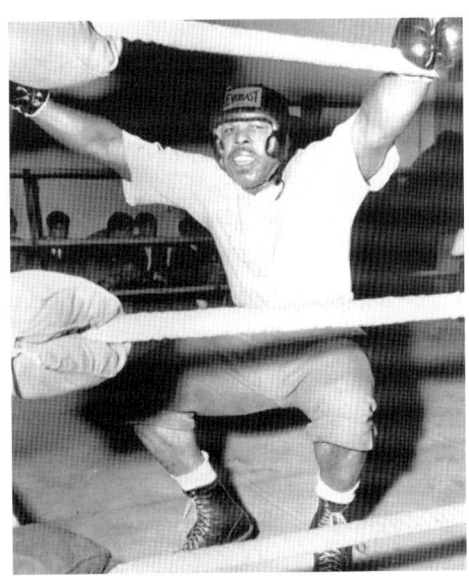

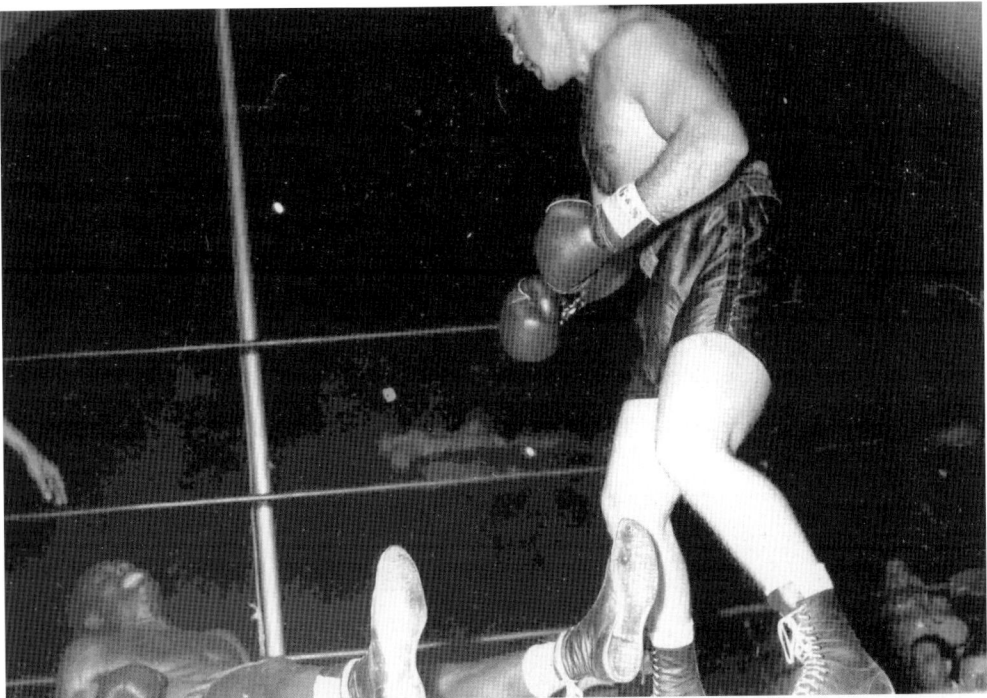

On July 14, 1947, Charles took on Hilton "Fitzie" Fitzpatrick at Crosley Field in Cincinnati. The Reds ballpark had a large fight crowd that night, and they saw a very unusual bout. Fitzpatrick was a tough customer, and in the second round, he knocked Charles down so hard Charles's feet flew in the air. The referee did a very slow count to nine, and after Charles made it to his feet, the referee held Fitzpatrick back until Charles indicated he was ready to go. Charles then scored a TKO over Fitzpatrick in the fifth round, and in a rematch held in Cleveland at the end of the year, Charles won on a TKO in the fourth. (Photograph courtesy of Larry Burton.)

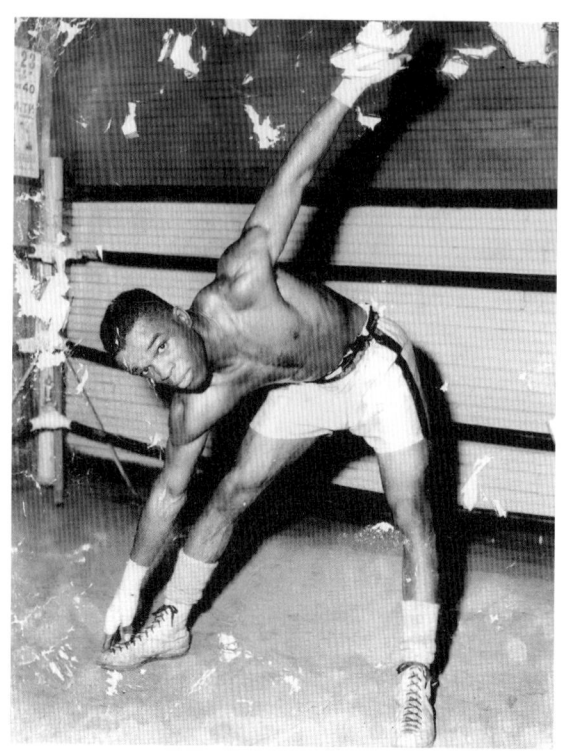

Bud Smith was a promising fighter in Sam Becker's stable. Born in Cincinnati in 1924, by the mid-1940s he was an excellent amateur lightweight who got his experience by tangling with some of the city's top pros and amateurs in local gyms. In 1948, he would win a spot on the U.S. Olympic boxing team. His later career years were marred by his management's involvement with organized crime, and he met a sad end himself. In 1973, while talking to a woman who was being threatened by her former boyfriend, Smith was shot in the head and killed. (Left, photograph courtesy of Buddy LaRosa.)

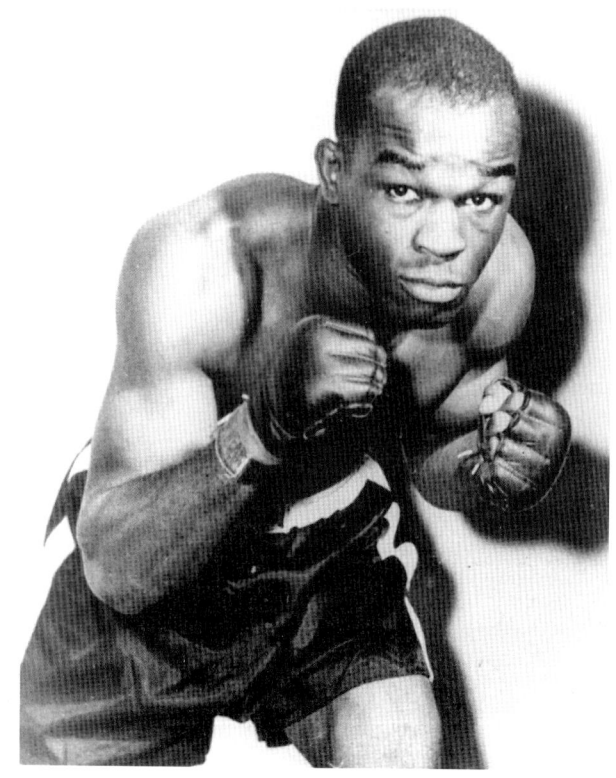

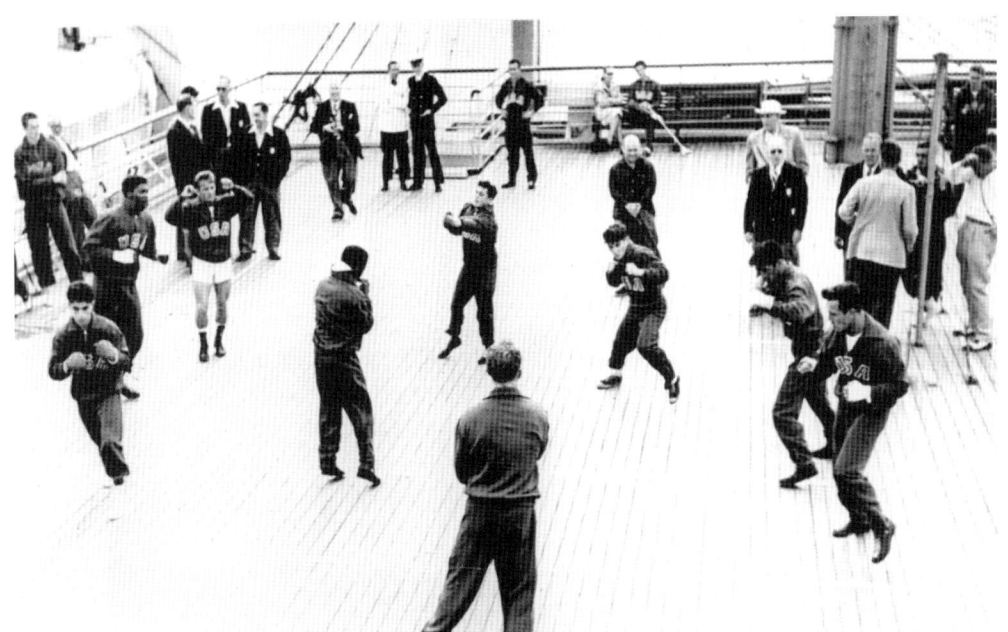

The Olympiad in 1948 was held in London, so the teams sailed to England in July. On the voyage over, the boxing squad worked out on the ship's deck, exercising and sparring a bit to stay sharp until landfall, as seen in the photograph above. To the right is the program for the matches, in which Smith won the bronze medal in the lightweight division. Smith was the first Cincinnati boxer in the Olympics and was followed by Tim Austin (1992, Barcelona), Larry Donald (1992, Barcelona), Ricardo Williams Jr. (2000, Sydney), Dante Craig (2000, Sydney), Rau'Shee Warren (2004, Athens), and Ron Siler Jr. (2004, Athens). Two other Cincinnati fighters, Ray Phillips (1960, Rome) and Tony Tubbs (1980, Moscow), were slated to fight but did not compete.

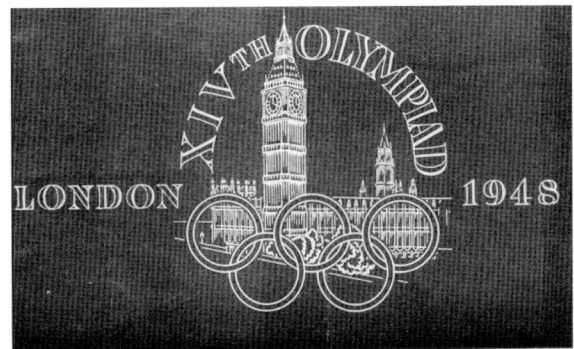

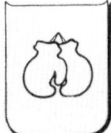

BOXING
at the
EMPIRE POOL WEMBLEY
FRIDAY AUGUST 13TH 1948

OFFICIAL PROGRAMME · ONE SHILLING

CINCINNATI BOXING

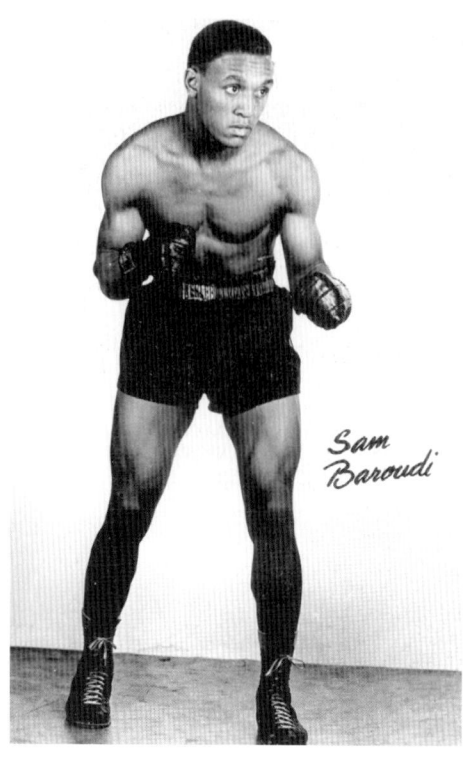

Sam Baroudi was Ezzard Charles's opponent on February 20, 1948, when they met up in Chicago. A month earlier in Cleveland, Charles knocked out Archie Moore, his sixth in his last seven fights. Charles was well on his way to a title shot, with a record of 54-5-1. Baroudi was a light-heavy from Akron and had had some success in a young career. But Charles was coming into his own, and while he did not have a devastating knockout punch, he was one of the harder hitters in the sport. Charles kept up a steady barrage of punches to Baroudi throughout the fight. In the 10th round, he knocked him out. Prone on the canvas, Baroudi could not be revived by his trainer, Izzy Klein.

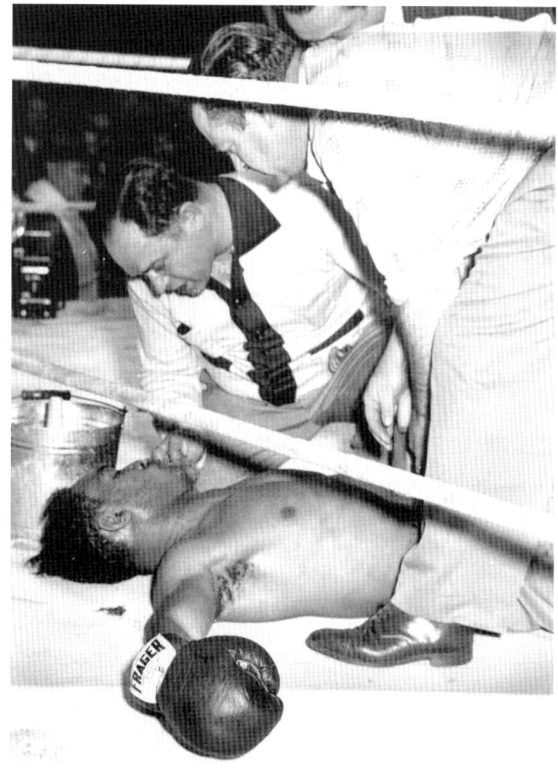

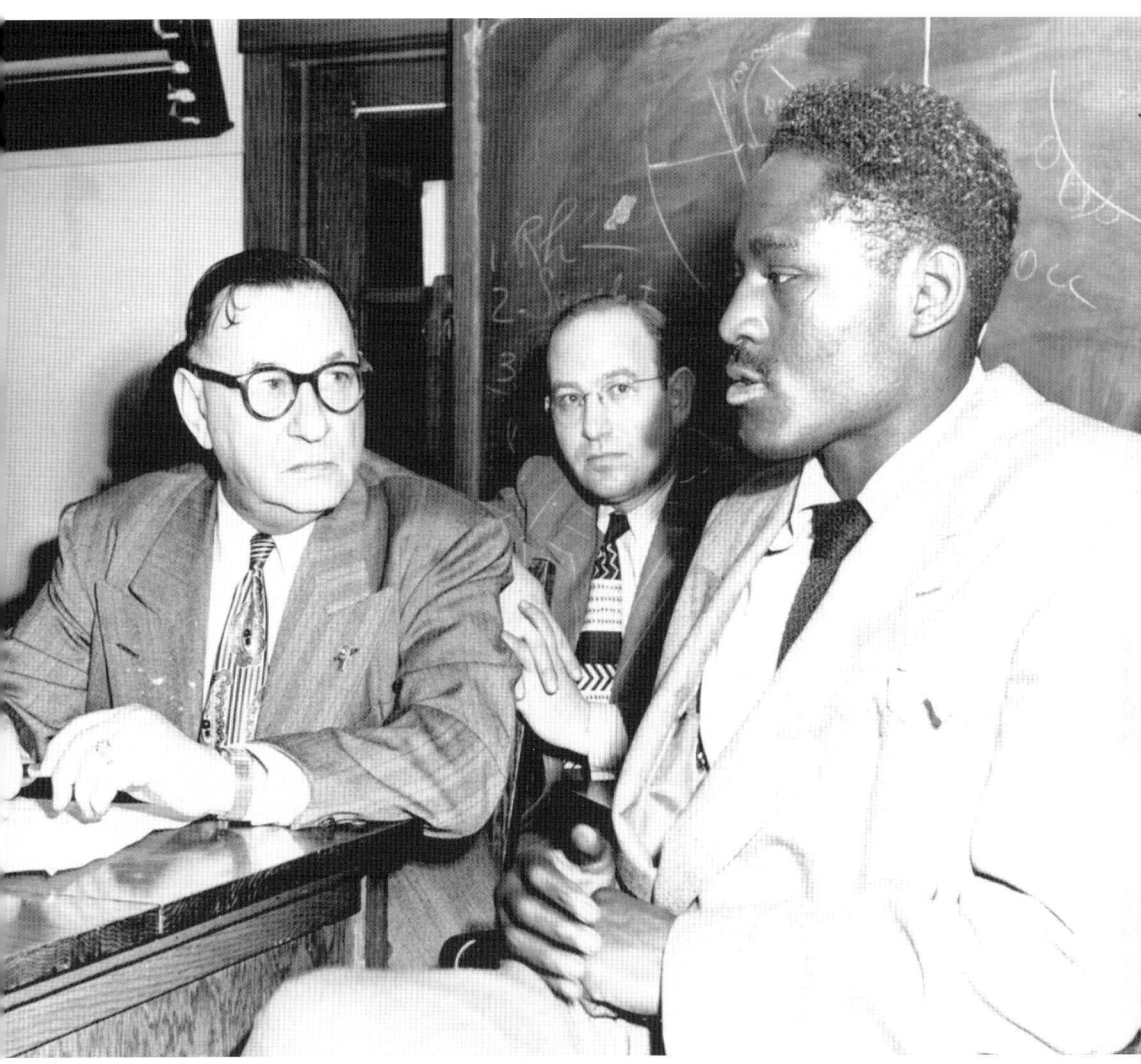

Baroudi was carried unconscious from the ring and taken to Chicago's Columbus Hospital, where he died the following morning. He was 20 years old. The State of Illinois immediately called a halt to all boxing matches, pending an investigation. An inquest was held on the 21st, and Charles was called to testify before coroner Thomas Brodie, shown at the left. The death was ruled an accident of the ring. Charles would be forever affected by it. Baroudi's father, Sam Crandall, met with Charles to tell him that it was a tragic part of the sport but that he must go on. Charles arranged exhibition bouts to raise money for Baroudi's widow and children, including the $5,000 purse from his next fight, but he never fought in the ring the same way again. He became a bit cautious and careful with his punches. Now boxing was a business he pursued to make a living. Ironically, in a bout six months previous in Massachusetts, Baroudi had fought Glenn Smith, who died of injuries from the match.

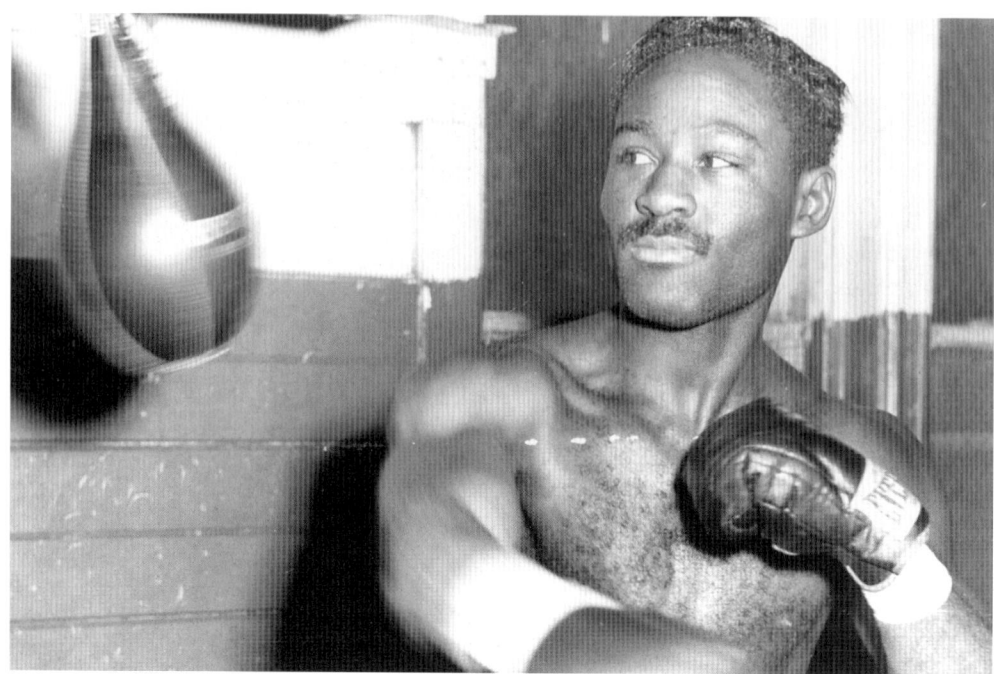

For the most part, Ezzard Charles was still fighting as a light heavyweight. When he finally moved up to the heavyweight class, he would still be an undersized one for the rest of his career. Charles stood six feet tall but was a light 180–185 pounds. In this image, he prepares for a light-heavy bout against Joe Baksi on December 10, 1948. Charles clocked him in the 11th round.

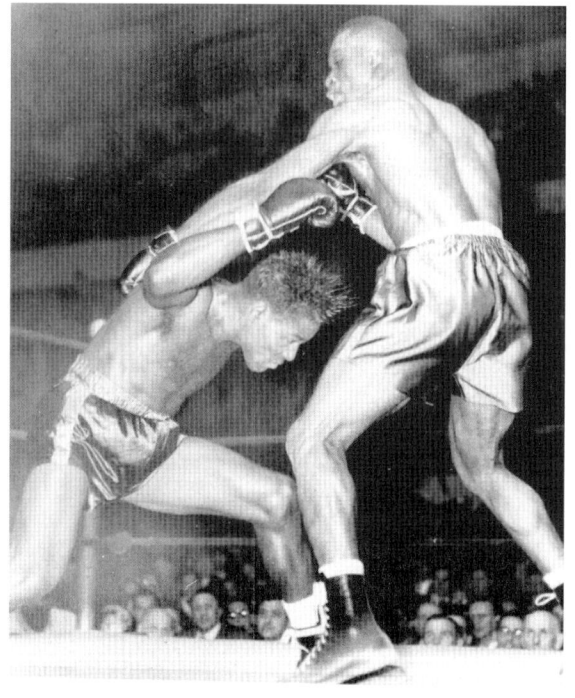

By the beginning of 1949, Ezzard Charles was considered a leading contender for the vacated heavyweight crown. Early in the new year, on February 7, Charles took on Johnny Haynes in Philadelphia. In this photograph, Charles ducks under a left thrown by Haynes and then comes up with a counter of his own. In the eighth frame of the 10-rounder, Charles knocked Haynes out.

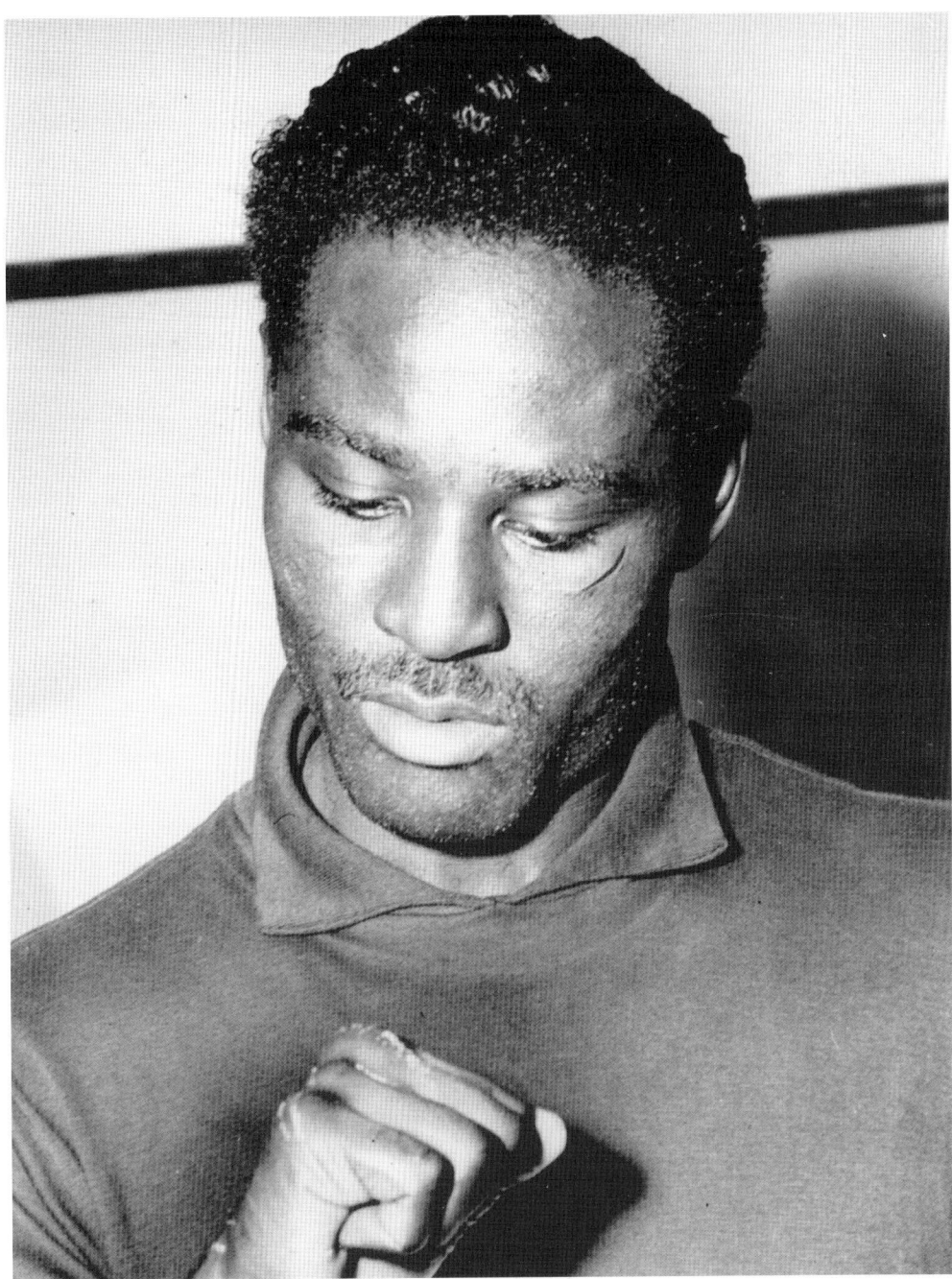

A title fight was set in June 1949. Ezzard Charles and Jersey Joe Walcott would fight for the vacant NBA heavyweight championship "box-off" in Chicago's Comiskey Park. The match was set for June 22. Charles set up camp outside Chicago in Momence, Illinois, but shortly after camp began, he suffered a gash under his left eye taking a punch from a sparring partner. He vowed, though, that he would be ready on the designated night for his big shot at boxing glory.

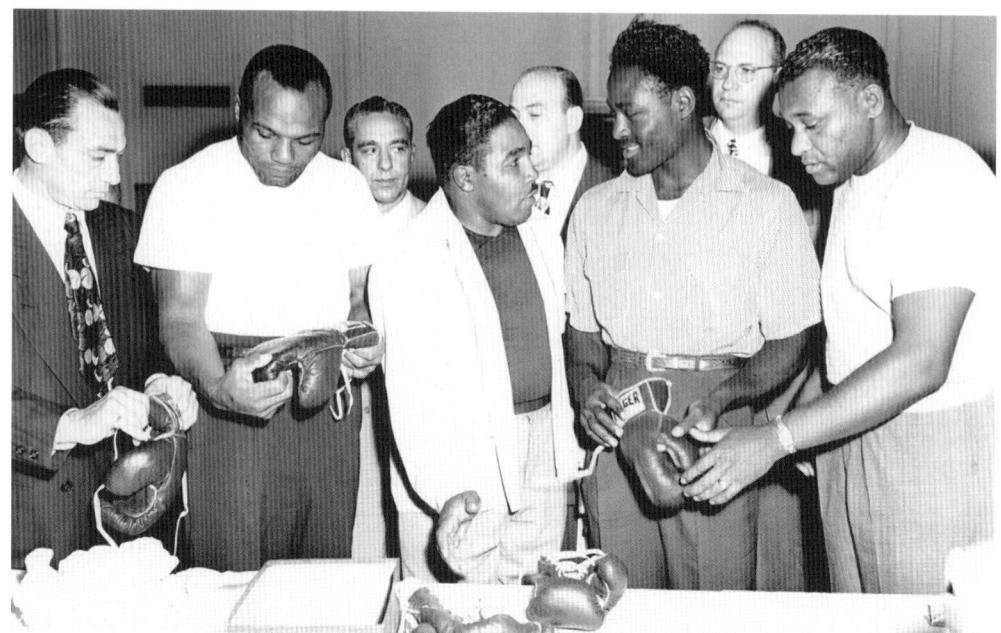

The two boxers and their representatives came together to choose the gloves for the match. Jersey Joe Walcott stands to the left, examining the glove he holds in his hands. Ezzard Charles is smiling at his friend, trainer, and occasional sparring partner, Jimmy Brown.

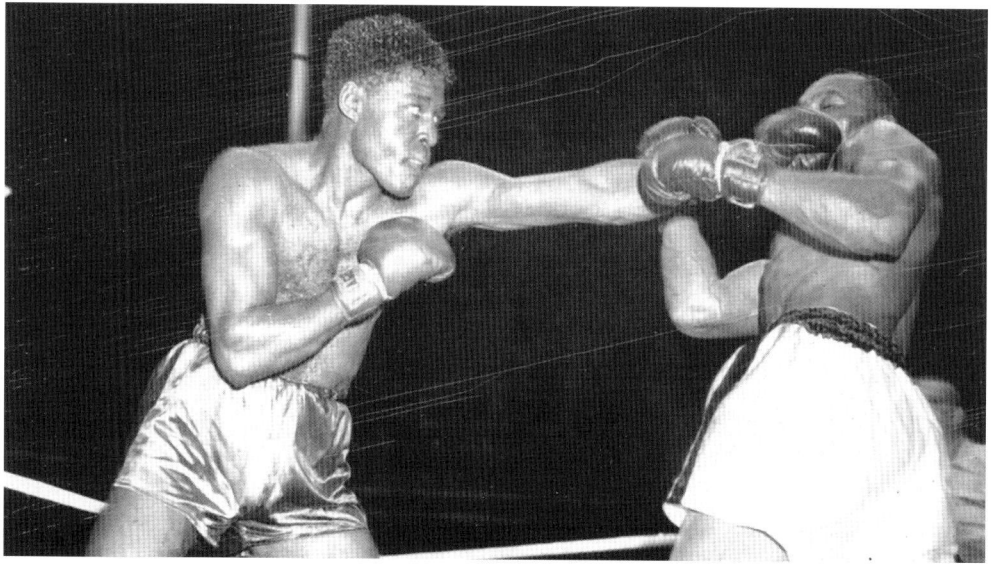

Walcott came into the fight with a 45-13-1 record. The boxers traded punch after punch, Charles trying to keep a short distance between them, effectively working his jab and, in this image, driving home a solid left to Walcott's jaw. In the seventh round, Jersey Joe wrestled down the Cincinnati Cobra by superior weight, but the referee did not rule it a knockdown. The fight went the distance of 15 rounds, Charles winning a unanimous decision with scores from the three judges of 78-72, 78-72, and 77-73.

Both men had fought a hard, incredible fight, and at its conclusion, the name of the winner was still in doubt for the fans. Oddly, boxing may be the only sport where the fans have no idea who is winning as the contest goes along. A crowd jumped into the ring as the decision was announced that the Cincinnati Cobra was the new heavyweight champion of the world. In the background of the photograph to the right, Charles can be seen with his arm being raised by the ring announcer, with his handlers Jimmy Brown, George Rhein, and Bobby Elkus to the left. The excitement was too much for Jake Mintz, his trainer. In the foreground, a crowd gathers around Mintz as he faints dead away, and in the image below, Mintz is revived with smelling salts.

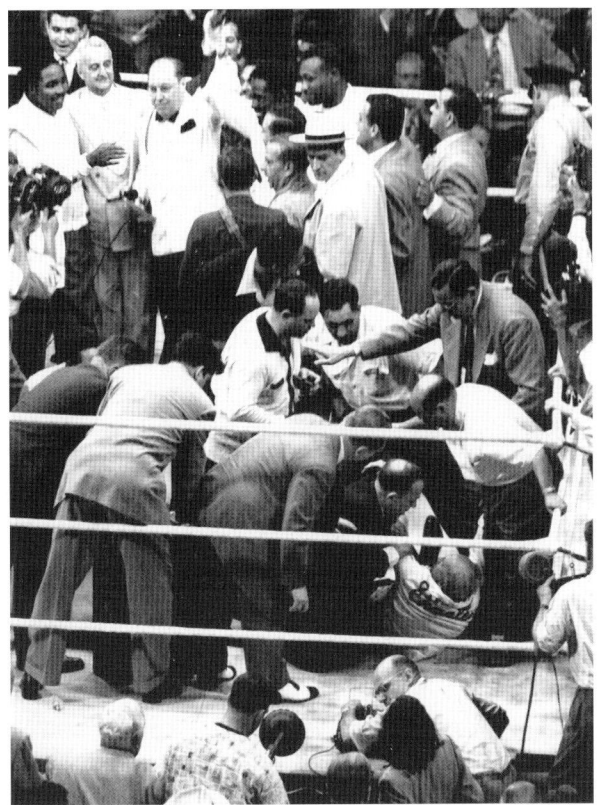

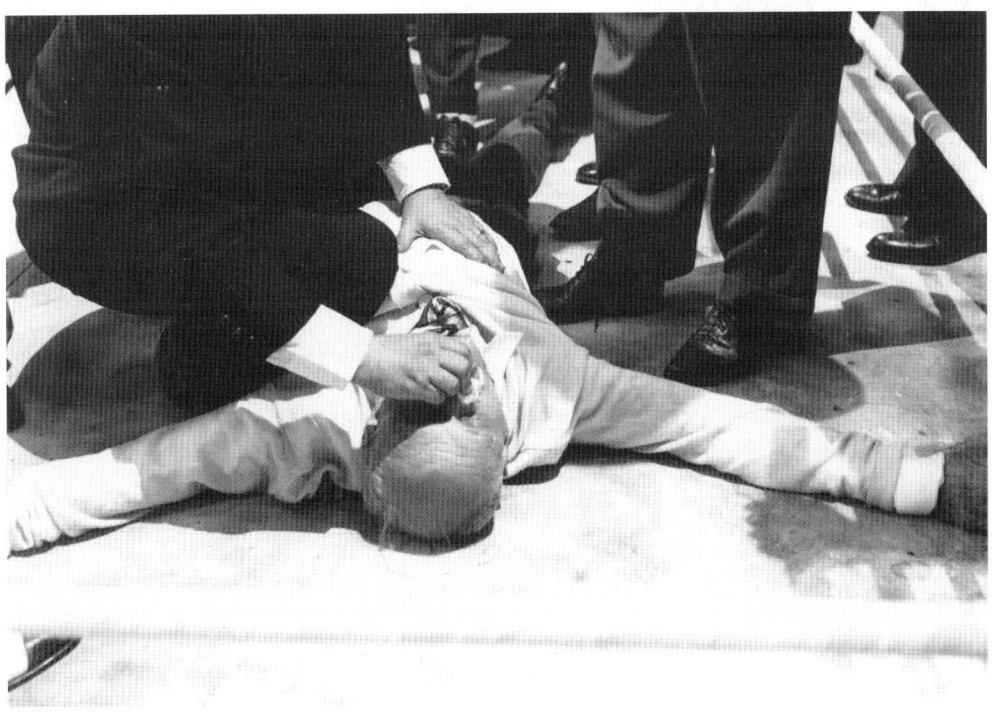

CINCINNATI BOXING

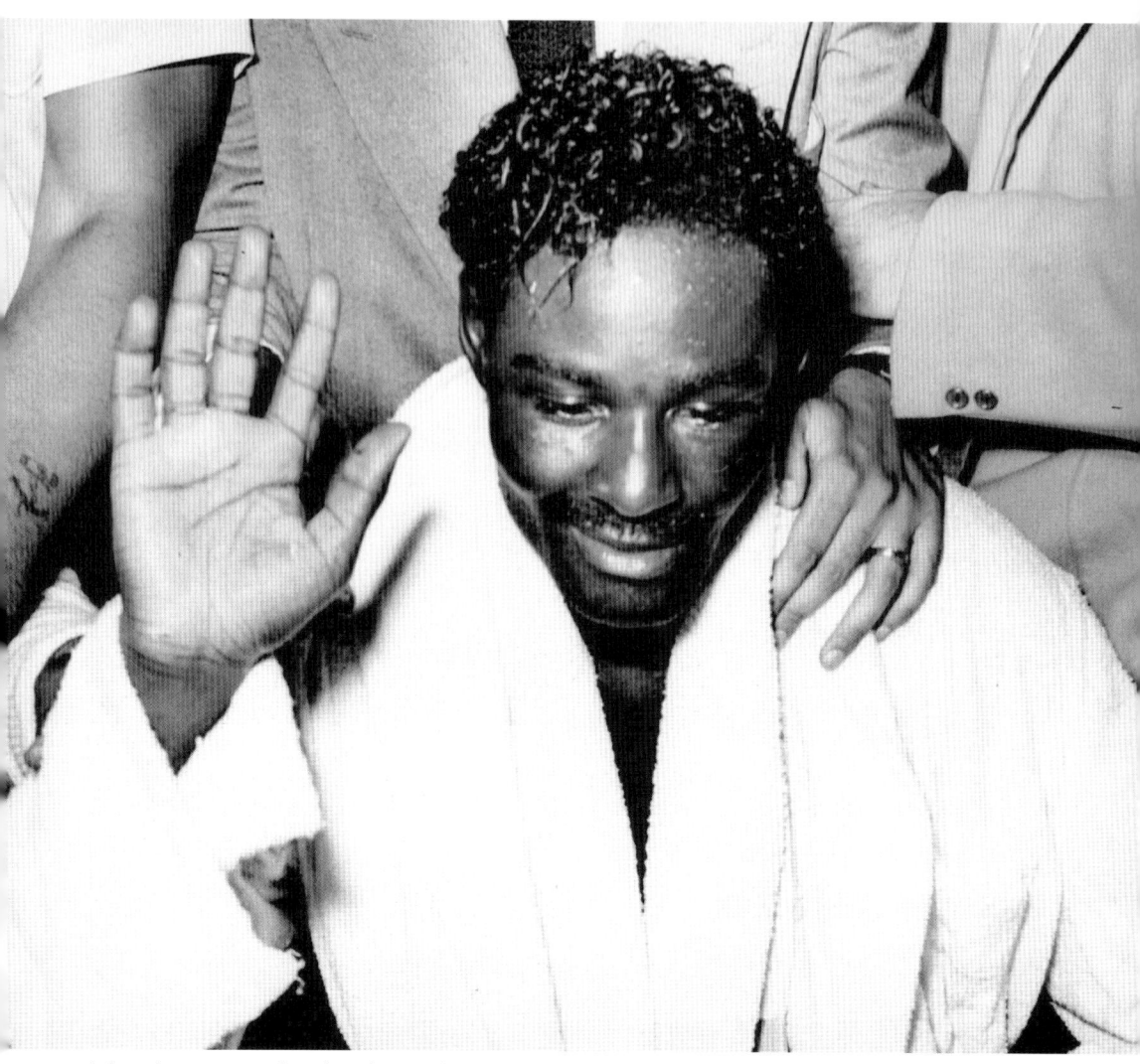

After the victory, the elated Ezzard Charles made his way back to the dressing room to shower and meet the press. It was the best fight of the year.

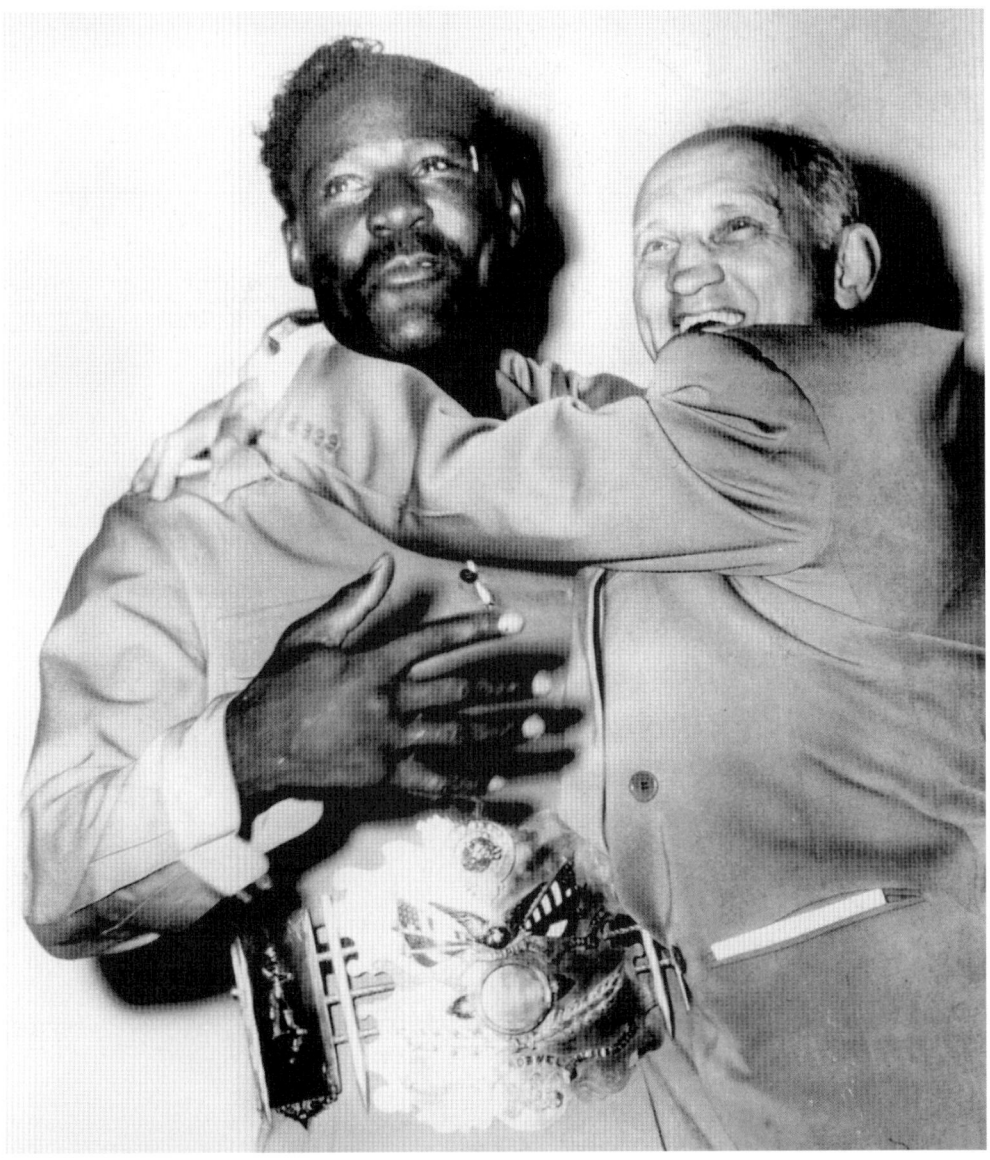

Fully recovered by the next day, Jake Mintz embraces the new world champion. At a ceremony held at a local hotel, Charles was awarded the *Police Gazette*'s heavyweight championship belt. It was a big payday for Charles: $53,857. However, many fight fans and officials would consider the Charles victory as only a part of a heavyweight crown until he could prove he was better than the retired Joe Louis.

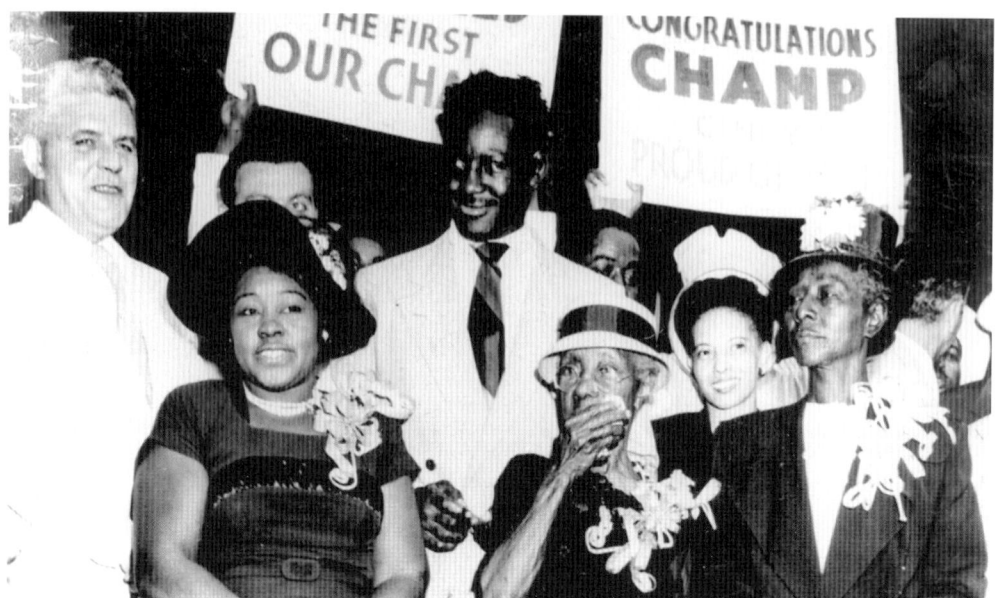

Ezzard Charles returned to Cincinnati and a hero's welcome. The city had its first heavyweight champion, the glamour division of the boxing world. At a reception in his honor, the dapper Charles stands with, from left to right, his mother, Alberta Moss; his grandmother Maude Foster; and his great-grandmother Belle Russell.

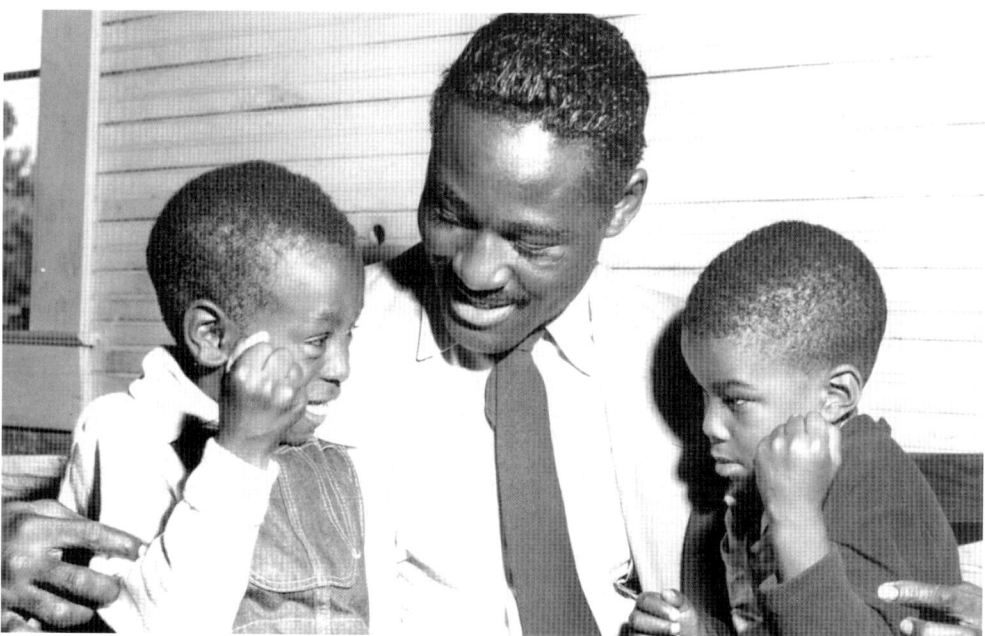

After winning the belt, Charles took a little time off in September to go back to his birthplace in Lawrenceville, Georgia, on his way to an exhibition bout in Atlanta. Excited to welcome back their hometown champion, the Lawrenceville school was dismissed two hours early. Here Charles dutifully appraises the biceps of two young boys.

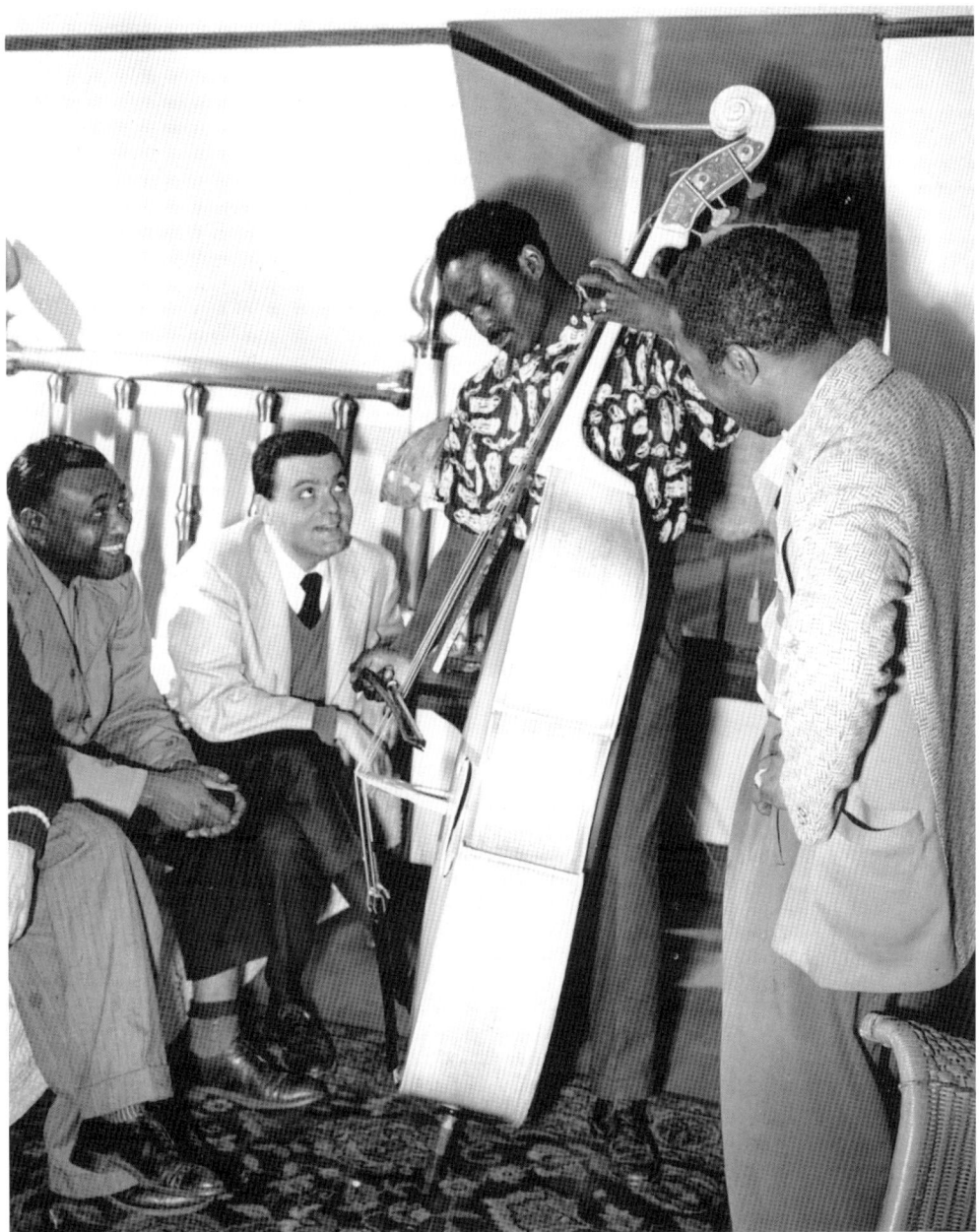

Like many boxers of his era, Ezzard Charles enjoyed the world of jazz and was even somewhat of a musician himself, playing the bass fiddle and taking lessons at Cincinnati's Cosmopolitan School of Music. In that way, he was like another heavyweight champion who also played the same instrument, Jack Johnson, although it may be safe to say neither played it very well! Charles would also spend large sums of money on his jazz record collection, of which he was very proud. Here he entertains the members of his training camp as they sit on a hotel room bed, including one of his managers, Gene Elkus.

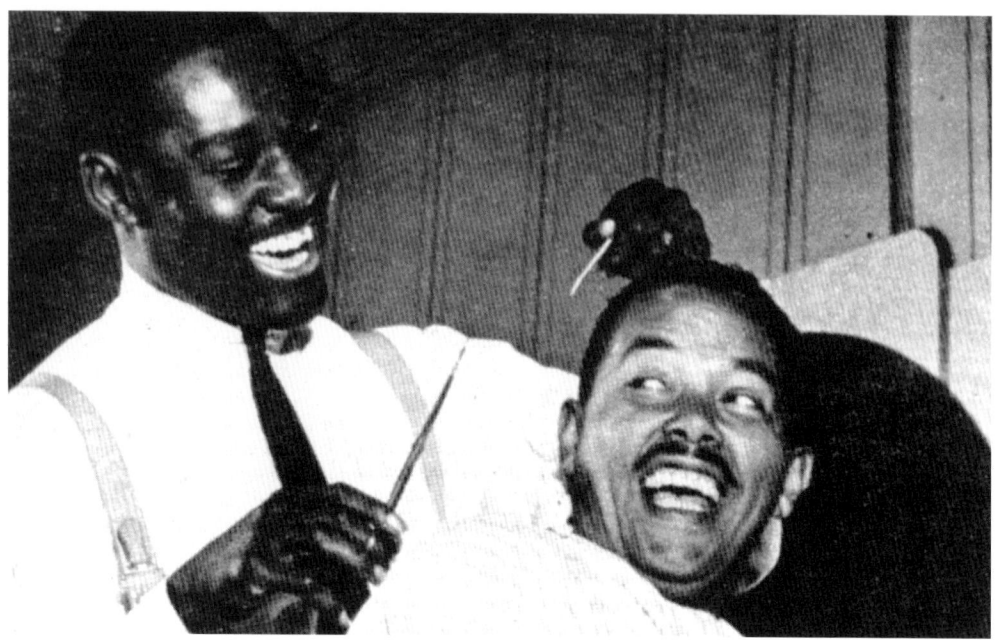

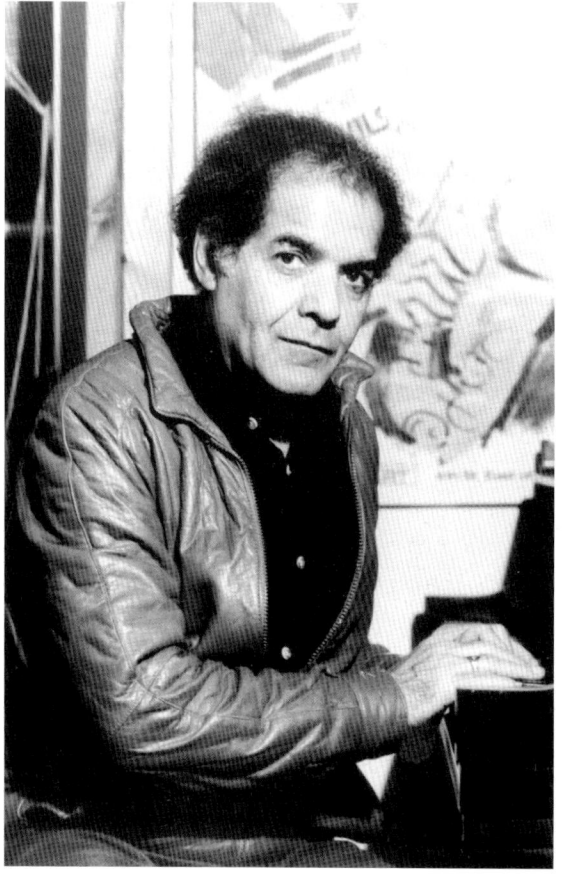

Whenever Ezzard Charles had a chance on his visits to various cities, he would slip away to local jazz clubs. And in many ways, the music complemented his elegant, precise boxing style, each punch and movement he planned having to join with improvisational counterpunches. And musicians admired boxers, their singular performances in the ring, their rhythmic execution of the "sweet science." In the photograph above, Charles jokes around with jazz great Billy Eckstine as he gives the musician a "haircut" during the musician's visit to Cincinnati. The image to the left is of noted jazz composer and fellow Cincinnati native George Russell. Russell has long been one of the most revered figures in jazz composition and teaching. In tribute to Charles, in 1951, he even composed a piece entitled "Ezz-thetics." (Left, photograph courtesy of Reggie Marshall and the Mars Jazz Booking Agency.)

Back on the ring circuit, Charles took on an excellent light-heavy in the person of Gus Lesnevich. Their fight was set for August 10, 1949, in New York's Yankee Stadium, and would be Charles' first defense of his title. The match came just two months after the Jersey Joe Walcott bout. Lesnevich trained outside New York on a farm near Summit, New Jersey, pausing occasionally to feed the sheep. Meanwhile, at Charles's training camp not far away in Pompton Lakes, Joe Louis paid a call. Louis retired undefeated, and it was the NBA portion of his crown that Charles now owned. The two shared a few laughs one afternoon, and then on the night of the match, Charles took on his foe.

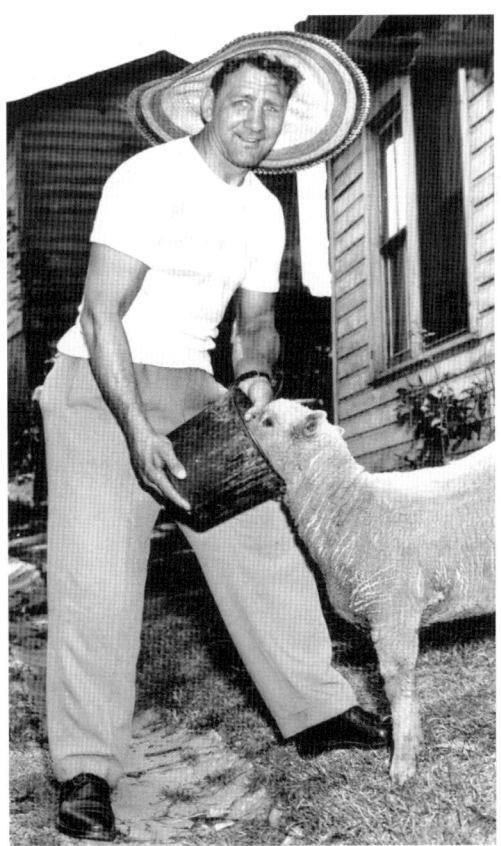

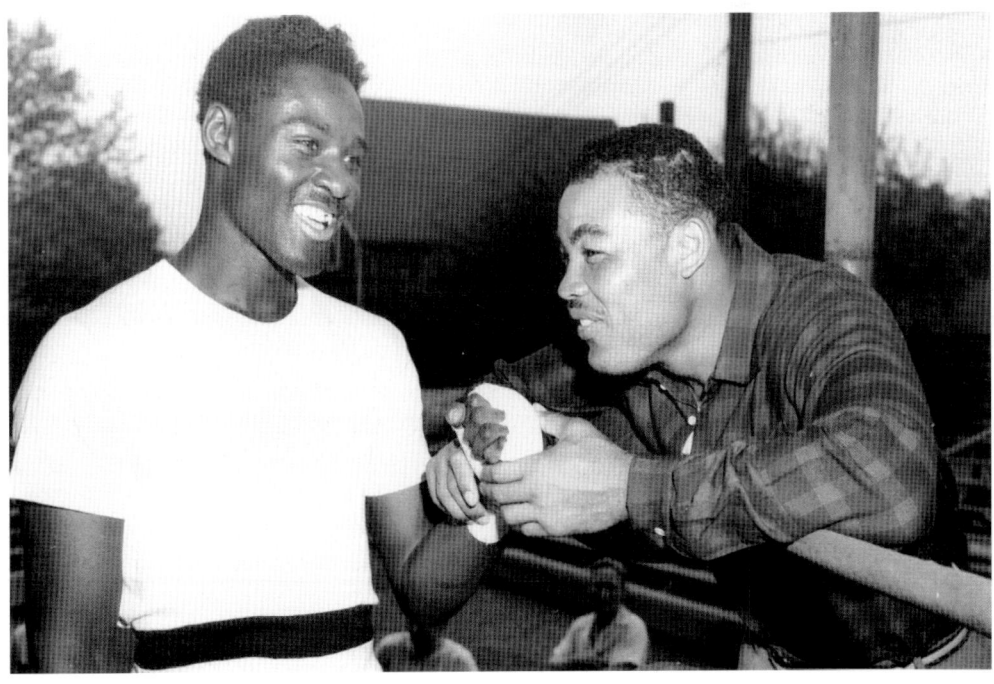

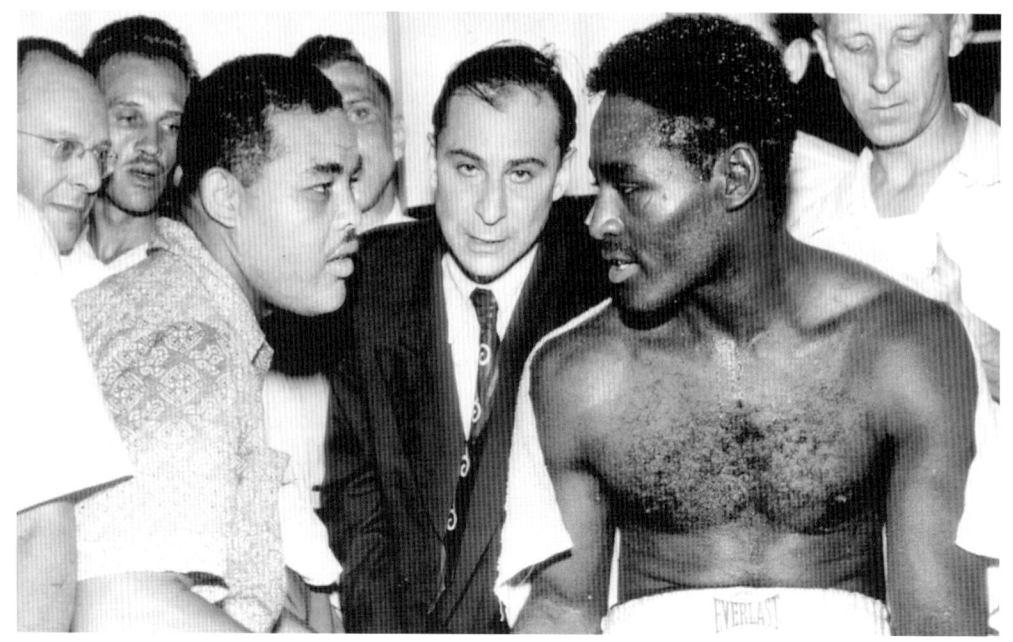

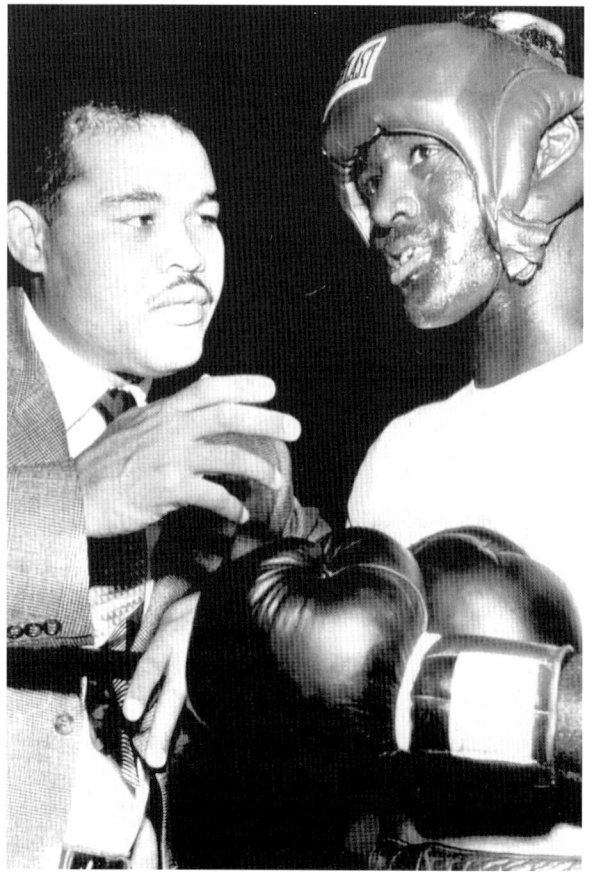

After the Gus Lesnevich fight, Joe Louis stopped by Ezzard Charles's dressing room to offer his congratulations. Charles had hammered the worthy Lesnevich pretty hard and was awarded a knockout when Lesnevich could not answer the bell for the eighth round. Six weeks later, Charles was across the country in San Francisco for a fight with Pat Valentino on October 14, and again Louis talked to him in camp. Louis was a hero to Charles, and in fact, they had sparred in an army exhibition during World War II. Between the Lesnevich fight and this one, Charles again fought two quick exhibitions in Chicago and Columbus against two guys named Joe Modzele and the Alabama Kid. Charles knocked out Valentino in the eighth round. Charles was still the NBA champ, but the Louis shadow was growing ever larger.

30—Cincinnati Garden, Cincinnati, Ohio

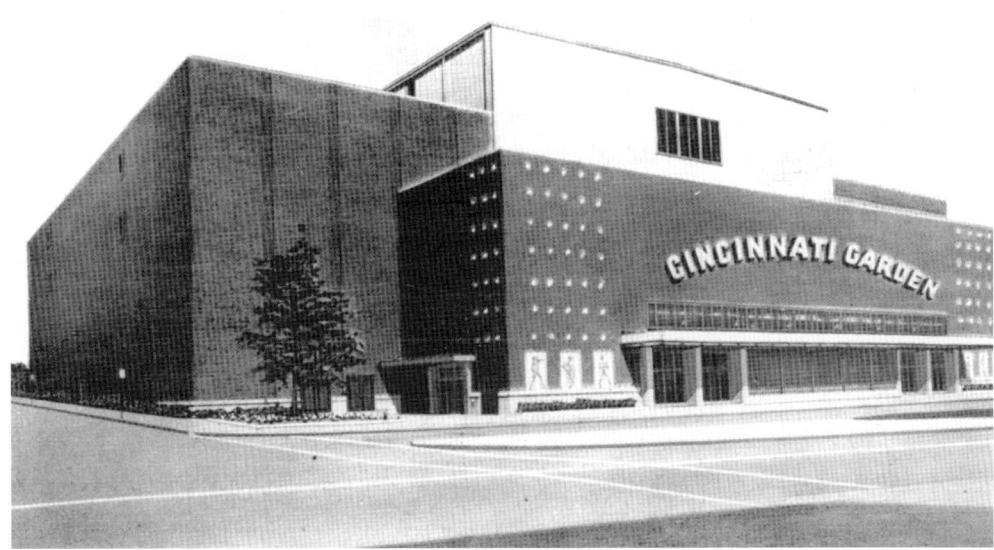

The Cincinnati Gardens in Bond Hill opened on February 22, 1949, and immediately began attracting basketball and boxing matches that might otherwise have had to be staged in Music Hall. The first event on the 22nd was a hockey exhibition game, but six days later, the heavyweight champion inaugurated the illustrious boxing history of the arena. Ezzard Charles may have been the NBA champion, but many of the country felt he really could not claim the heavyweight crown until he beat Joe Louis. Charles went to work building his résumé. More than 14,000 people packed the place that night to watch Charles battle with Joey Maxim. Both boxers were in great shape, but the fight was a long one, and Charles would not prevail until a decision was announced in his favor at the end of 15 rounds.

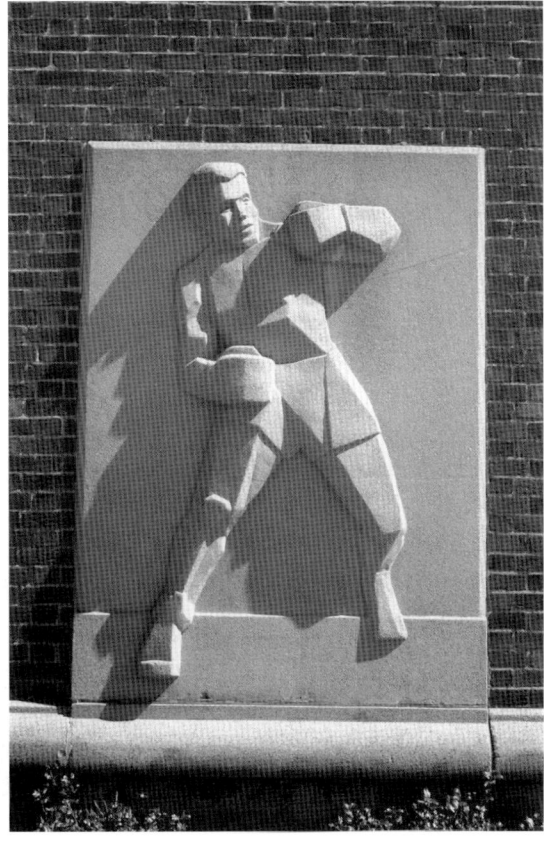

CINCINNATI BOXING

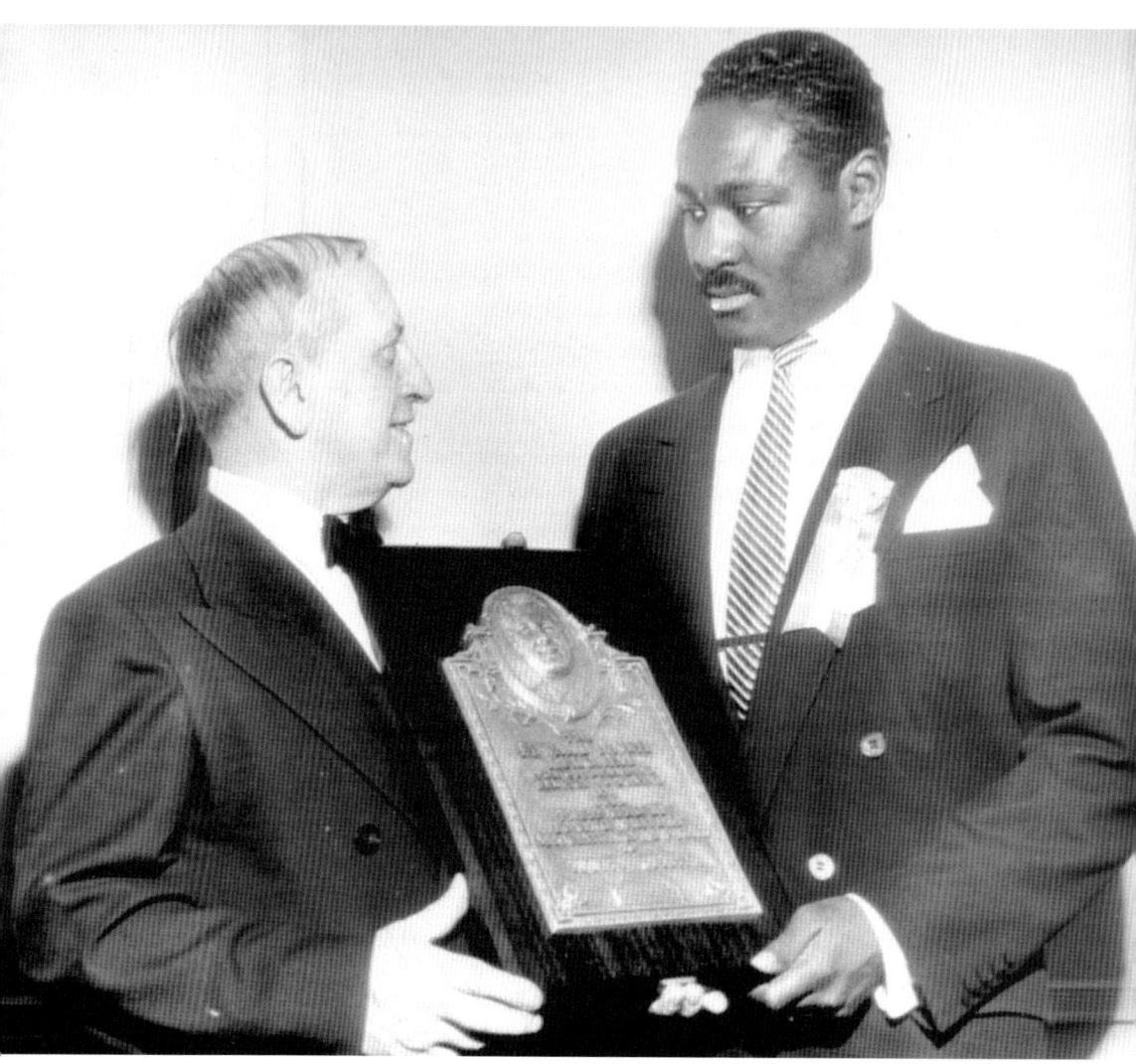

Ezzard Charles finished 1949 with five victories, three by knockout. He also fought 12 exhibition bouts. At the end of October, he took it easy and did not fight again for real until the following August. In the meantime, he journeyed to New York for a special presentation. On January 13, Charles was feted at the annual dinner of the Boxing Writers Association of New York, held at the Waldorf-Astoria. The association's president, and the editor of *Ring Magazine*, Nat Fleischer presented Charles with the Edward J. Neil Award for contributing the most to boxing in 1949.

Ezzard Charles was a gentle man by nature, very quiet and unassuming, although he liked late-night jazz clubs and mingling with fellow celebrities. But America had a certain image of a boxing life, and Charles did his best version of that visage with a penetrating frown at the camera. To sharpen his image, he was given the various nicknames of "Snooks," the "Cincinnati Cobra," the "Cincinnati Tiger," and the "Cincinnati Flash," but through it all, he was still the quiet Ezzard Charles from the West End.

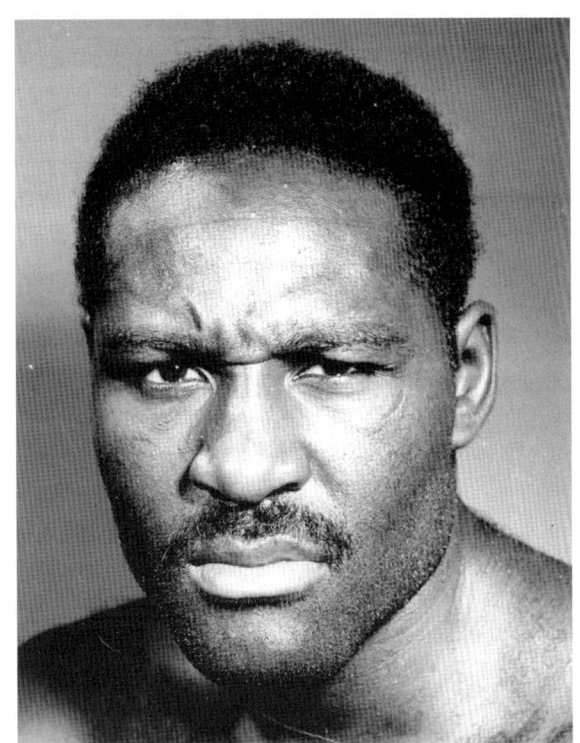

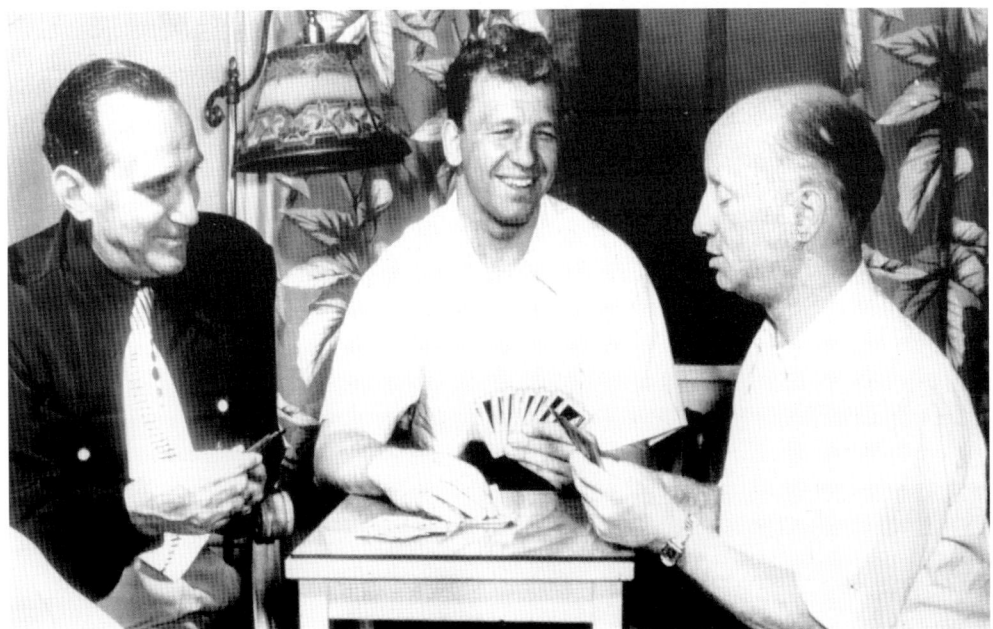

On August 15, 1950, Charles put his title on the line by fighting Freddie Beshore in Buffalo. Beshore relaxed with his manager, Ralph Gold (left), and his trainer, Whitey Bimstein, before the 15-round bout. Then he gave Charles all he could ask for until Charles knocked him out in the 14th round.

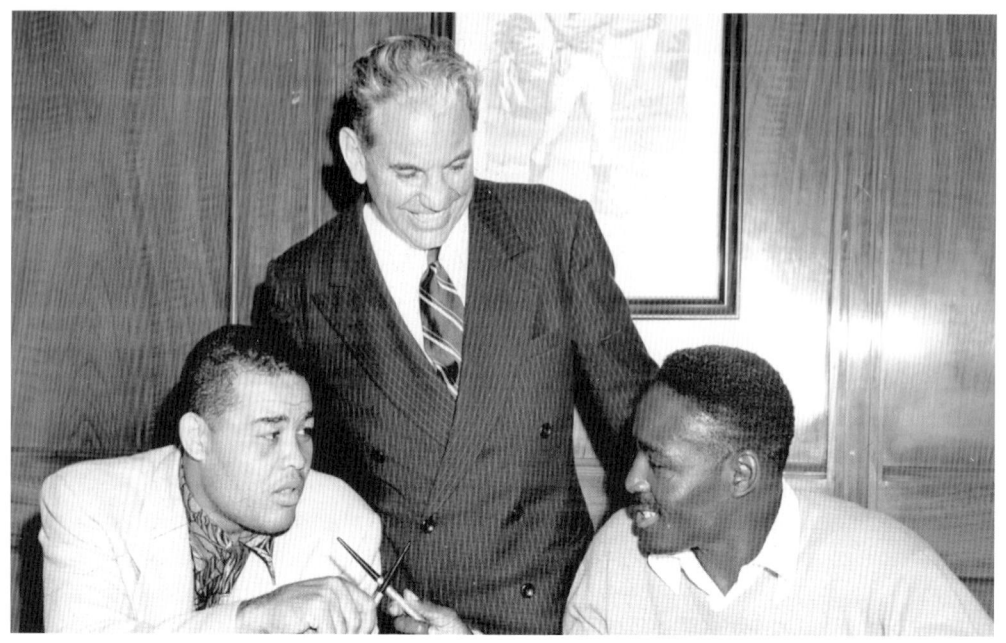

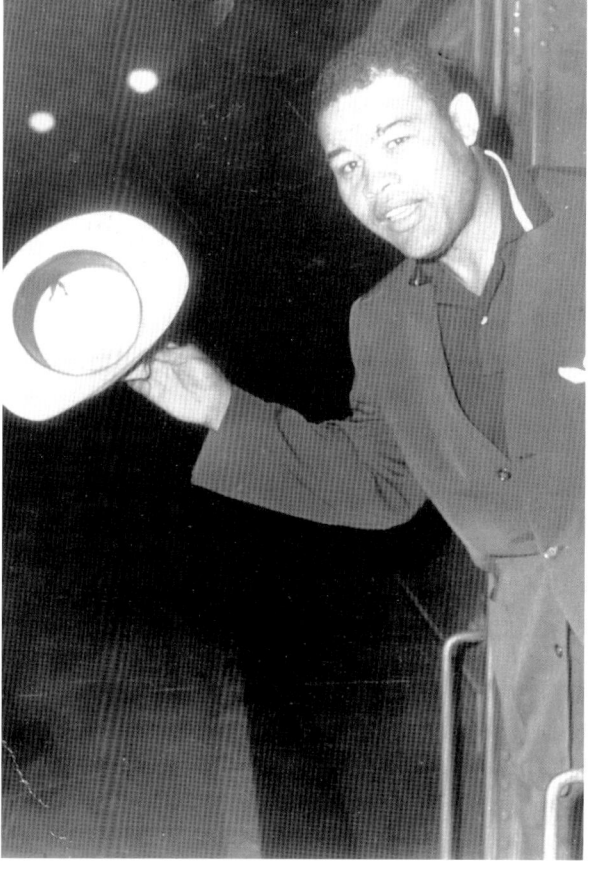

But eventually it had to be. The New York State Boxing Commission did not recognize Ezzard Charles as champion and neither did most of the European boxing world. American boxing writers and fans were divided. The only thing that would unite opinion would be Charles going up against the beloved Joe Louis. Louis had little choice in the matter himself. He needed the money, so he came out of retirement to fight Charles and to settle once and for all who was really the heavyweight champion of the world. In New York on September 11, 1950, Louis and Charles signed a contract before the state boxing commissioner, Edward Eagan. The match was set for September 27. Then the Brown Bomber boarded a train at Penn Station and left for Pompton Lakes, New Jersey, to set up camp.

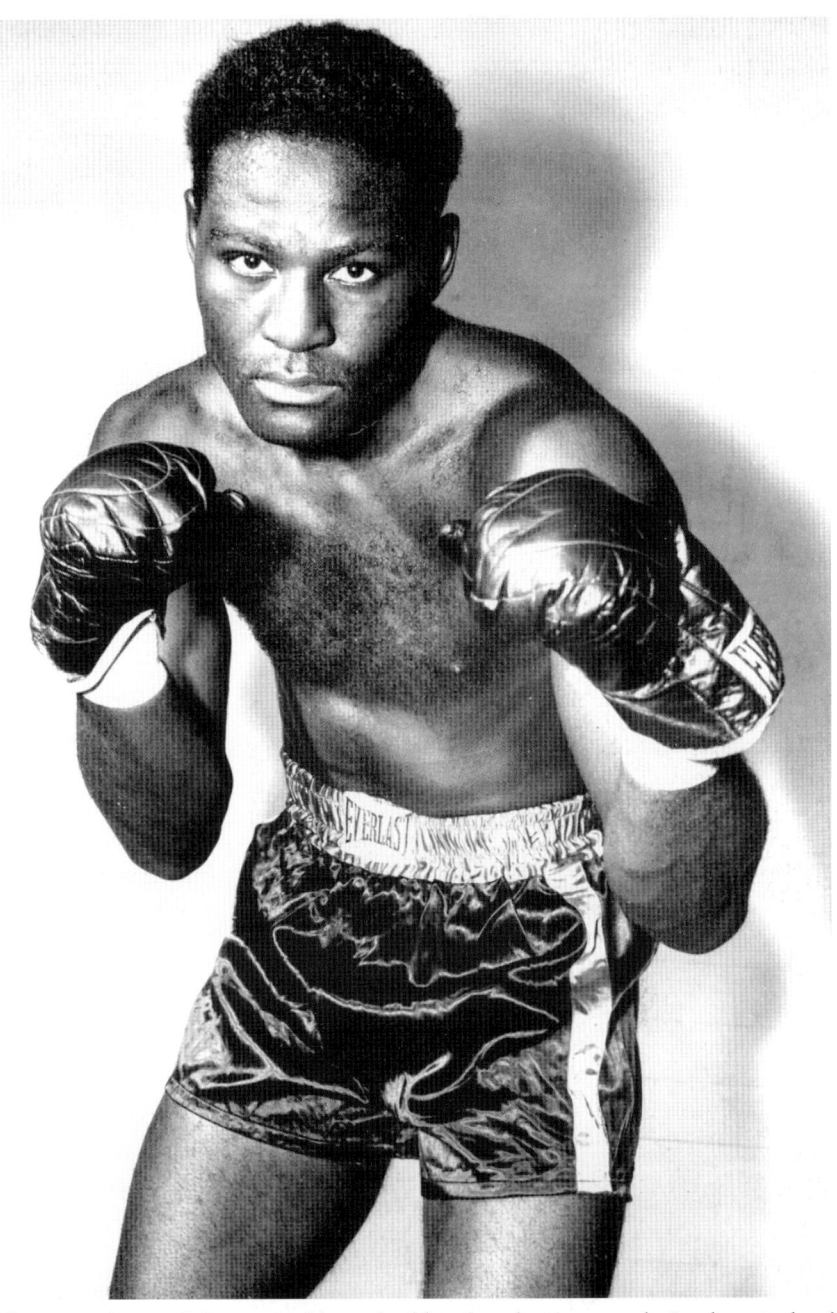

The fight would receive the year's biggest publicity buildup for a boxing match. In the minds of everyone connected to it—fans, officials, the media—there would be seemingly no doubt as to who was champion. Charles found himself conflicted: Louis was his hero. He had sparred with Louis during World War II, and for many years, he had kept a scrapbook of clippings on the Brown Bomber. But now he had to claim his own place in heavyweight lore. That July, doctors in Illinois examined Charles and cleared him to fight after he had suffered a bruised heart muscle while sparring. CBS would broadcast the fight to the nation at 10:00 p.m. on September 27.

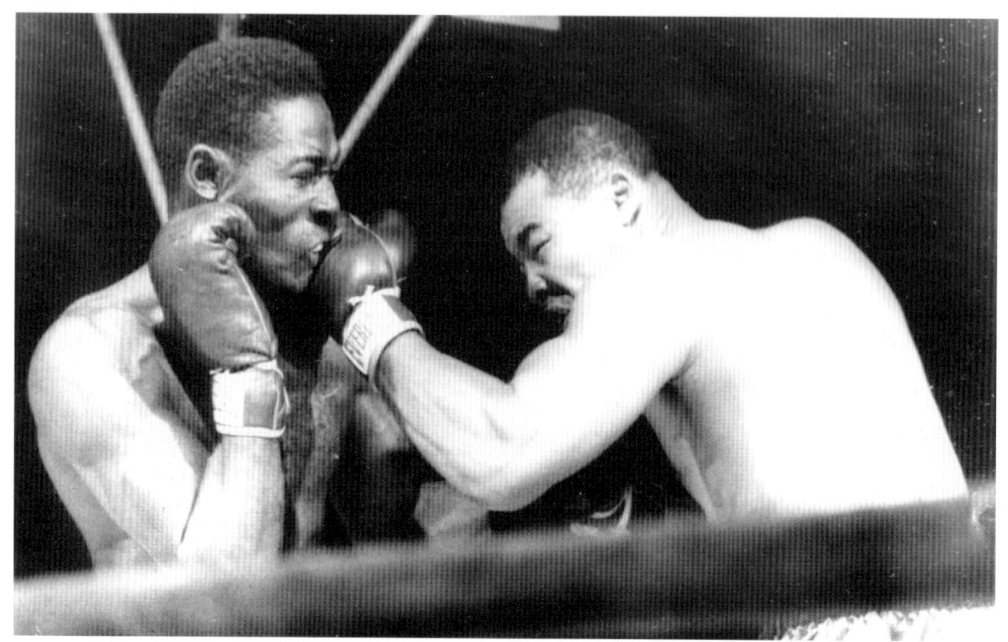

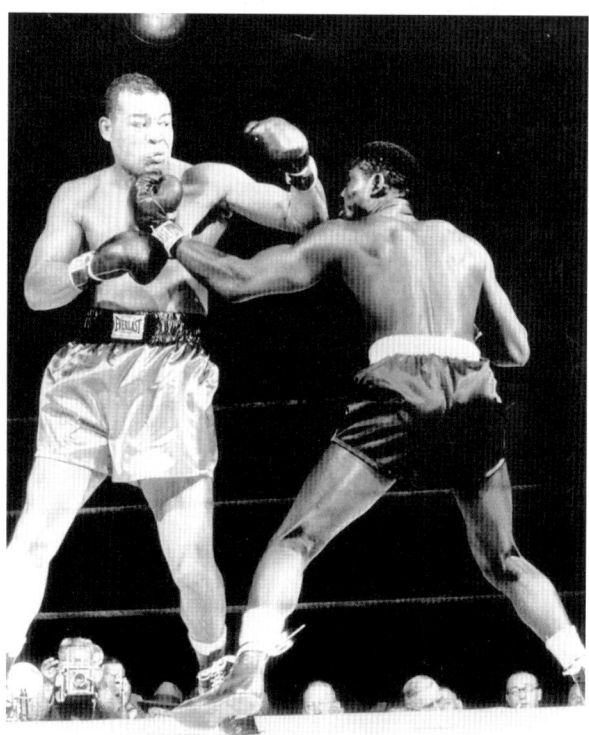

Both men were prepared for the fight, and although Joe Louis was said to be past his prime, Ezzard Charles later stated that in all his fights to that point, "no man ever hit me harder with a left. They told me I could hit him with a certain type of blow, but I found out I couldn't." But Charles kept battling, his stamina and skill—and his own excellent left—taking their toll on Louis. Charles bobbed and stuck and, as the rounds went on, began to hammer away at Louis, closing his left eye by the 13th. At one time, a tremendous left hook lifted Louis off his feet. The fight went the championship distance of 15 rounds, and at the end, there was no doubt in anyone's mind who had dominated the fight.

While the judges' scores were tallied at the final bell, Charles, his own face battered, had his gloves cut off and walked to the center of the ring. Announcer Johnny Addie raised his arm in victory. *Ring Magazine* had, perhaps prematurely to many in New York boxing circles, proclaimed Charles's international recognition as champion in its March issue, but by the end of the year, no one could say otherwise. Although he was never a man to complain, Charles remarked that "Louis took the bigger share of that purse even though he was retired and I was the official NBA champion. I only got 20%." There was still public sentiment, about which Charles said, "I've always recognized that following Joe Louis as a champion would be hard . . . After a man like that steps down, there's a natural reaction on the part of the public against the next man who comes along."

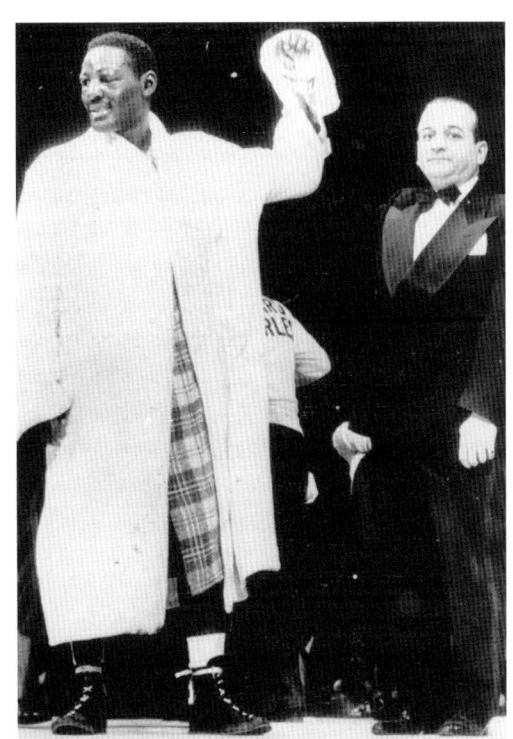

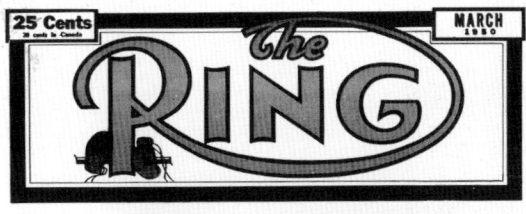

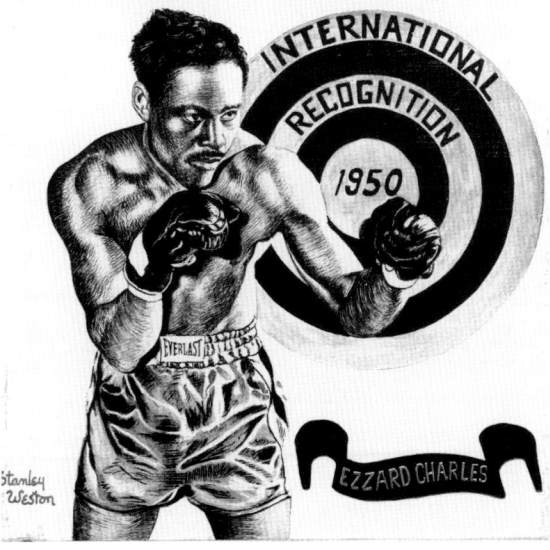

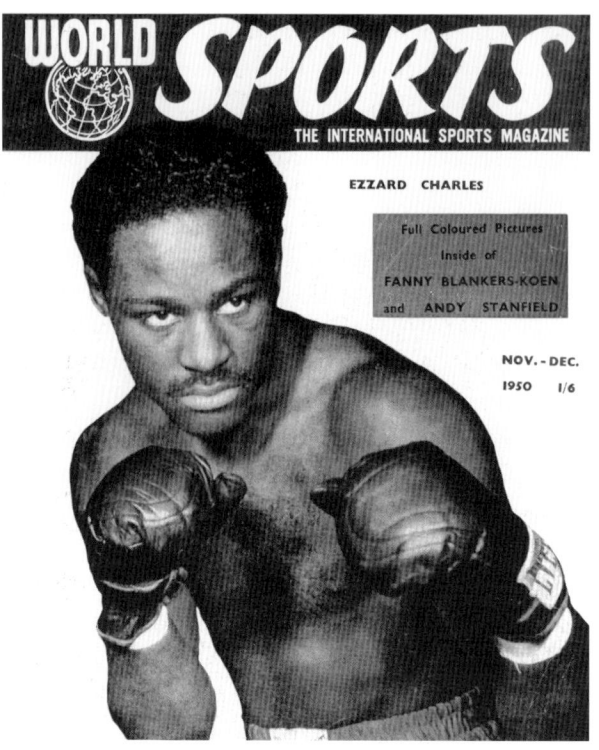

With the defeat of Joe Louis, Ezzard Charles was indisputably the heavyweight champion of the world. But if he thought no one could doubt his ring skills any longer, he was wrong. He was sometimes disparaged by many fans saying that he beat a Louis past his prime. Maybe, but he still beat him in a championship match. England's *World Sports* featured Charles on the cover, with a story about how he was not a "utility" champion but one truly deserving of the boxing world's acclaim. Even a comic book story was published, telling the life story of Charles and his defeat of Joe Louis. The gist of it all was that Ezzard Charles was a true champion.

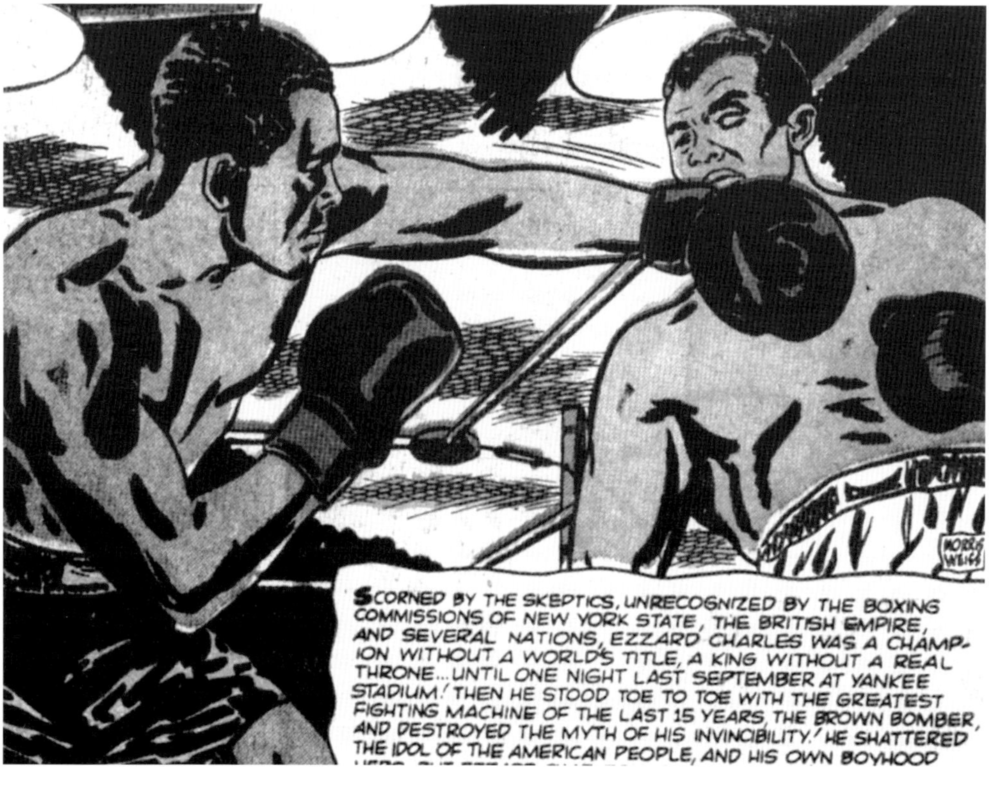

SCORNED BY THE SKEPTICS, UNRECOGNIZED BY THE BOXING COMMISSIONS OF NEW YORK STATE, THE BRITISH EMPIRE, AND SEVERAL NATIONS, EZZARD CHARLES WAS A CHAMPION WITHOUT A WORLD'S TITLE, A KING WITHOUT A REAL THRONE...UNTIL ONE NIGHT LAST SEPTEMBER AT YANKEE STADIUM! THEN HE STOOD TOE TO TOE WITH THE GREATEST FIGHTING MACHINE OF THE LAST 15 YEARS, THE BROWN BOMBER, AND DESTROYED THE MYTH OF HIS INVINCIBILITY! HE SHATTERED THE IDOL OF THE AMERICAN PEOPLE, AND HIS OWN BOYHOOD

In the April issue of *Ebony* magazine earlier that year, Charles made the cover and talked in an article on how he planned to beat Joe Louis. Charles was weary of always being in Louis's shadow, justifying his skills to an African American community that had made Louis a national icon. His unified belt did little to dispel the shadow, however.

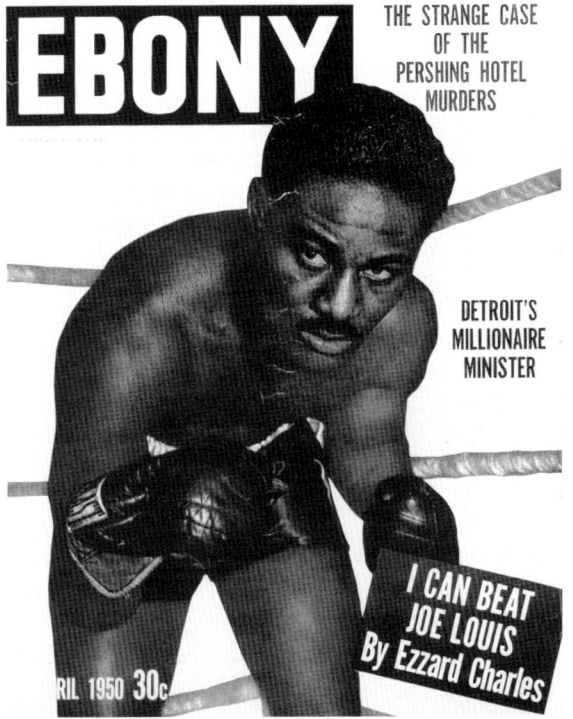

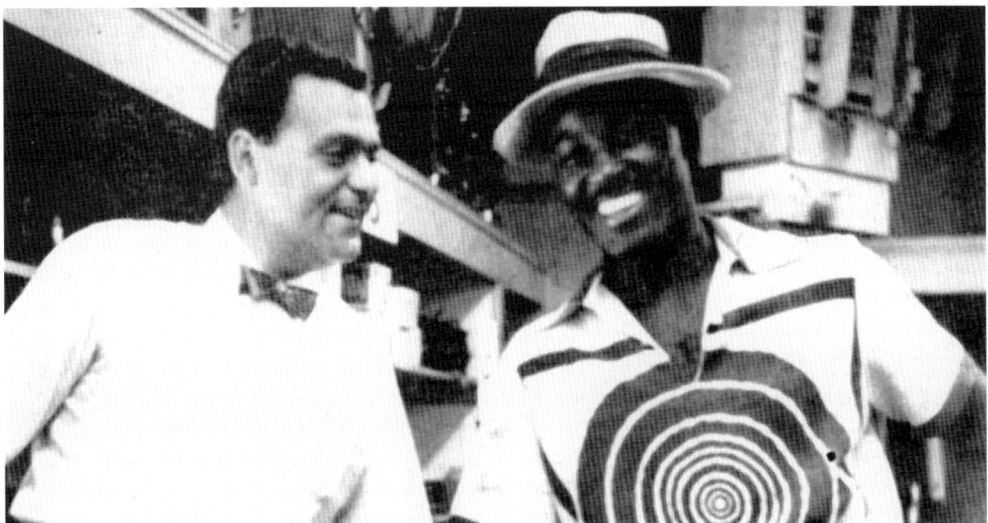

Back home in Cincinnati, Charles visited with one of his old managers. When Charles was a high school student, Max Elkus, a clothing merchant and pawnbroker, gave him a job in the clothing store while he managed his boxing career. Located at Seventh Street and Central Avenue in the West End, the store had a jingle that local fan Stuart Hodesh still remembers, "One block, two blocks, three or maybe four. Walk a little further down to Max's Clothing Store. Finest clothing, sportswear and slax, you really save your money when you buy from Max." After Elkus died, his sons Bobby and Gene (posing here with Charles) took over Charles's management.

CINCINNATI BOXING

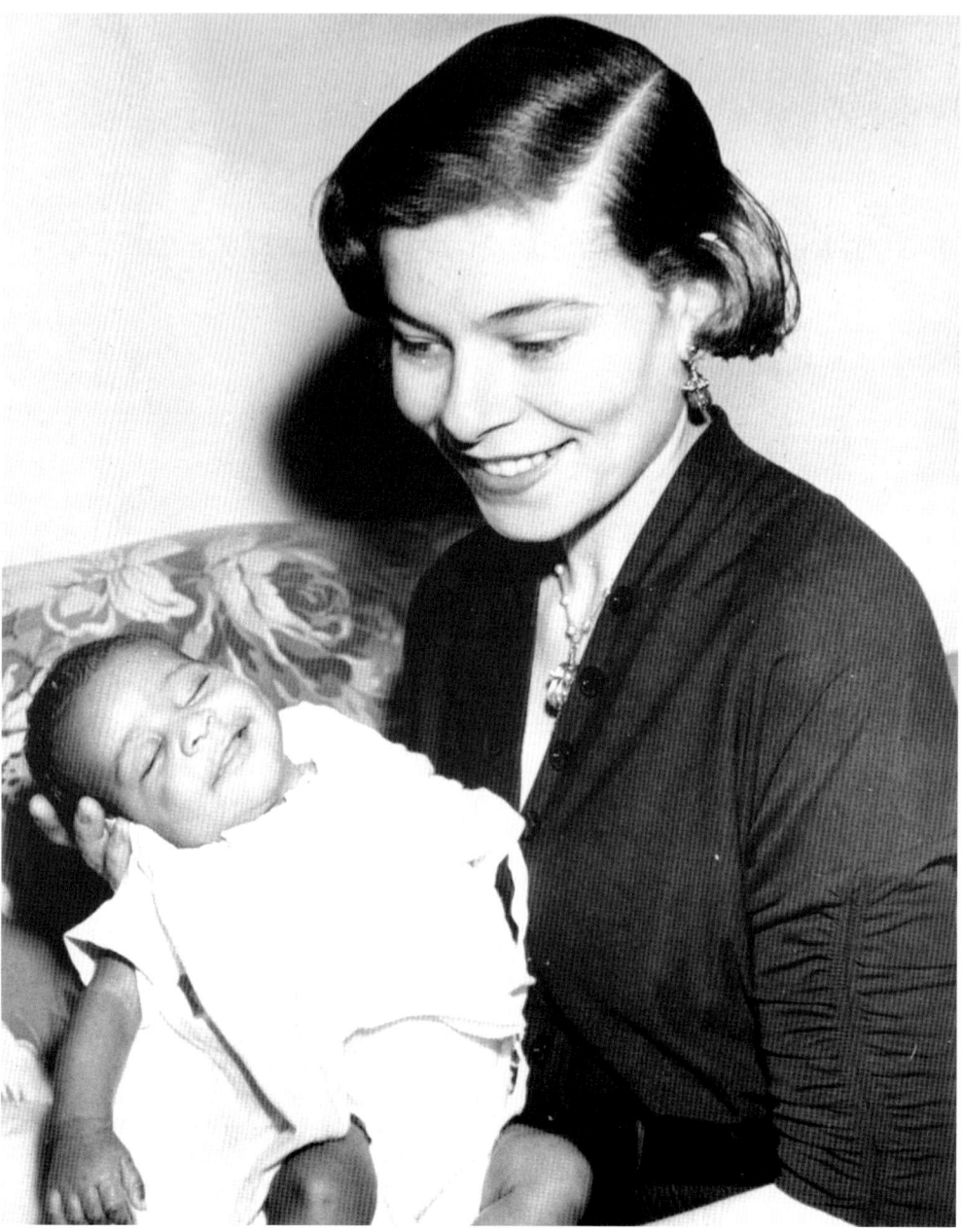

Even with the considerable publicity of being a heavyweight champion, Ezzard Charles still remained a very private person in many ways. In New Kensington, Pennsylvania, on December 30, 1949, he married Gladys Gartrell of Cincinnati. Yet they did not announce their marriage for several months. And when their daughter Deborah was born on February 13, 1951, Ezzard and Gladys only permitted a few photographs of the event. By this time, they were living in the Pittsburgh area, but they also maintained a residence in Cincinnati so they could be close to relatives and so Ezzard could train.

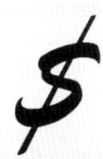

After defeating Jersey Joe Walcott twice, Charles gave him a third opportunity to beat him when the two met in Detroit in 1951. On January 12, Charles had successfully defended his title with a 10th-round knockout of Lee Oma and then followed that with two exhibition matches in Louisiana, one with his longtime sparring partner, Jimmy Brown. In Detroit, the fighters locked up at the legendary Olympia, and Charles retained the championship with a decision in 15 rounds.

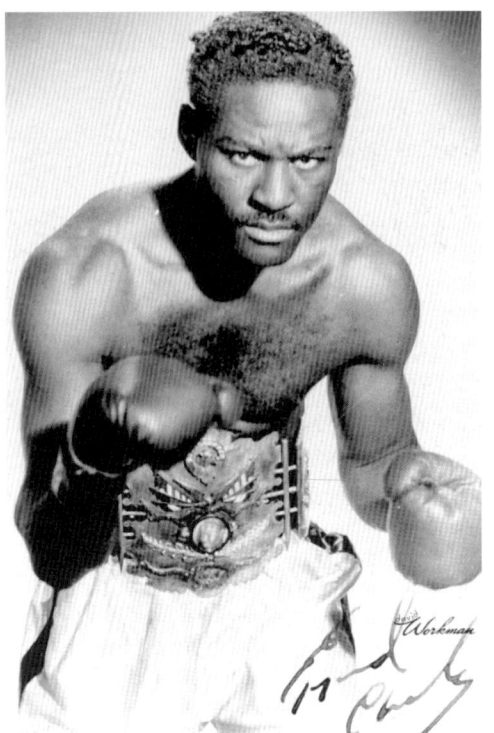

Seeing a scowl on the face of Ezzard Charles was a very unusual occurrence, and, in fact he reserved it for the publicity shots. Even then, he had to be strongly encouraged to do so. His constant smile was one of the memorable things about him. However, for postcards to be autographed for his fans, Charles did strike a menacing pose. (Photograph courtesy of Stuart Hodesh.)

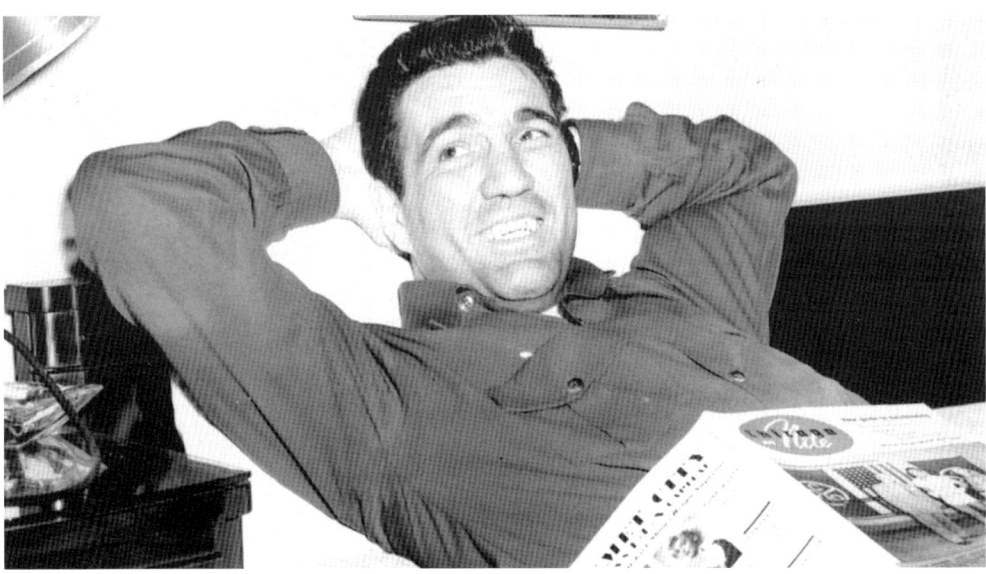

Before Joey Maxim went into the army during the war, Charles fought him twice in 1942, decisioning him in 10 rounds in both fights. Their rivalry picked up again in 1949 when Charles won in 15 rounds in the Cincinnati Gardens. On the eve of their May 30, 1951, matchup in Chicago, Maxim looks positively relaxed, but Charles beat him again in 15 and then once more in San Francisco on December 12. However, he was never able to knock out the very tough Maxim.

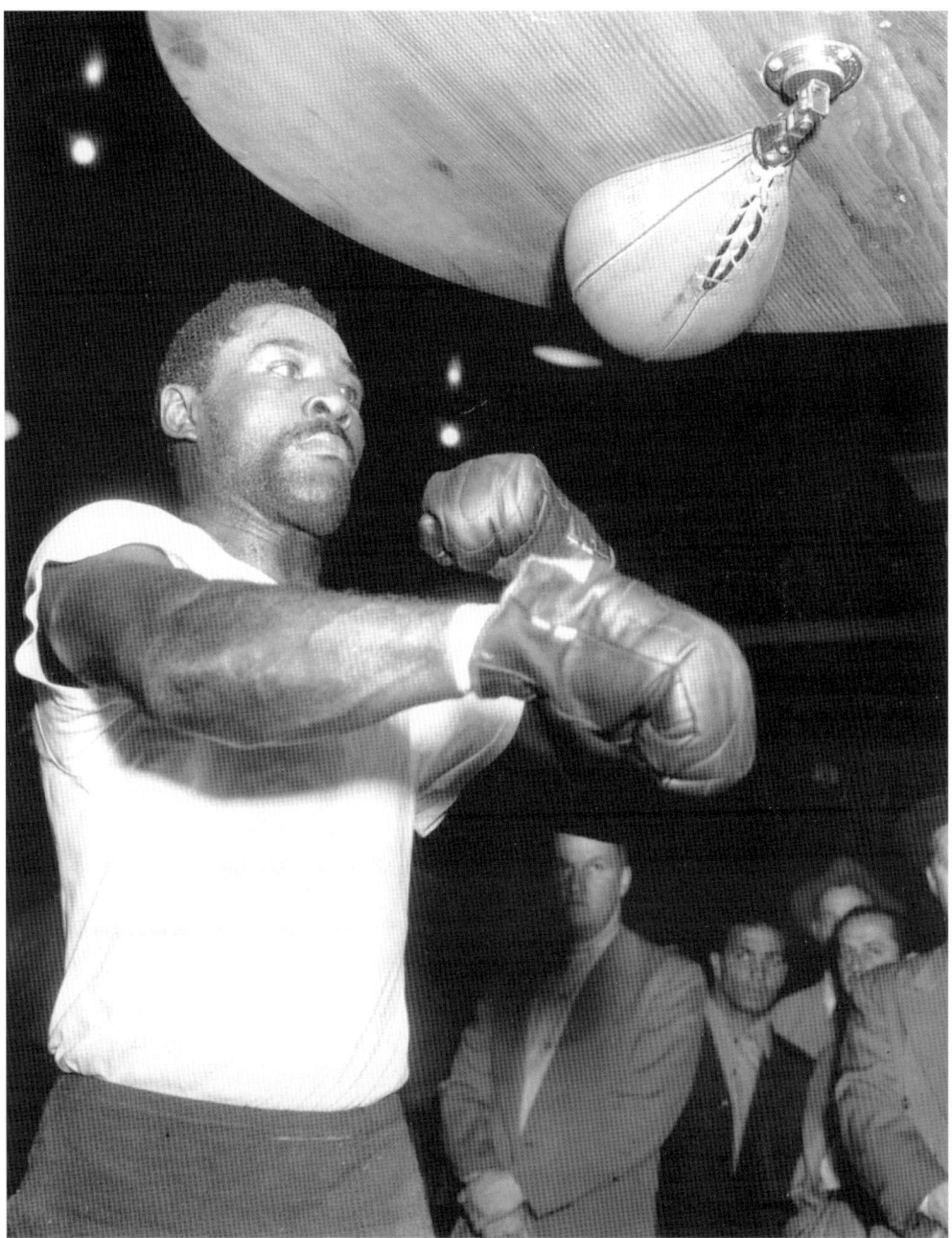
Charles trained for the 1951 Maxim match with his usual steady approach and concentration. Hitting the speed bag in this photograph, the handsome Charles decided to try for a little more fierceness in his demeanor by growing a beard. A British reporter once remarked that the most colorful thing about the publicity-bland Charles was his moustache.

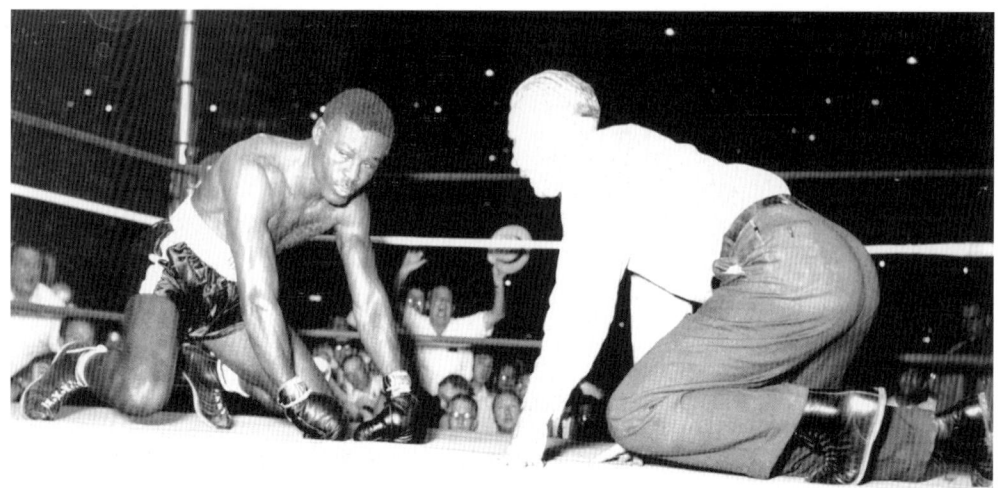

Ezzard Charles beat Jersey Joe Walcott in Chicago and in Detroit, but their third matchup in the summer of 1951 would not yield the same result. Fighting on July 18 at Forbes Field in Pittsburgh, the Charles-Walcott fight was the first heavyweight championship match to be held in that city. Both men were in excellent condition for the hot outdoor bout, but Walcott was far more aggressive in seeking to wrest the title from Charles. In the seventh round, Walcott flattened him, and although Charles struggled to his knees, he could not make it. Referee Buck McTiernan counted Charles out, and Jersey Joe was the new champion of the world. It was voted the "Fight of the Year" by *Ring Magazine*.

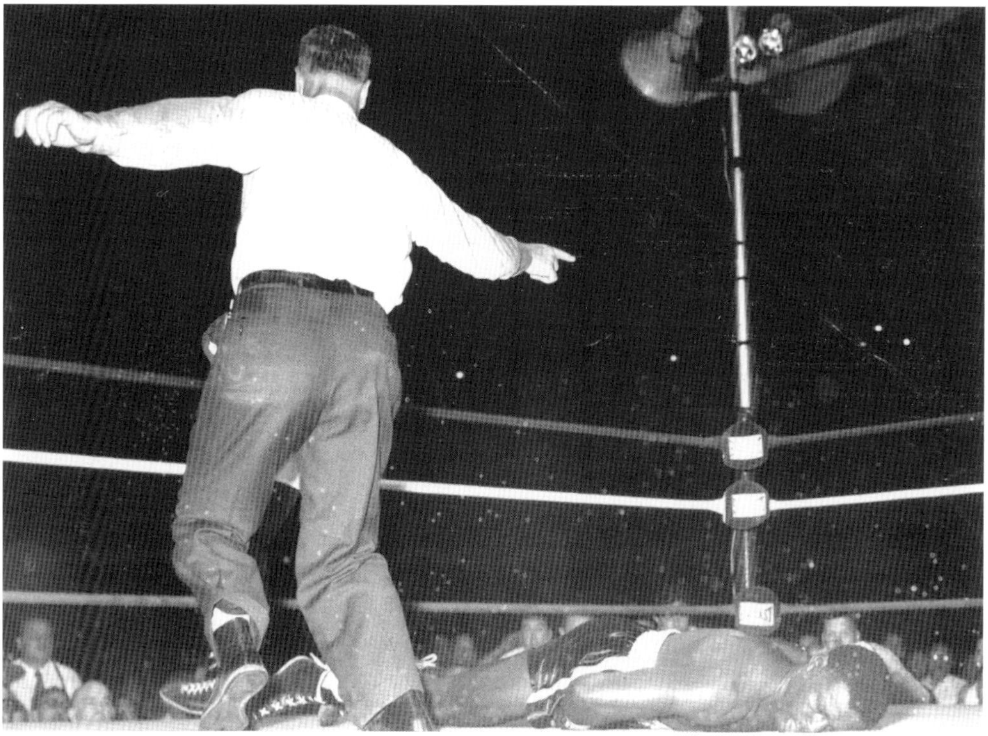

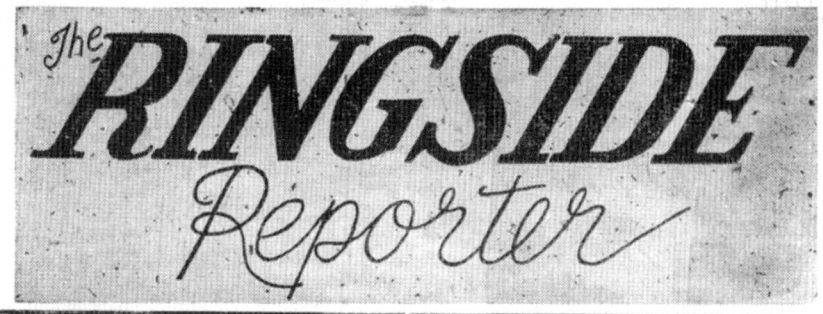

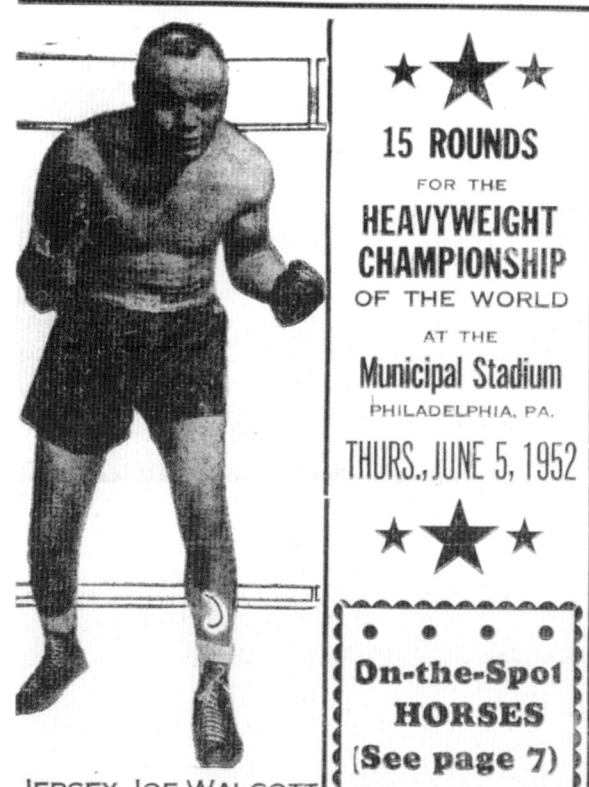

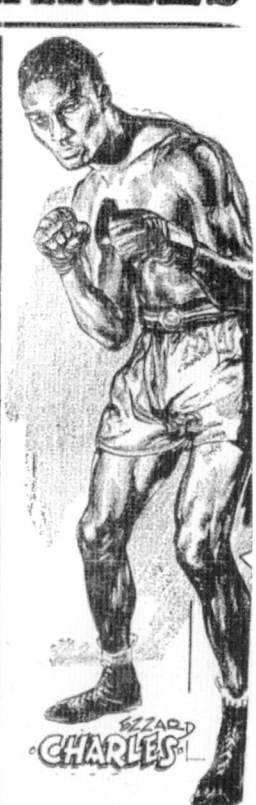

There would be a fourth bout between the fistic rivals. The next year, on June 5, 1952, Charles tried to regain his crown from Walcott in Philadelphia but lost again, in a 15-round decision. The fight was notable also for being the first heavyweight fight to be refereed by an African American, Zach Clayton. Walcott and Charles finished their careers 2-2 against each other. Three months later, Walcott lost the belt to the "Brockton Blockbuster," Rocky Marciano. Marciano successfully defended a rematch with Walcott the next year, knocking him out in the first round in what was Walcott's last fight.

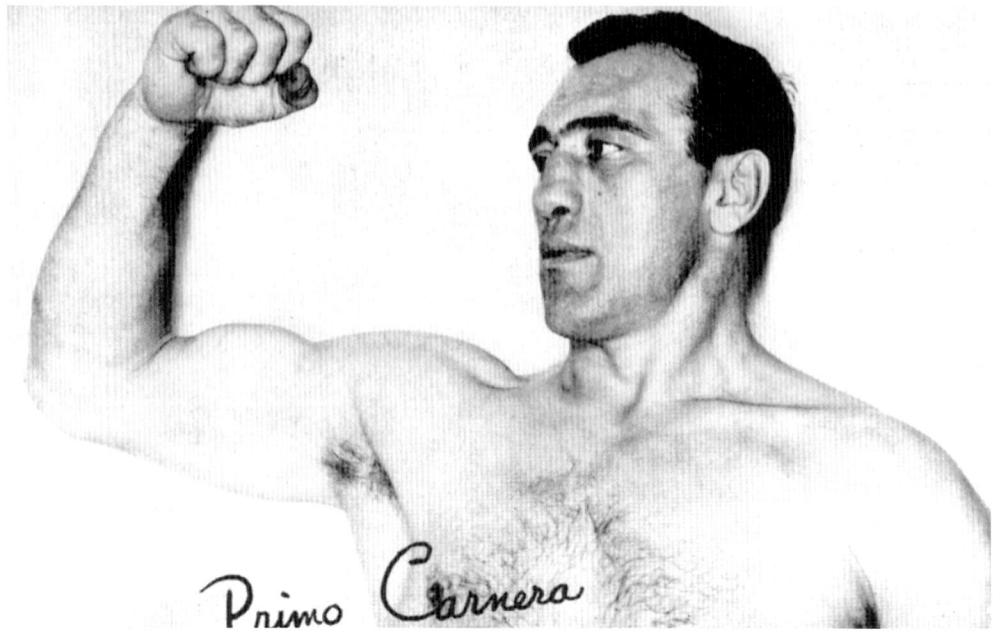

Primo Carnera, the "Ambling Alp" from Italy, was world heavyweight champion from 1933 to 1934. Known more for his massive size than for any real ring skills, Carnera became a professional wrestler after leaving the boxing game. In January 1955, the former fistic champion showed up in the Cincinnati area when he participated in a wrestling show in Newport.

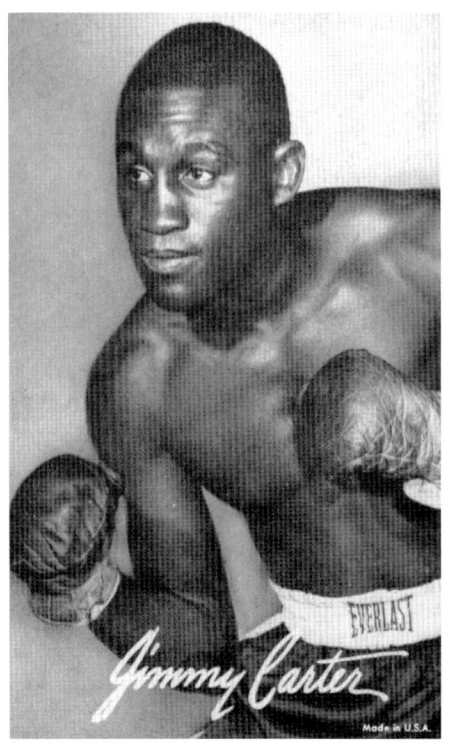

Bud Smith turned pro after the 1948 Olympics and had his first match at Music Hall on November 29 that year. He knocked out Torpedo Tinsley in the first round. From that point, his career steadily progressed. On June 29, 1955, in Boston, he avenged a 1950 loss to Jimmy Carter (pictured here) at Music Hall by decisioning him in 15 rounds to claim the world lightweight championship. Four months later, at the Cincinnati Gardens, Smith defended his title in a rematch with Carter, again winning as the fight went the distance.

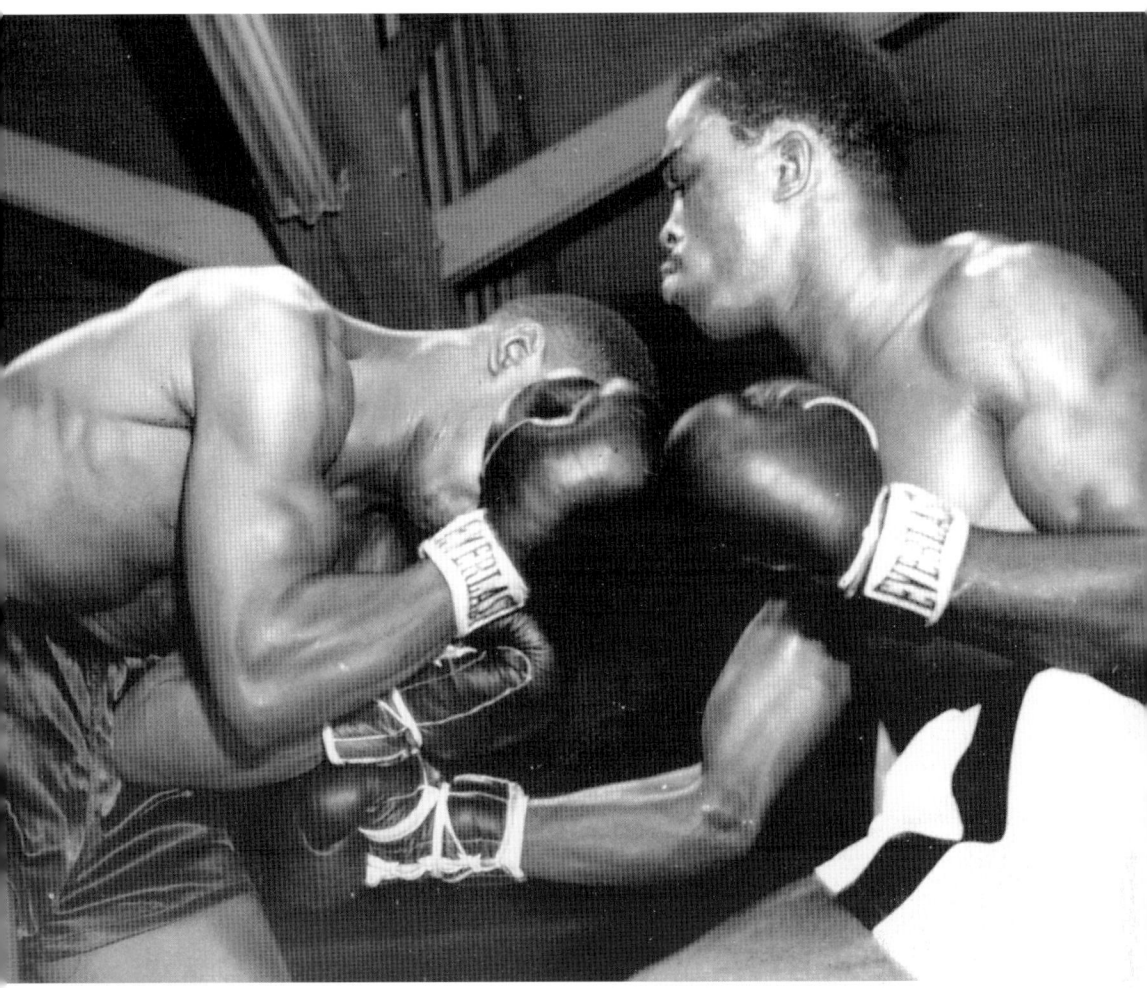

Back in the ring just three weeks after a TKO of Carl Coates, Bud Smith (left) had a match on August 24, 1953, against Charley Spicer. A 10-round welterweight bout, the fight seemed to be Smith's from the very beginning as the Cincinnati boxer continued the rise that would lead him to the lightweight championship two years later. With a series of left hooks to the head and some strong right uppercuts, Smith staggered Spicer in the sixth round. As he sat on his stool at the end of the round, Spicer's corner threw in the towel.

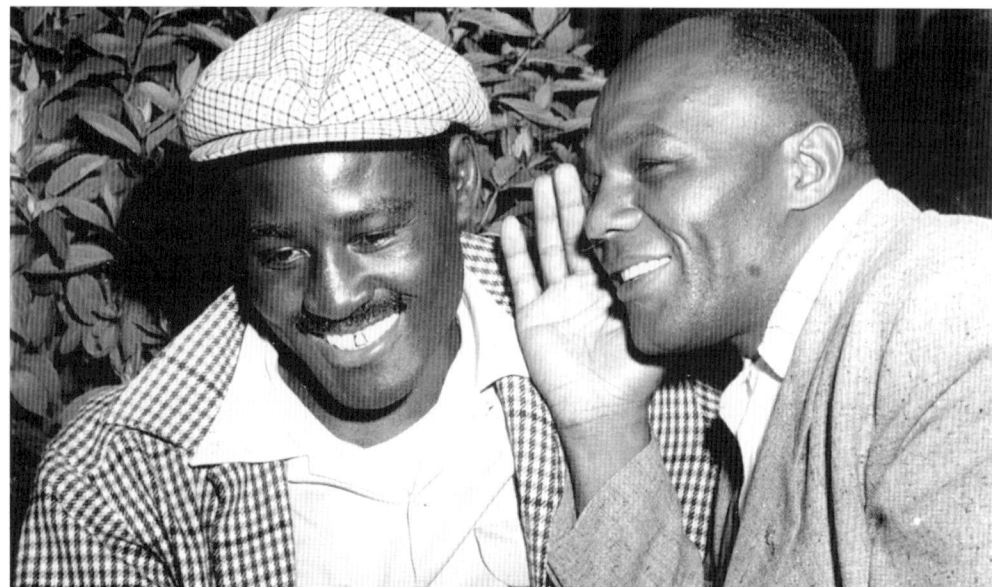

Fierce formal rivals, by the time Charles was training for his fight with Rocky Marciano on June 17, 1954, both he and Jersey Joe Walcott were ex-champions. In this image, Walcott (right) visits Ezzard Charles in camp, sharing a few laughs with him.

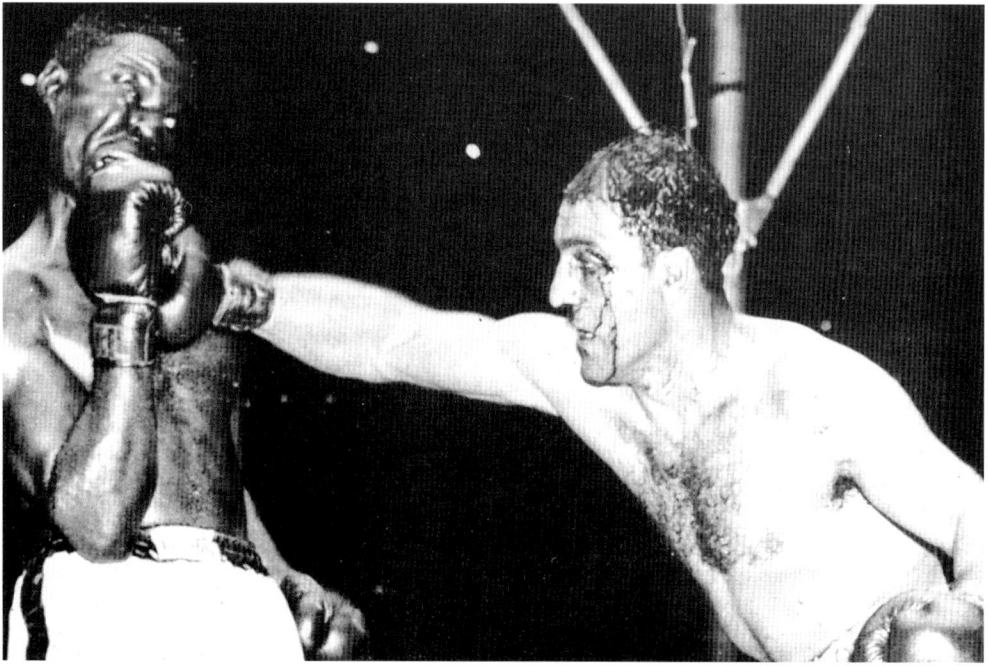

Charles weighed in at 185.5 pounds to Marciano's 187.5, and the fight was a long, drawn-out punching match. Charles circled and stabbed, trying to establish his right hook. Marciano just kept boring in on him and landed his hammerlike punches whenever Charles left him an opening. The fight went the distance of 15 rounds, and Marciano won the unanimous decision.

The publicity machine was in high gear for that first Charles-Marciano bout. *Ring Magazine* featured the fighters on the cover, the former champion seeking to reclaim his title by besting the new and seemingly unstoppable champion. Many fans would see the fight on closed-circuit television, but once the fight was over, the newsreel footage would let all of America view the action at their local theaters. Prizefight films had a long tradition in the United States, and this particular fight in Yankee Stadium would further that heritage. Six large cameras, along with smaller handheld cameras, captured every angle and important moment. Within hours of Marciano's victory, many theaters were showing the film.

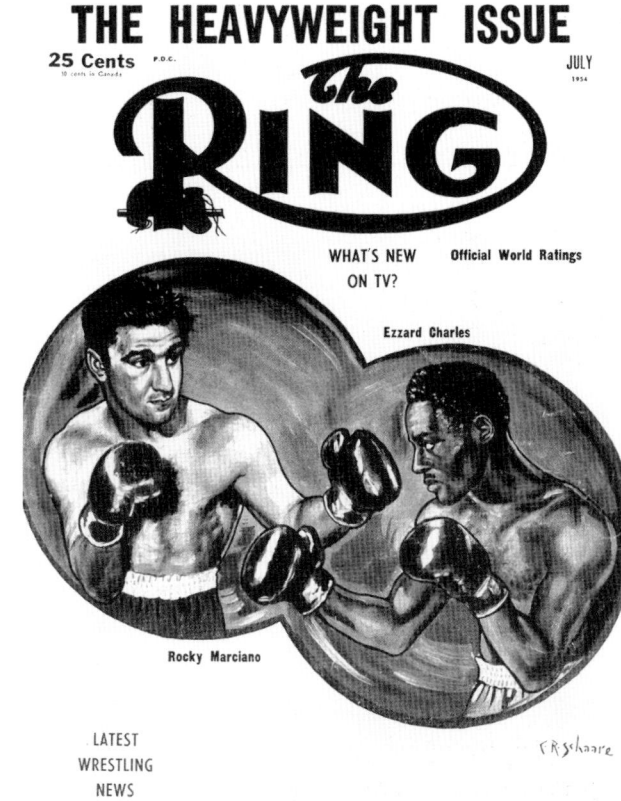

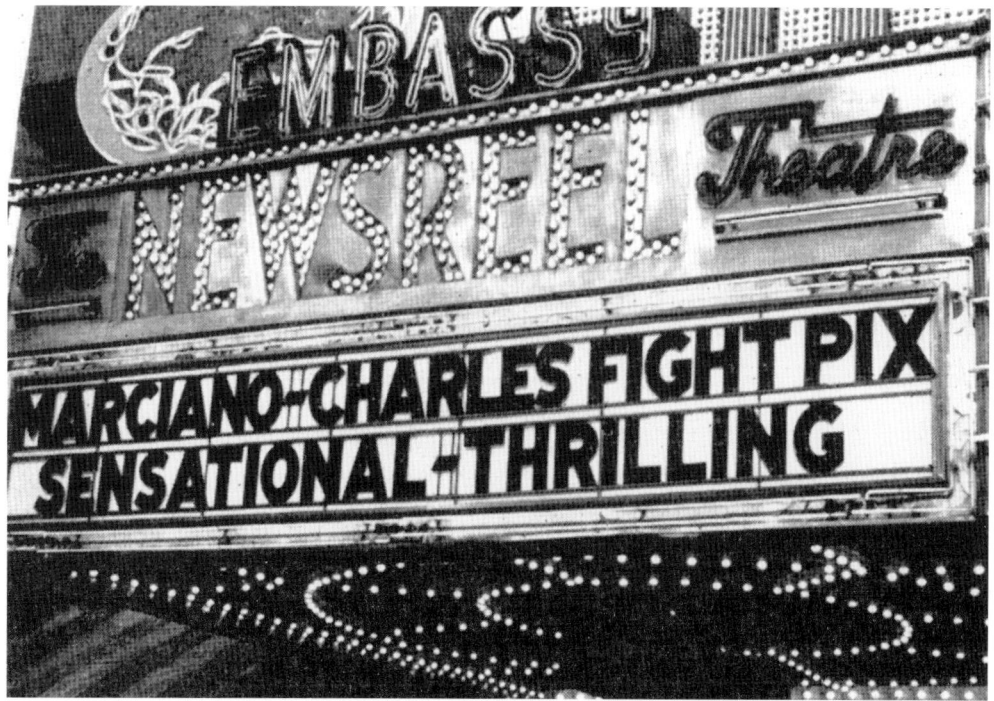

CINCINNATI BOXING

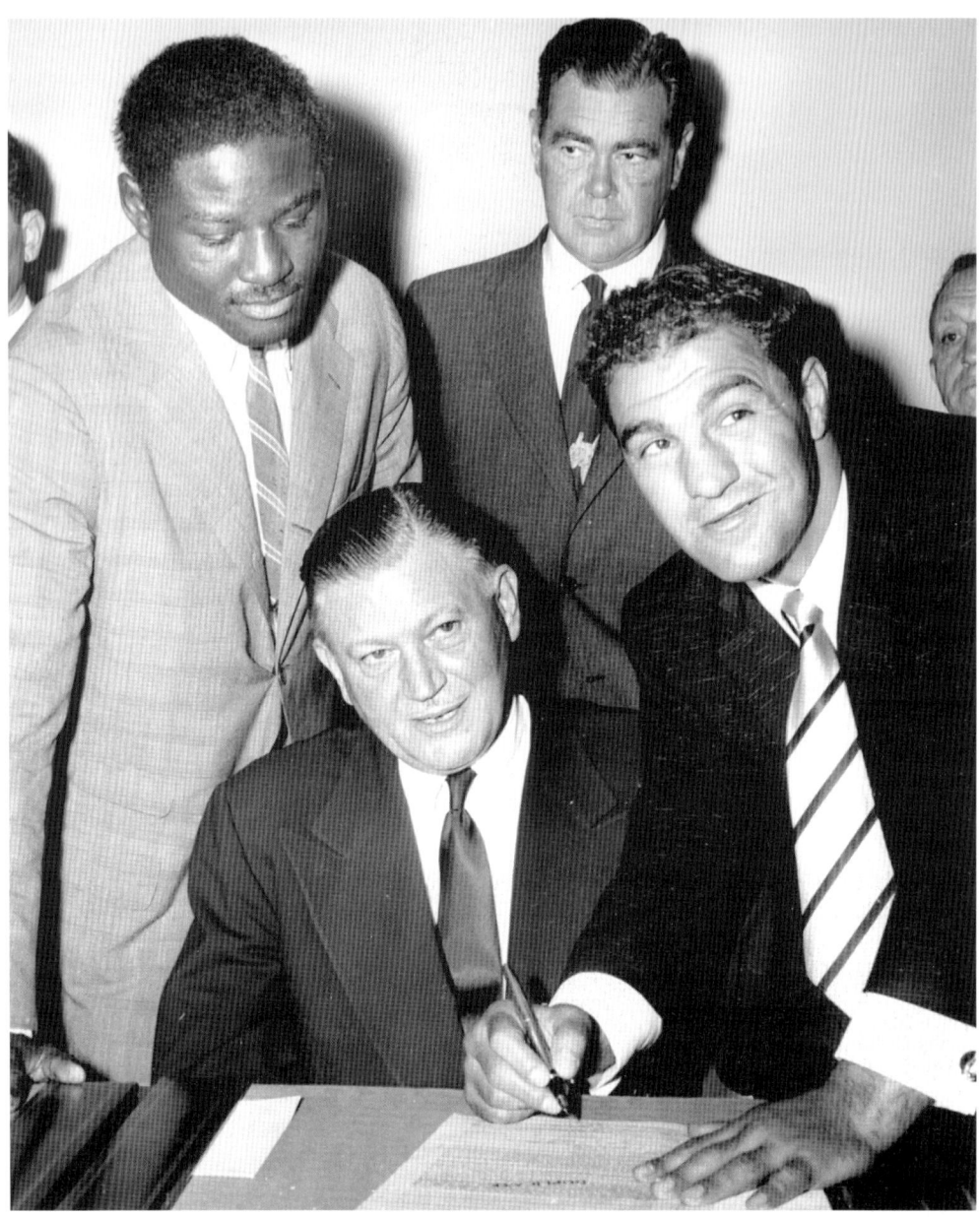

Ezzard Charles wanted a rematch. Rocky Marciano, too, was all for it. Another bout with Charles meant not only a great fight for the fans but an excellent payday as well. On August 3, the two pugilists met at the office of Robert Christenberry (standing at rear), the chairman of the New York Boxing Commission. Seated is Jim Norris, president of the International Boxing Commission and a key figure investigated during the boxing scandal trials of the 1950s. A sedate Charles looks on as Marciano puts his signature on the contract. This would be Charles's third attempt to recapture the championship.

Setting up camp at Kutsher's Country Club, a resort in Monticello, New York, Charles got to work on preparing for the upcoming fight. This was an intense, serious time for Charles. If he were ever to become champion again, he would have to mentally overcome the first defeat at the hands of Marciano and conquer him in the rematch. With hands taped, Charles stretches as part of his training routine. On the September 15, however, rain delayed the fight, but Charles kept up his preparations.

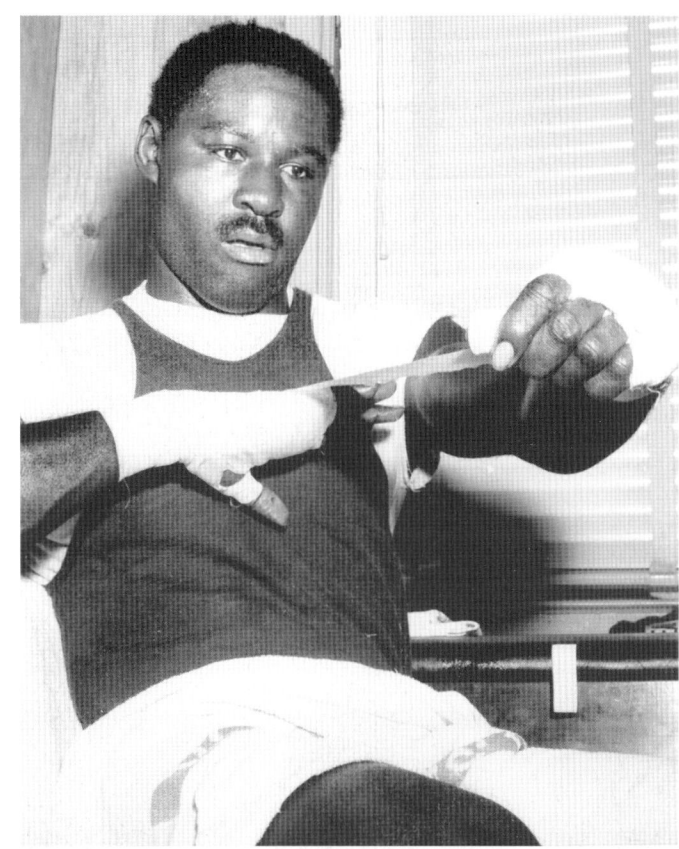

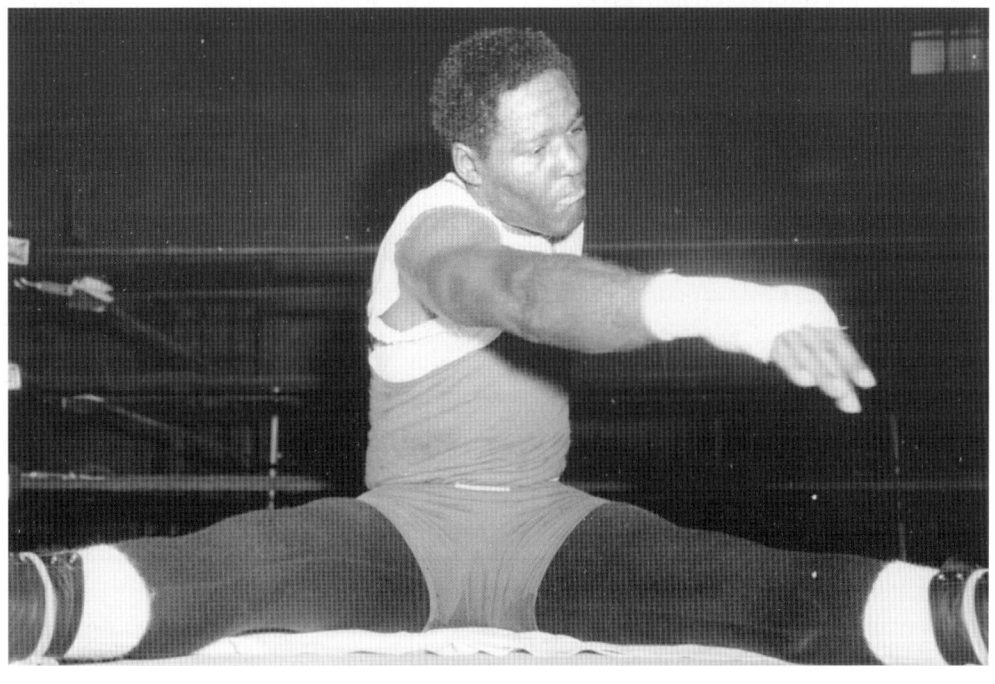

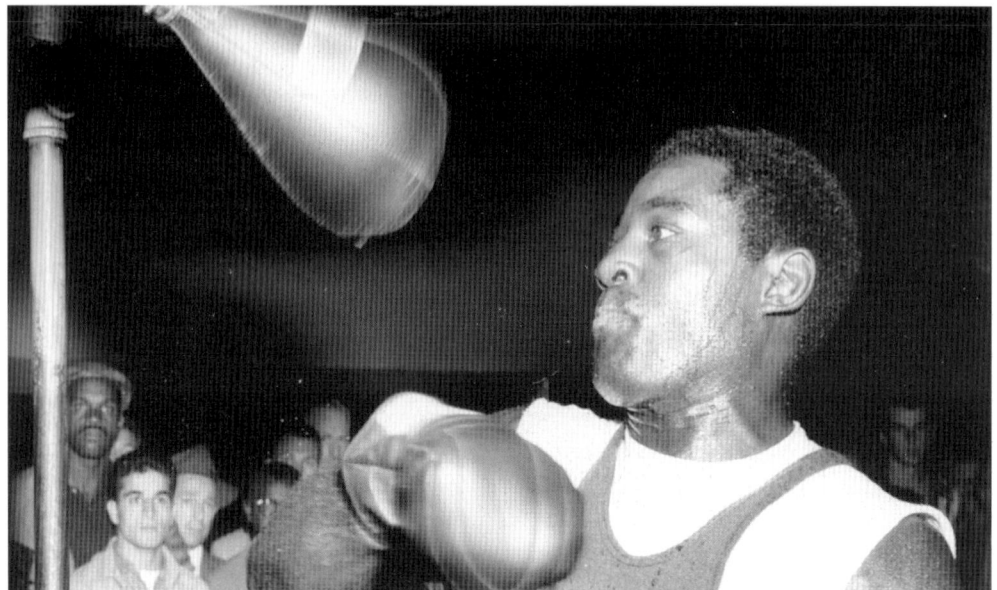

Rain postponed the outdoor bout at Yankee Stadium for a second time on the September 16, but Ezzard Charles stayed sharp by working out at the famous Stillman's Gym in New York City.

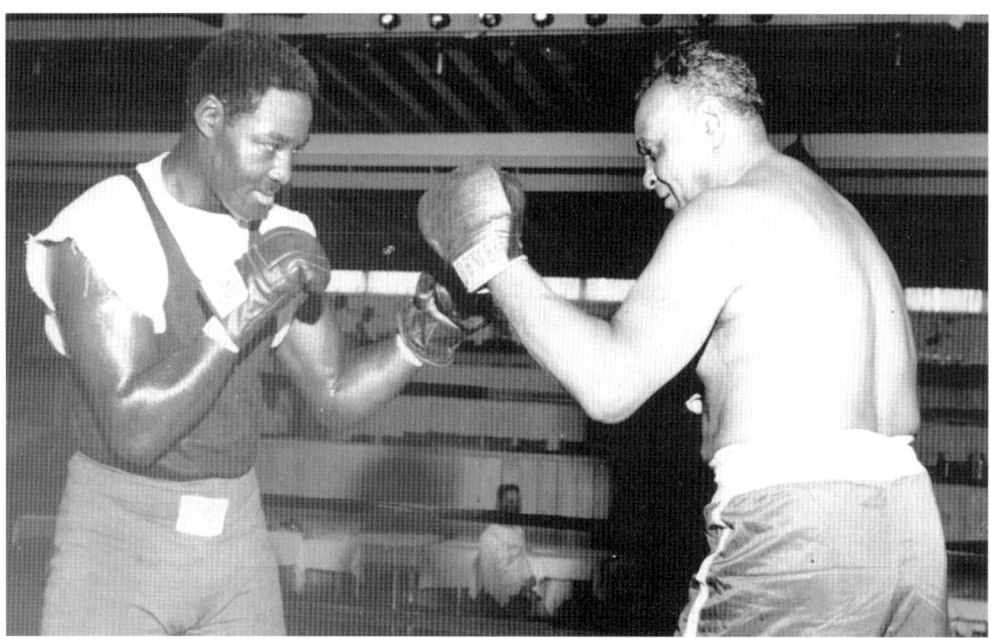

Former heavyweight boxer Harry "Black Panther" Wills earlier showed up in the Charles camp on September 3 in Upstate New York to talk with Charles and spar a bit in the ring with him. Wills was one of the greats of the heavyweight division, fighting over 100 bouts from 1911 to 1932. However, he was of that generation of fine African American fighters who were prevented from legitimate shots at the belt in the wake of Jack Johnson. Wills made his mark by fighting such other black legends as Sam McVey, Joe Jeannette, and Sam Langford.

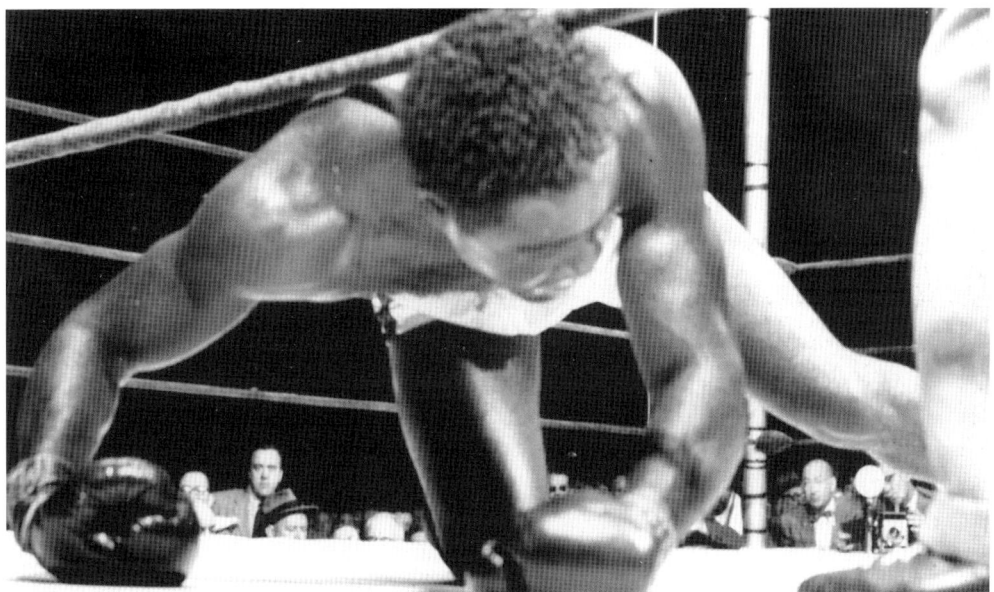

The fight finally came off on September 17. Charles started off with his usual ring aplomb, fighting a strategic fight and peppering Rocky Marciano with counterpunches. But in the eighth round, Marciano got to him and knocked him down. Charles rose from the canvas but a few seconds later was knocked out. Two days later, Charles and his wife, Gladys, met with the press in a Yankee Stadium dressing room to talk about the fight. His wife was subdued, but Charles, his face visibly swollen by Marciano's sledgehammer punching, was relatively animated and of good cheer. He knew what his mistake had been: although he was known for "boxing" rather than "punching," he tried to out slug Marciano and forgot his own strategy.

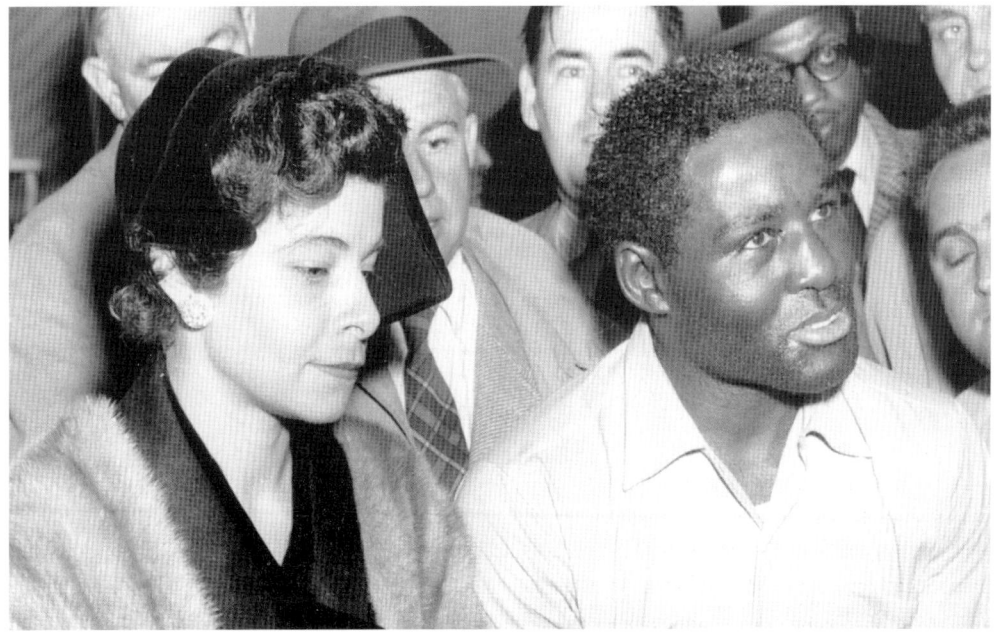

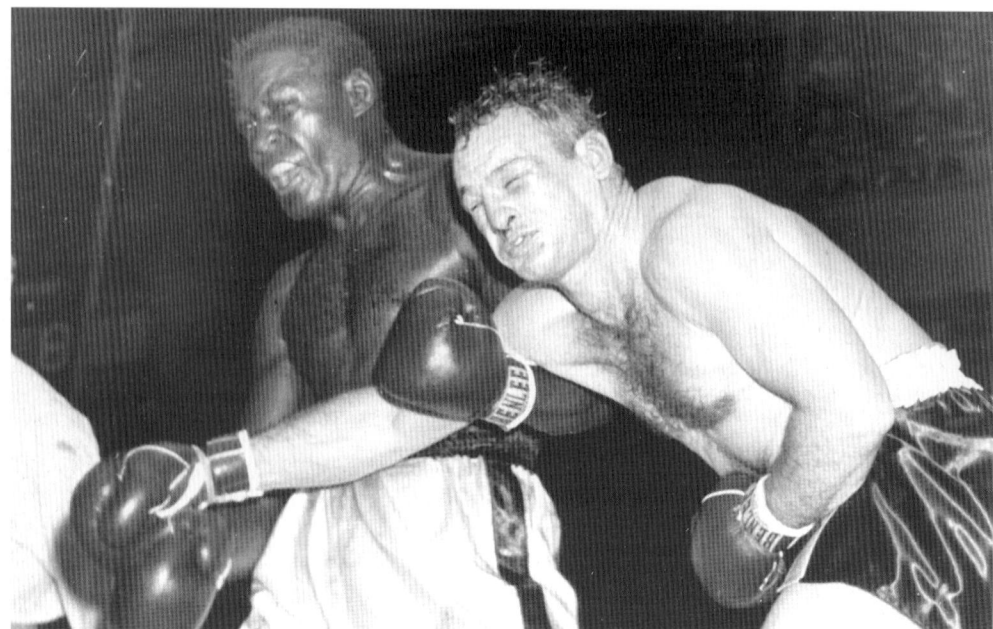

Ezzard Charles's first fight after Rocky Marciano was on February 18, 1955, against Charley Norkus at Madison Square Garden. Although he had dropped the two slugfests to Marciano, Charles was a drawing card because of his solid punching and ring finesse. By this time, though, he was 33 years old, and he had been fighting for a very long time. The ninth round of the Norkus fight was a dramatic one. After punching Norkus, Charles got tangled up in the arms of his opponent, and a few seconds later, he unleashed a stinging right to the chin of Norkus, sending him to the canvas for the only knockdown of the fight. Norkus stood at the five-count, but his awkward, lumbering style led to a unanimous decision for Charles.

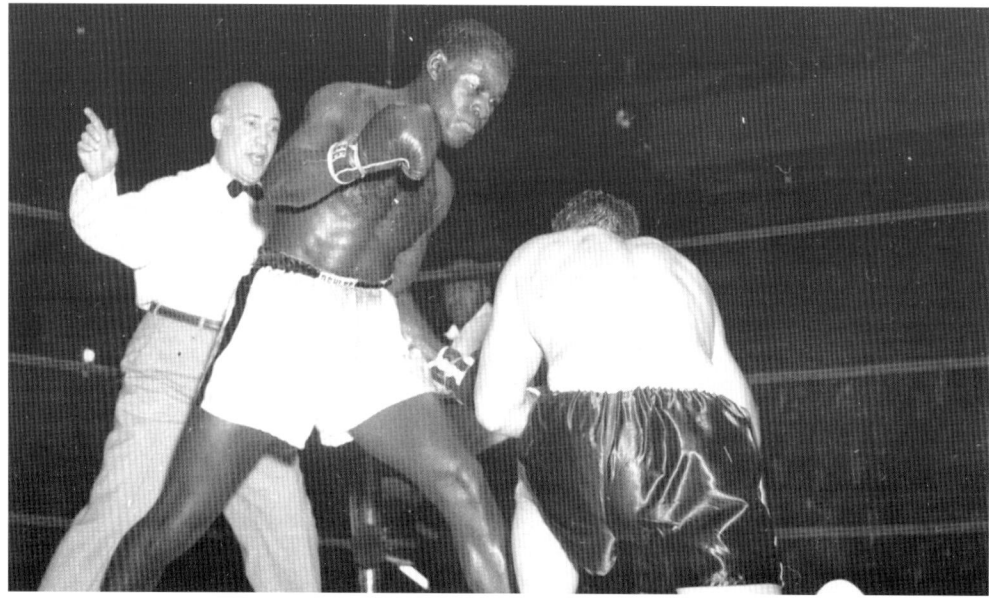

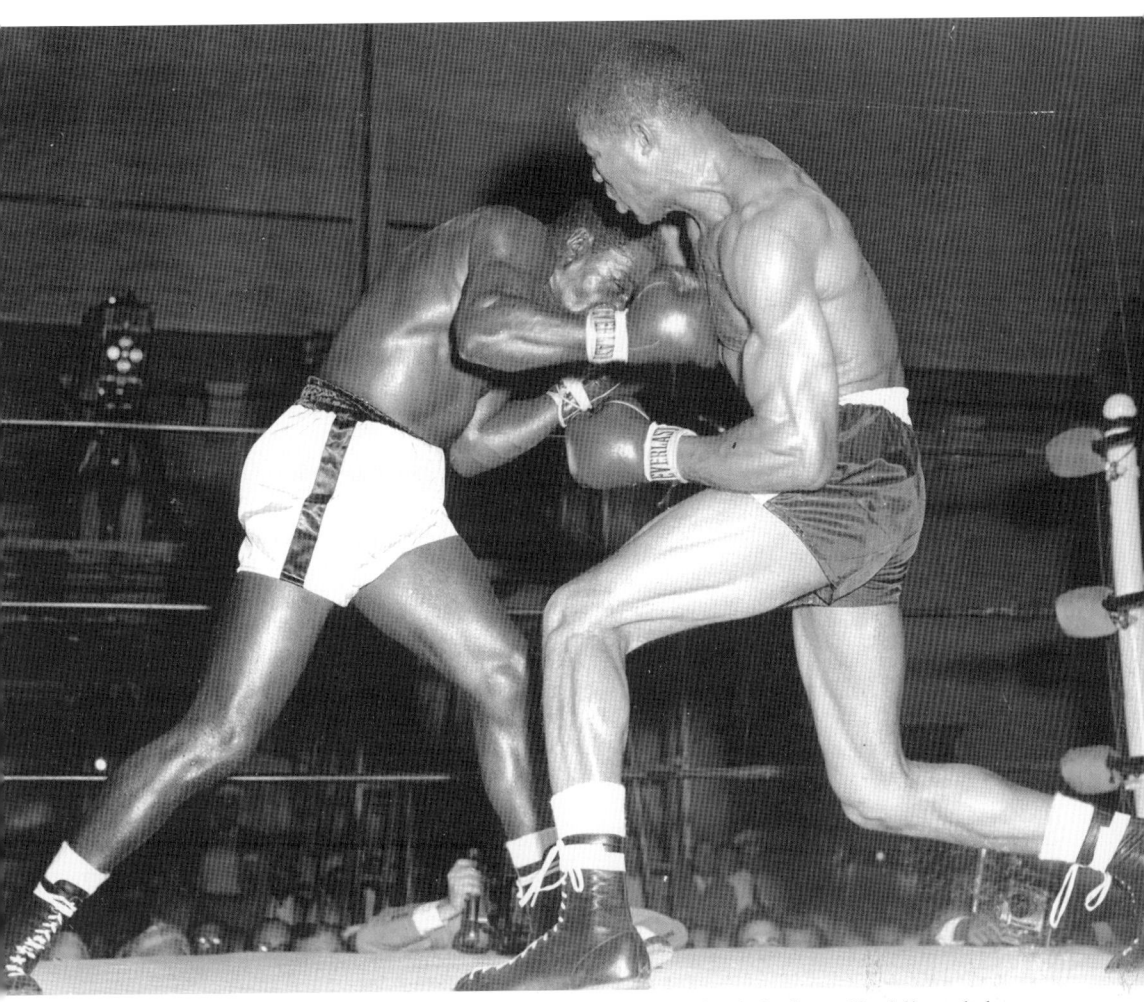

Charles hoped the victory over Norkus would signal a comeback for him. He followed that win with one over Canadian Vern Escoe and then two fights with John Holman. However, in the first match, Holman knocked Charles down in the first and again in the ninth. As Charles staggered around the ring, the referee called a halt and awarded Holman a TKO. In the rematch in Cincinnati's Music Hall on June 8 (shown here), Charles pounded out a 10-round decision. That fight, perhaps, was his last hurrah. Fighting a variety of tomato cans, Charles lost his next three fights, won a few, and then lost some more.

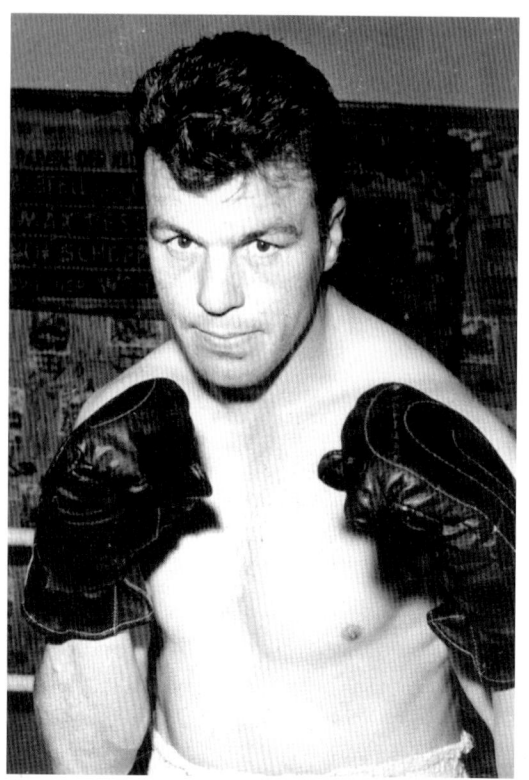

On the downside of his career by 1956, Ezzard Charles was just holding on and hoping for a few more paydays. He was coming off losses to a couple of journeymen and decided to take a fight in London against the Welshman Dick Richardson. Still somewhat of an attraction, Charles drew the British reporters and photographers to his training sessions for his fight against a fairly good heavyweight. But fighting Richardson on October 2 in the Harringay Arena, Charles just did not have it anymore. He was disqualified in the second round for persistent holding. On December 1, Charles announced his retirement. He stayed retired in 1957, but, in need of money, he came back in 1958. Charles would only have six more fights, winning two and losing four, one of which was a TKO against Cincinnatian Dave Ashley, the "Lockland Milkman," in what was his final local bout.

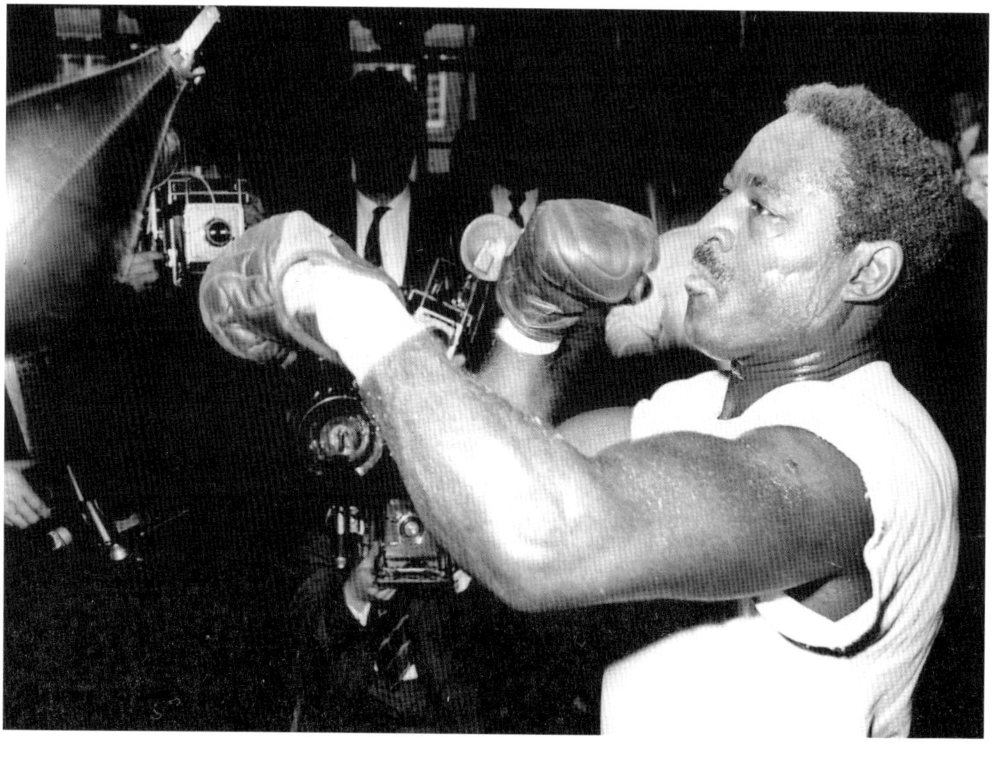

5

Contending for a Dream

1961–1990

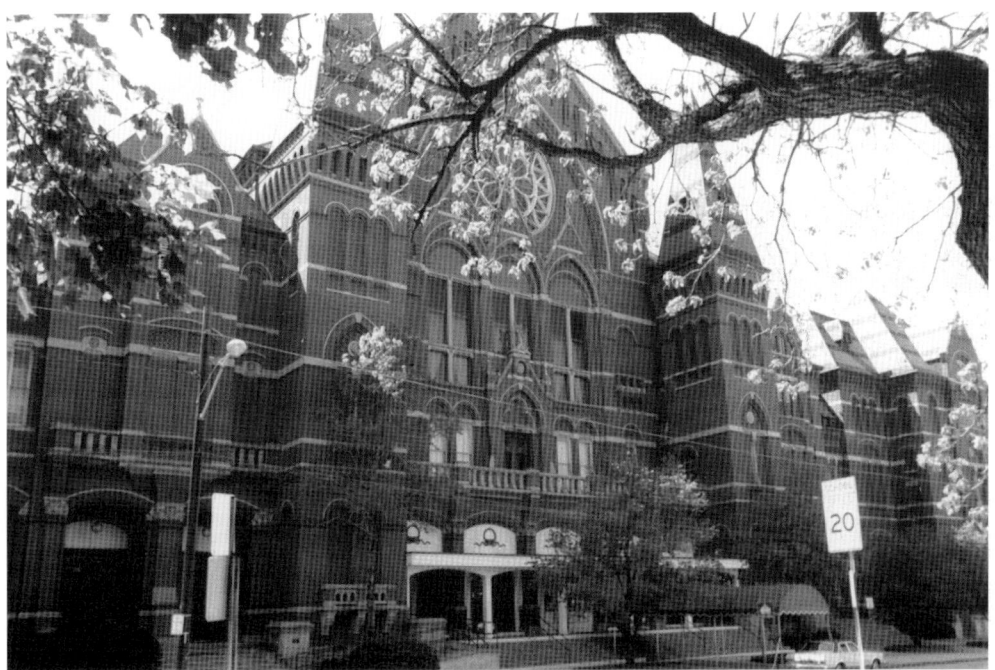

For decades one of the premier Cincinnati venues for professional fights, Music Hall had the odd distinction of straddling the neighborhoods of Over-the-Rhine and the West End, both of which were at one time heavily German and Jewish. Even after World War II, this aspect of its heritage was still somewhat evident. In 1954, German champion Hein ten Hoff knocked out Ralph Schneider here. Stuart Hodesh, a young Jewish boy attending the fight with his father, remembers being shaken by the rhythmic chanting and cheers from Hoff's German supporters in the balcony.

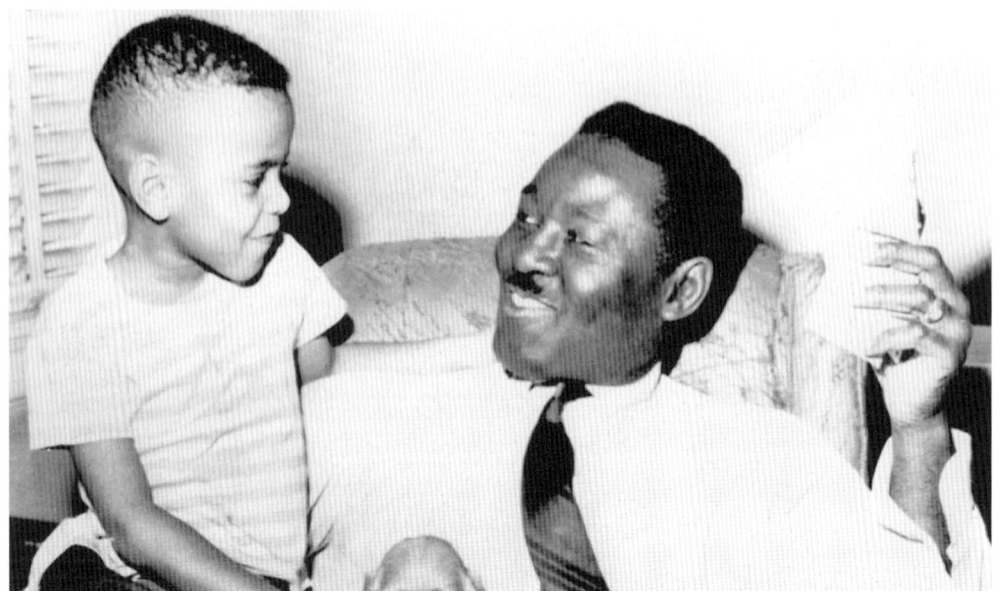

At the end of his career, Ezzard Charles was broke. Although he had made more than $1.5 million during his life of boxing matches, poor investments had taken every penny he had. The thing about Ezzard Charles was, however, that he never made excuses. He knew he had lost his money, but he was determined to pay off his debts and live his life. At first he did like so many other former boxers had done, trying the clownish circuit of professional wrestling, but he could not do it. He was a greeter at the Club Alibi in Newport for a while. In the photograph above, he poses for the camera with his son, Ezzard II, mulling over job offers. By the mid-1960s, Charles and his family were living in Chicago, where he had worked for youth welfare, public recreation, and later for the automobile license bureau. He had erased all his debts and was living simply with his wife and children.

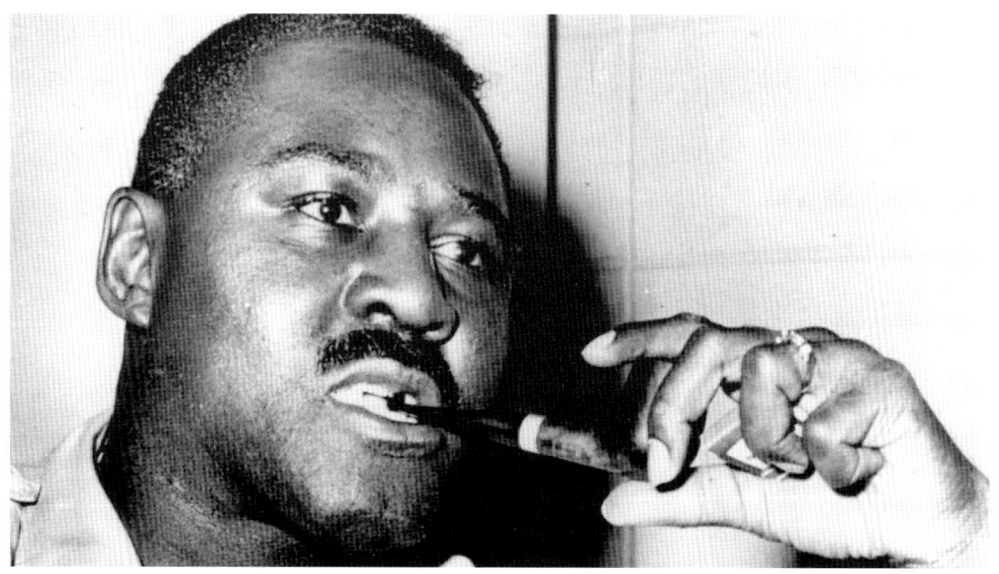

CONTENDING FOR A DREAM

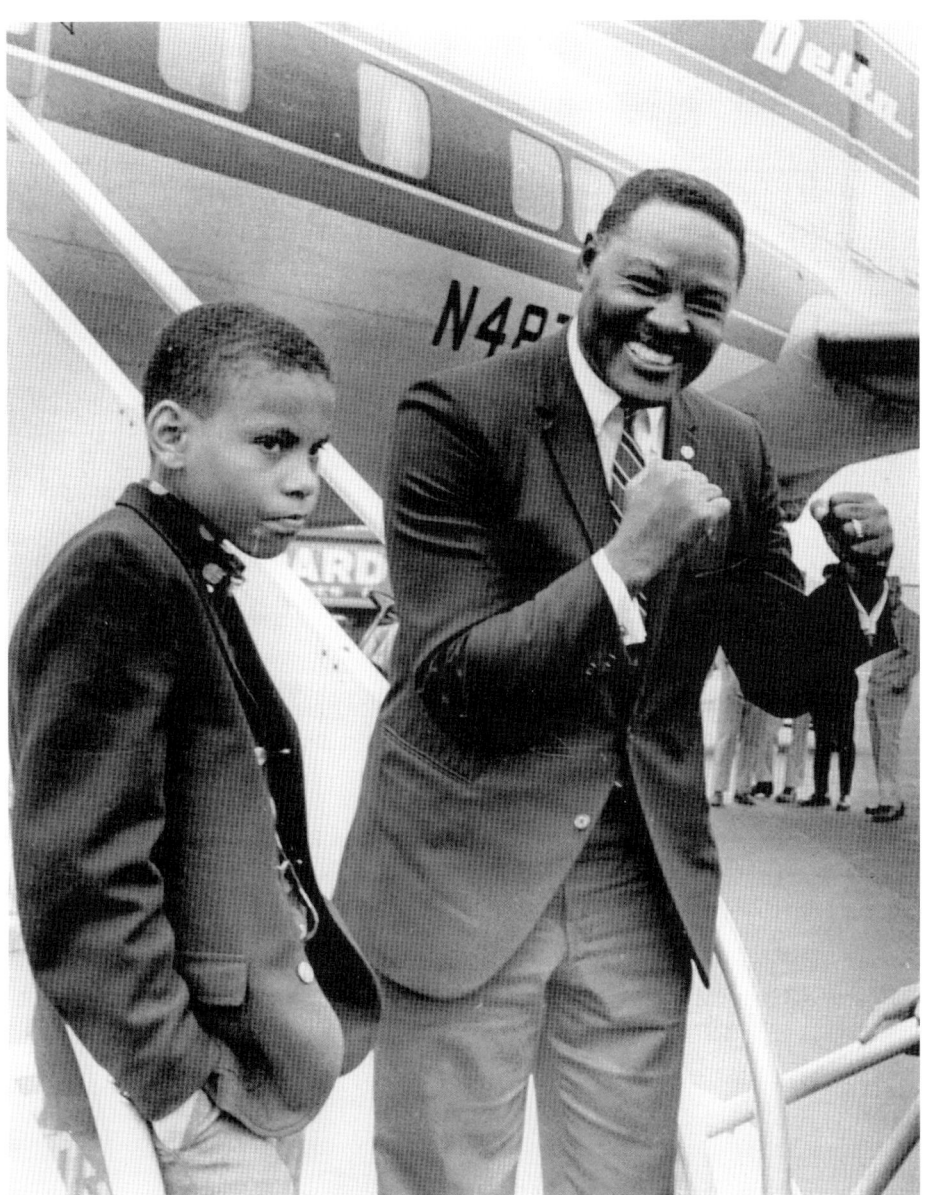

Occasionally he would make it home to Cincinnati, particularly for the reunions of the Woodward High School class of 1942. This photograph is of Charles and his son landing at Lunken Airport prior to attending the 25-year reunion. He strikes a familiar pose, but things were turning grim. In 1967, Charles was diagnosed with amyotrophic lateral sclerosis, Lou Gehrig's disease. His muscles were gradually weakening and failing him. In subsequent years when he visited Cincinnati, he would proudly refuse the arms extended to assist him, but he would place a hand on an available shoulder to steady himself. Soon he was confined to a wheelchair. Benefits were held for him in Chicago as former foes and current boxers came together to raise money for his care. On May 27, 1975, the Cincinnati Cobra died and was buried in Burr Oak Cemetery just outside Chicago. (Photograph by Jack Klumpe.)

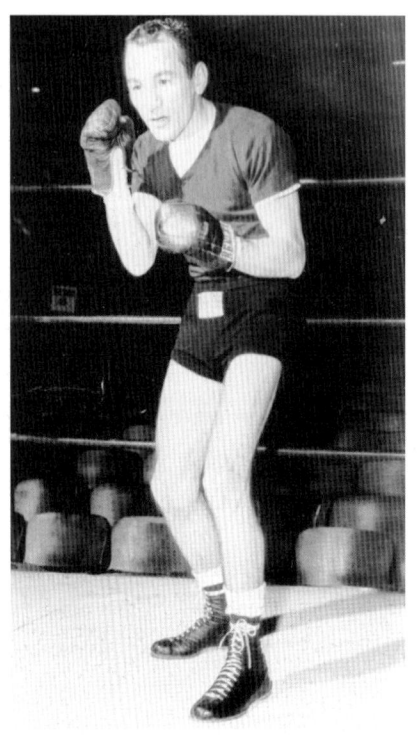

Carmen Iacobucci, the brother of Pat, was a flyweight whose career stretched from 1947 to 1970. He fought mostly locally, and mainly on the undercards of bigger fights. Carmen had a pretty good knockout punch but had to use it in the very early rounds. As fights went on in length, he tended to wear out but rarely was he knocked out. Instead he kept throwing—and stubbornly taking—punches, losing on points. Still he was a crowd favorite for his gameness. In a 1966 Music Hall bout copromoted by Ezzard Charles's old friend Richard Christmas, Carmen tangled with Gene Young and lost a 10-round decision. Carmen followed that fight with three quick knockouts of his opponents in his next trio of bouts but lost two after that and retired.

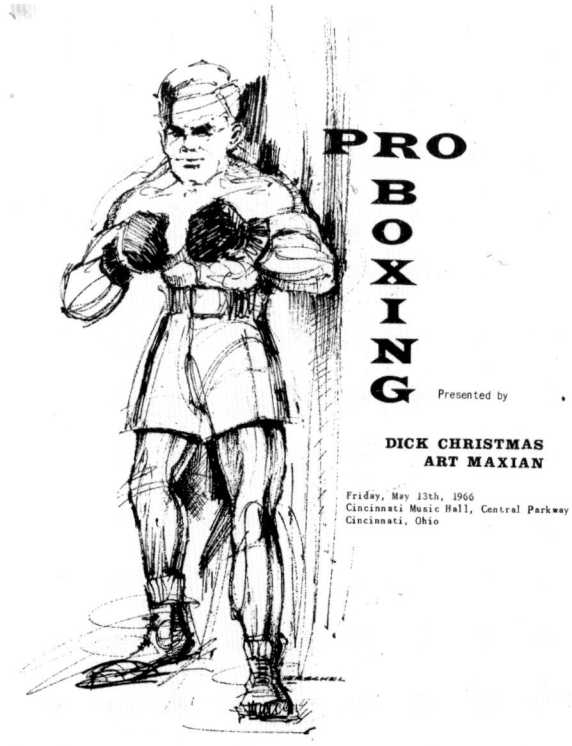

HELD UNDER THE SUPERVISION OF THE CINCINNATI BOXING & WRESTLING COMMISSION

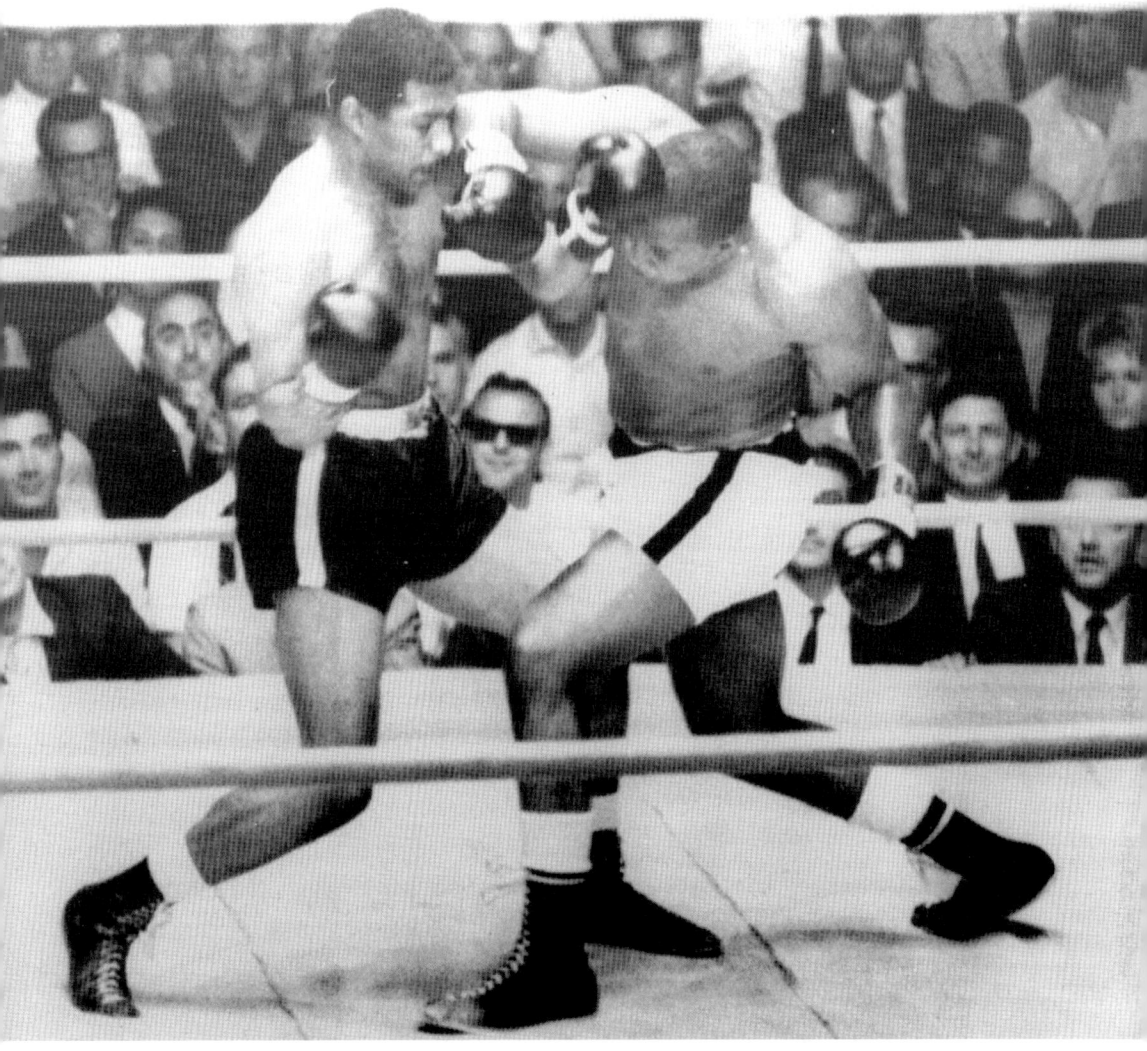

The Joiners are Cincinnati's first family of boxing. Brothers John and Herschel started the Joiner involvement in the sport in the 1930s. In fact, in his first professional bout, Herschel was the last opponent faced by champion Freddie Miller in his career. On April 1, 1940, Herschel knocked him out in the eighth round. After their own careers were over, both brothers trained professional and amateur fighters in Cincinnati for four decades, including lightweight champion Bud Smith. John's sons, Billy and John Jr., also had illustrious amateur careers with John Jr. winning state AAU belts and Billy a national Golden Gloves championship. In this photograph taken during Billy's professional career, he fights the "Bear," Sonny Liston (left). The May 24, 1968, bout in Los Angeles saw Billy fighting a former champion who was still a formidable opponent. Liston scored a TKO in the seventh round.

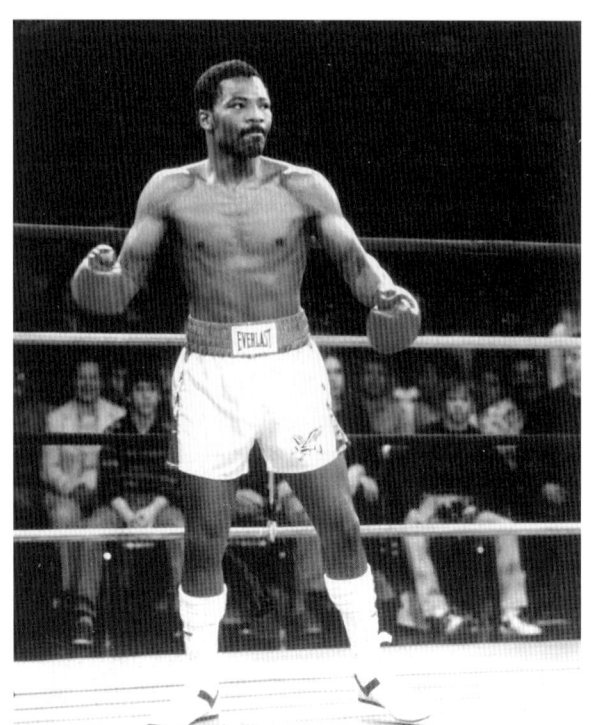

Aaron "the Hawk" Pryor was born in Cincinnati in 1955. He began boxing at a young age and had an amateur record of 204 wins and just 16 losses, including a 1972 National AAU belt, and a shot at the 1976 boxing team for the Olympics in Montreal. After he fell short in the Olympic trials, serving as an alternate to Howard Davis. He turned pro with Buddy LaRosa as his manager.

Frankie Williams Jr., a friend of Pryor's, decided to turn pro at the same time and, like Pryor, came under the wing of LaRosa. Williams Jr. had something of a pedigree—his father, Frank Sr., was a longtime sparring partner of Ezzard Charles and one of the champion's earliest professional opponents in 1940. A heavyweight like his father, Williams Jr. fought from 1977 to 1979.

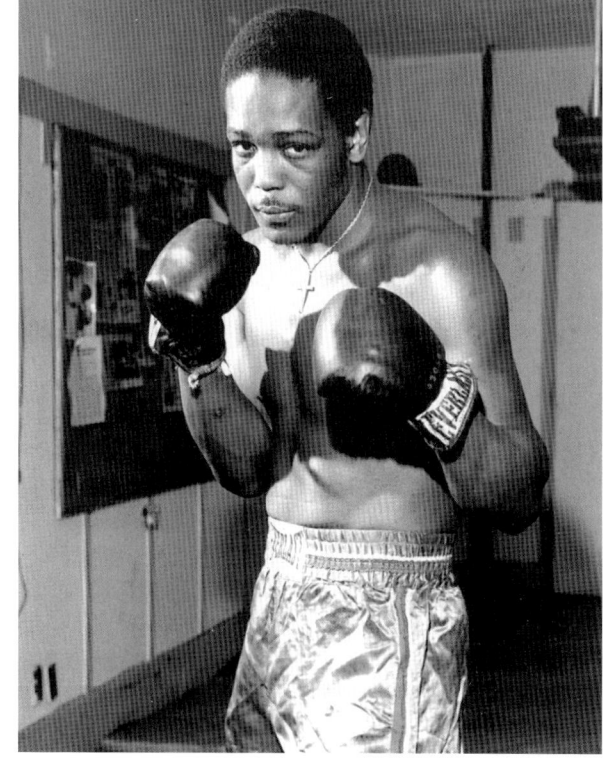

By 1980, Pryor's rise to the light welterweight championship looked inevitable. On August 2, 1980, he faced off against Antonio Cervantes at Riverfront Coliseum in Cincinnati. Pryor pounded at Cervantes, but the incumbent champion was ahead on the judges' scorecards through the third round. In the fourth, Pryor knocked him out to take the crown. However, it was Pryor's defenses of his belt with Alexis Arguello in 1982 and 1983 that became the stuff of fight legend. The two fights, the first in Miami's Orange Bowl and the second at Caesars Palace in Las Vegas, established the real fame of the champion. Both fights were notable for the boxers' skills and unrelenting punching power. In the first matchup, Pryor TKO'd Arguello in the 14th round, but not without controversy. It was said that his trainer, Panama Lewis, allegedly slipped Pryor something to drink after the 12th round to revive him. The bout was later named the "Fight of the Decade" by *Ring Magazine*. In their rematch in Vegas, again it was an excellent fight, and again Pryor won on a TKO, this time in the 10th round. Pryor finished his career in 1990 with a record of 39-1.

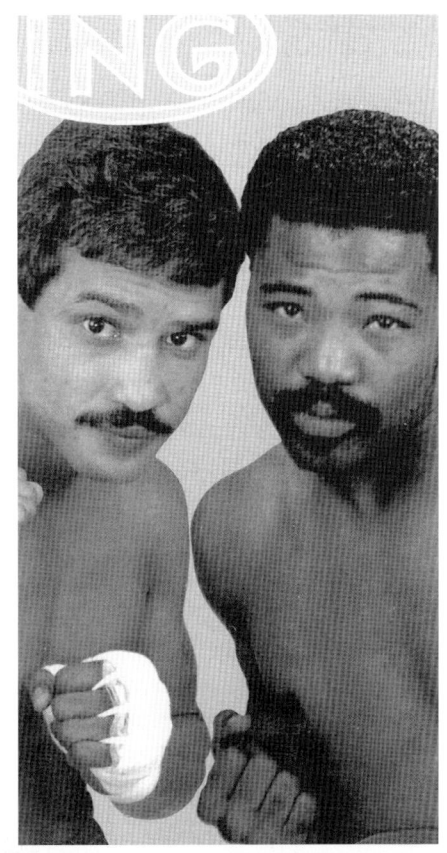

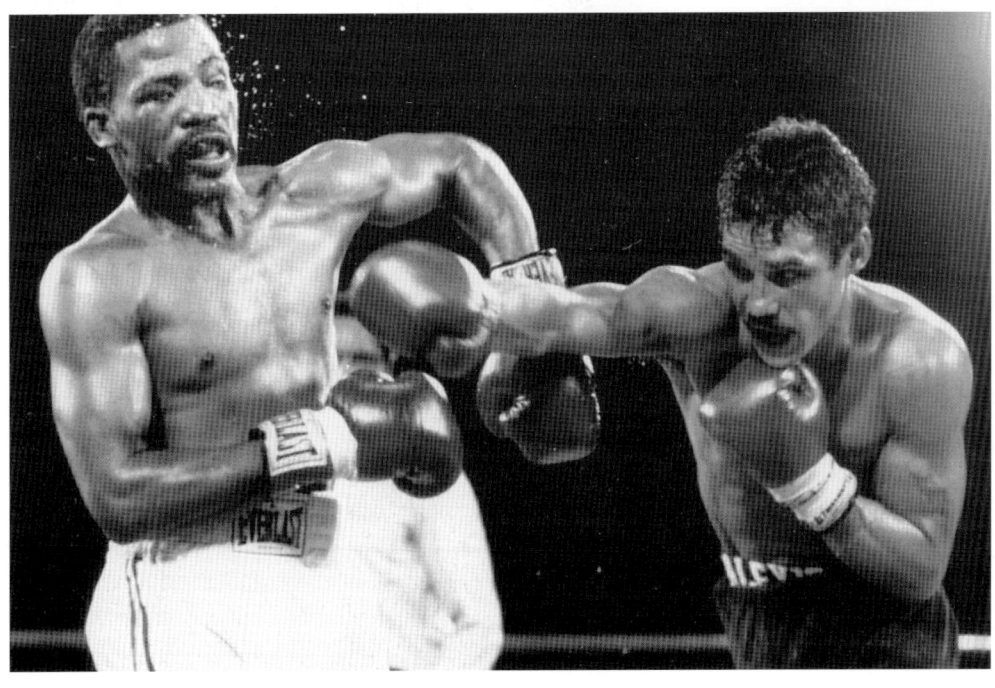

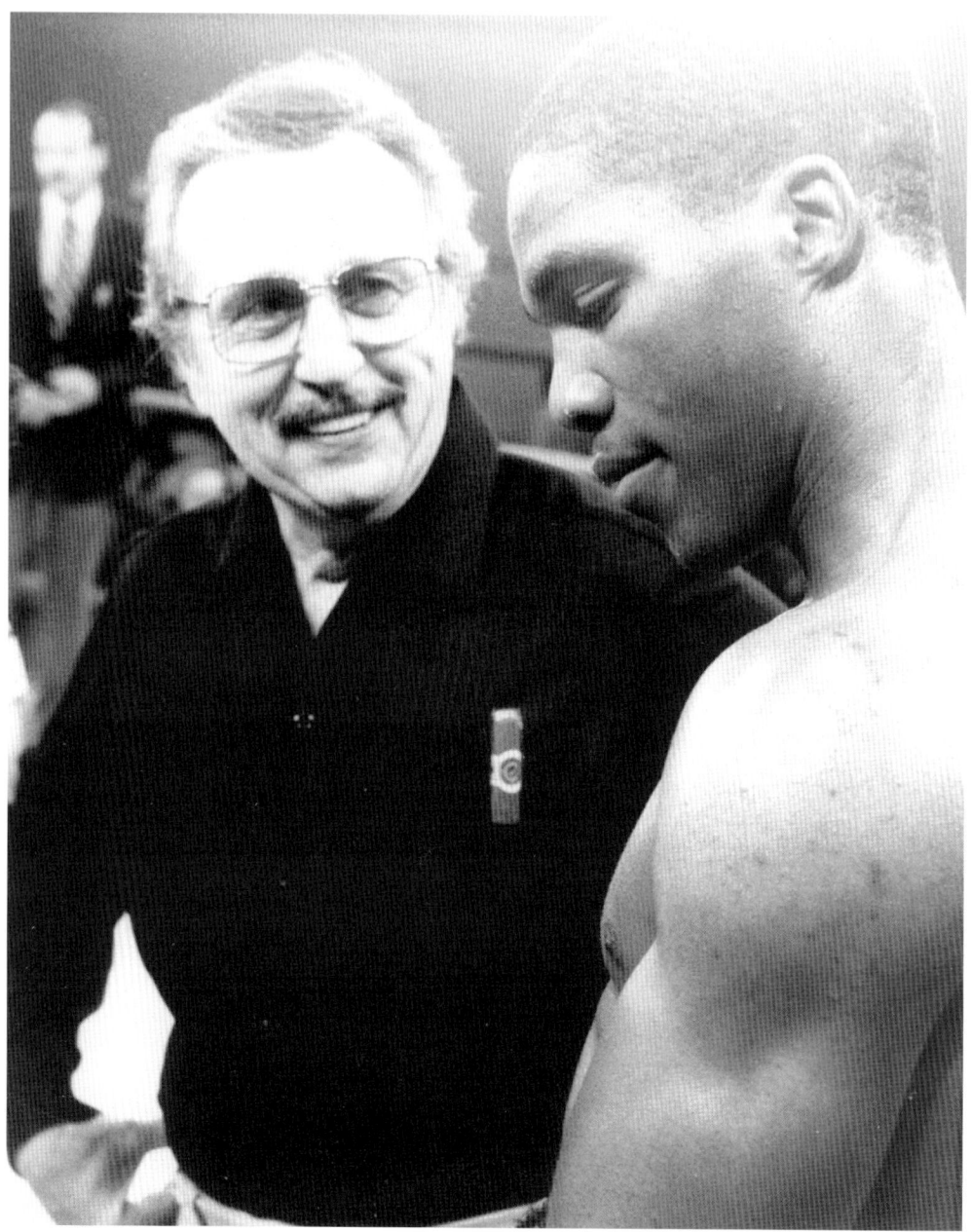

Pictured here with manager Buddy LaRosa, Tommy Ayers began his professional boxing career in 1981. During his career, he fought for welterweight titles on three separate occasions, winning the North American Boxing Federation (NABF) title in 1987 with a fourth-round TKO over Luis Santana. After suffering defeats in two straight fights, including a second-round stoppage to James "Buddy" McGirt in Atlantic City, Ayers retired as a fighter in 1990. However, he has continued on as a trainer with Ricardo Williams Sr. of top local amateurs at the Mount Auburn Community Center.

Rollie Schwartz was one of the individuals responsible for reviving the Golden Gloves program in Cincinnati, where he worked closely with the local club amateurs in addition to coaching boxing at Xavier University. Schwartz was a licensed referee for the 1968 and 1972 Olympiads and the coach for the 1976 Olympic team that brought home five gold medals, including one by Sugar Ray Leonard. Schwartz is said to be responsible for establishing the rule requiring headgear for amateur boxers.

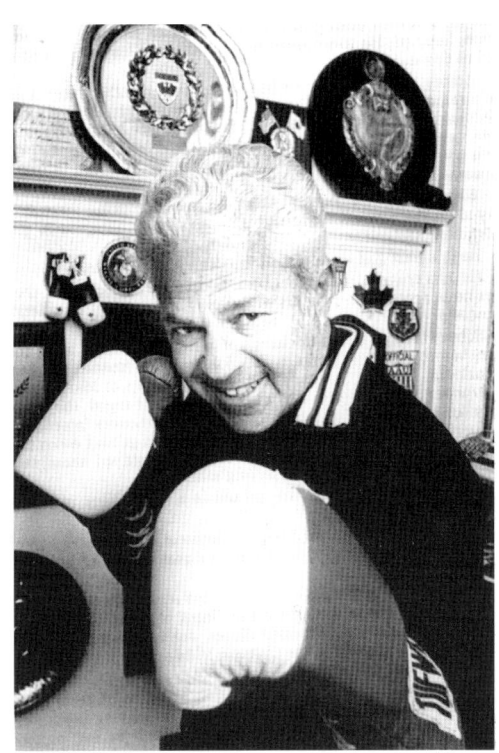

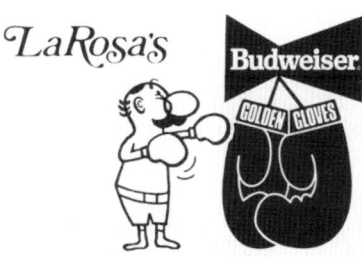

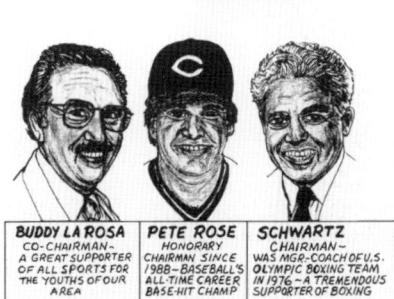

CINCINNATI REGIONAL GOLDEN GLOVES CHAMPIONSHIP

Saturday, April 28, 1990 — Cincinnati Gardens
— 12 CHAMPIONSHIP BOUTS —
Winners Go To National Golden Glove Championship

Presented by Budweiser and LaRosa's for the benefit of
Cincinnati Golden Gloves for Youth Foundation

SOUVENIR PROGRAM

Schwartz, Buddy LaRosa, and Phil Smith helped restore a Golden Gloves franchise in Cincinnati, and the city has been a hotbed of competition. In 1990, the regional championships were held at Cincinnati Gardens, with the winners of 12 bouts going on to the national championships. Cincinnati fighters have won more than 30 national titles, beginning with the inimitable Ezzard Charles winning the 160-pound championship in 1939.

CINCINNATI BOXING

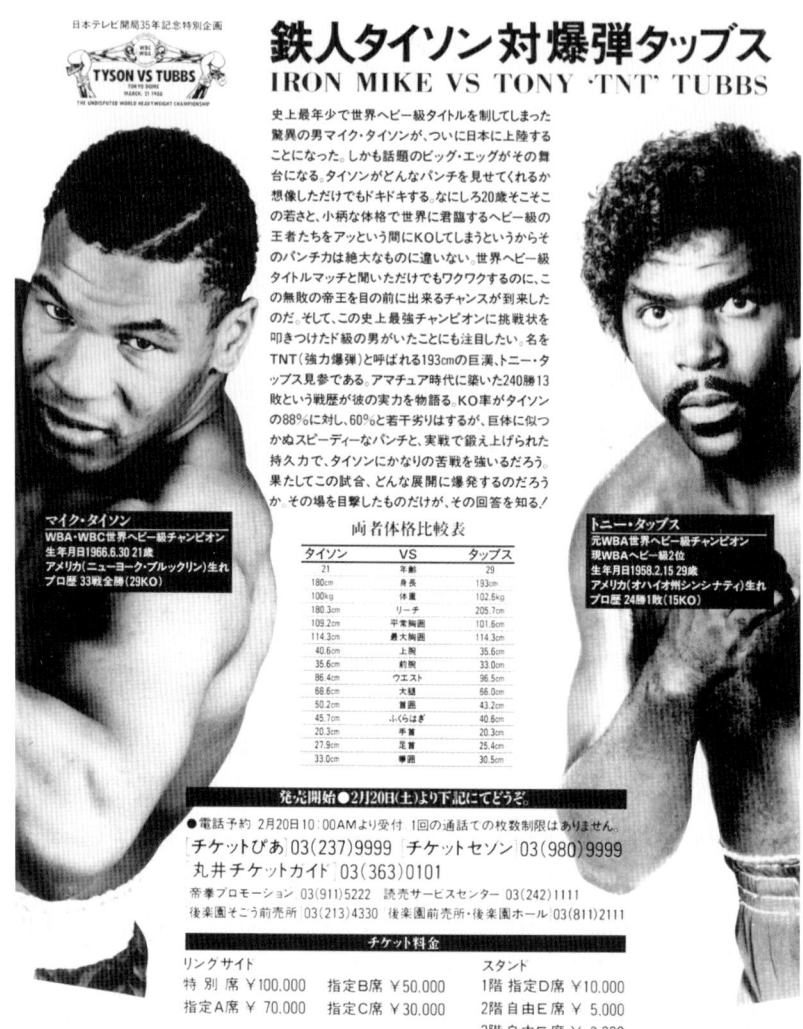

Despite an excellent amateur career and being the favorite to win gold for the United States in the heavyweight division, Tony Tubbs was unable to display his boxing talents for the entire world until turning pro. While preparing himself to represent his country in 1980, it was announced that the United States would boycott the Olympics, which would be held in Moscow. Once shedding his amateur status, Tubbs rose through the heavyweight ranks to win the World Boxing Association (WBA) Heavyweight belt. On March 21, 1988, Tubbs took on undisputed champion Mike Tyson in Tokyo for the unified heavyweight title. In front of a politely quiet Japanese crowd, Tyson dropped Tubbs late in the second round with a devastating left hook that stopped the fight. Well, at least Tubbs walked away with both his ears intact. Today Tony Tubbs and his brother, Nate, run a gym in the West End and continue to stay active as both fighters and promoters on local boxing cards.

6

BUILDING ON A HERITAGE

1991–2006

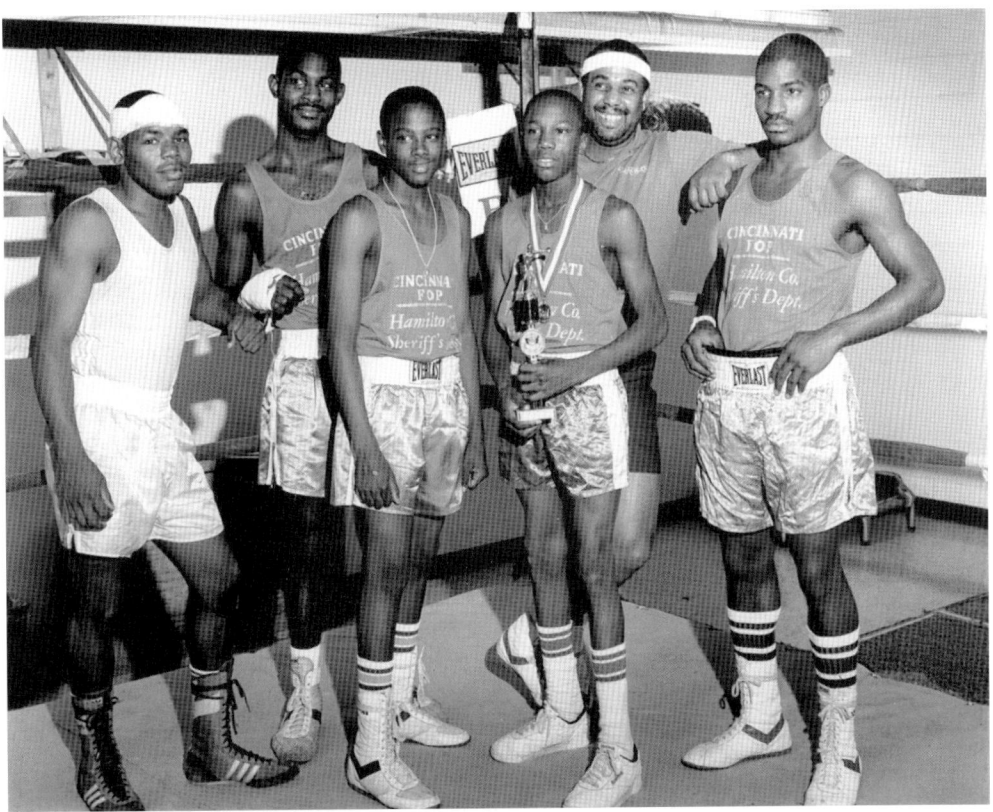

Pictured in the center of this photograph with other local amateurs, Tim Austin began in the amateur ranks putting together victories in bunches and winning more than 100 fights. Following his Golden Gloves and Goodwill Games championships, Austin made the journey to Spain in 1992 for the Barcelona Olympics and secured the bronze medal for the United States. He turned pro that year and in 1997, "the Cincinnati Kid" captured the International Boxing Federation (IBF) Bantamweight title with a knockout of Mbulelo Botile. Despite lackluster promotion, Austin successfully defended his belt for nearly six years, remaining undefeated before succumbing to the power of Rafael Marquez in early 2003. (Photograph courtesy of Buddy LaRosa)

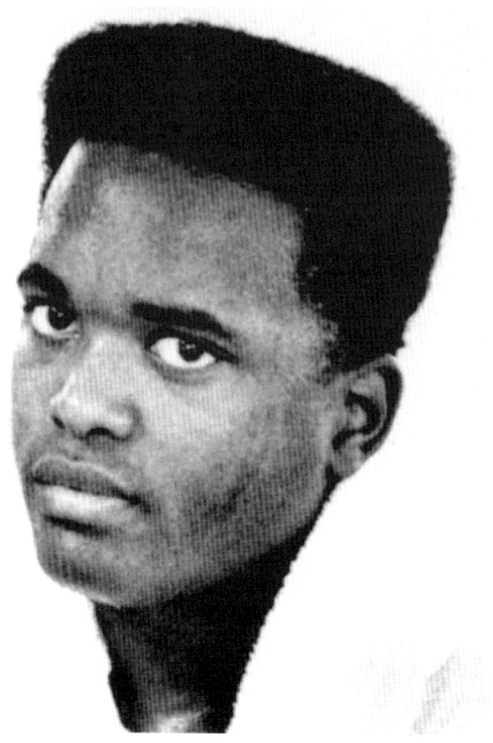

After competing in the 1992 Olympics with fellow Cincinnatian Tim Austin, Larry Donald turned pro in early 1993. Over the years, Donald has stepped into the ring with noted heavyweights Riddick Bowe, Vitaly Klitschko, and the seven-foot-tall Nikolay Valuev. In 2004, Larry "the Legend" defeated five-time heavyweight champion Evander Holyfield by unanimous decision. Donald continues to fight his way through the division in an effort to position himself for another title shot.

Journeyman heavyweight Greg Page began his career in 1979 in his hometown of Louisville, Kentucky. Over the next 22 years, Page fought the likes of Cincinnatian Tony Tubbs, James "Buster" Douglas, James "Bonecrusher" Smith, and Razor Ruddock, winning heavyweight titles with the United States Boxing Association (USBA) and WBA, the latter of which he lost to Tubbs. At the age of 42, Page stepped into the ring at Peel's Palace in Erlanger, Kentucky, to fight Norwood heavyweight Dale Crowe. Following 10 hard-fought rounds, Page went down, his head landing on the bottom rope. Page was taken to a hospital where he lay in a coma for months following a series of strokes. The former champion continues to battle medical problems as a result of the injuries suffered from the fight.

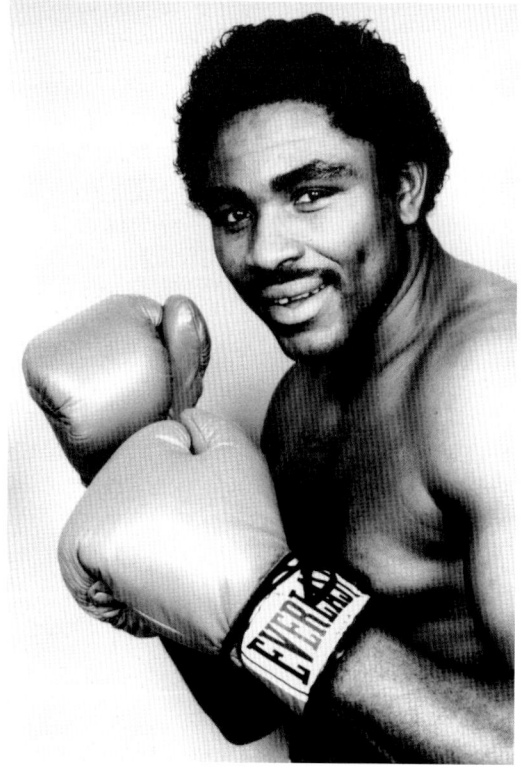

BUILDING ON A HERITAGE

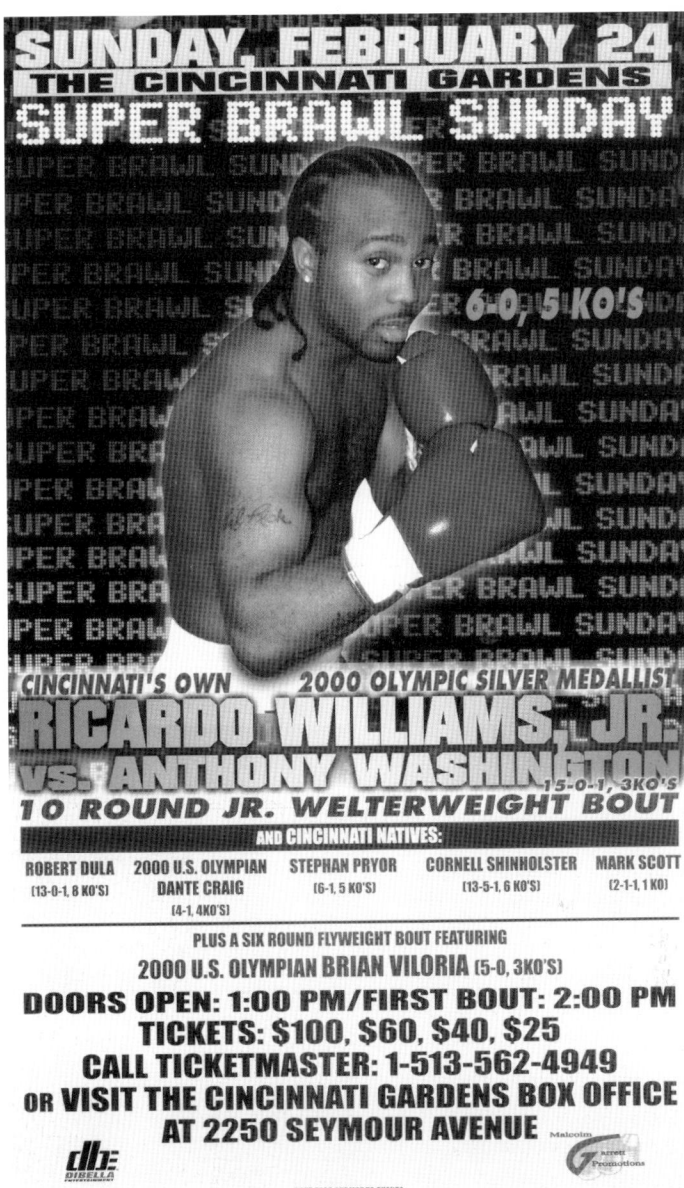

One of the most ballyhooed prospects to come out of Cincinnati in recent years, Ricardo Williams Jr. brought a stellar amateur background and *Sports Illustrated* profile to the Sydney Olympics in 2000 as the United States' best hope for an Olympic medal. Williams brought home the silver medal and turned pro under the promotion of Lou DiBella. The Taft High School product brought boxing back to Cincinnati in 2002 as the headliner of an ESPN2 card at the Cincinnati Gardens, in which Williams was victorious. Another local boxer, Dante Craig, joined Williams in Sydney. Following his first-bout win over Fadel Showban of Egypt, Craig was defeated by Bulent Ulusoy of Turkey in his second fight and failed to medal. Shortly after the Olympics, Craig turned pro, and despite losses early in his professional career, he has continued to fight his way up the junior middleweight ranks.

The Cincinnati Museum of Athletics

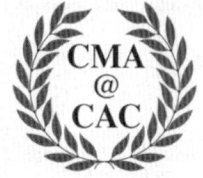

at
The Cincinnati Athletic Club

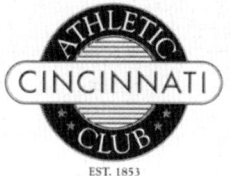

in conjunction with

Buddy LaRosa and the Cincinnati Golden Gloves -
Greater Cincinnati Police Athletic League

Proudly Presents the

Inaugural Dedication of the Cincinnati Museum of Athletics

and

"Friday Night at the Fights"

Featuring Special Guest

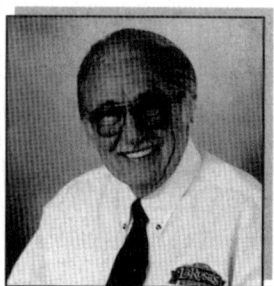

Buddy LaRosa

On March 3, 2006, the venerable Cincinnati Athletic Club (CAC) staged a fund-raiser to inaugurate the Cincinnati Museum of Athletics. Dubbed "Friday Night at the Fights," the event featured amateur bouts through the Cincinnati Golden Gloves and the Greater Cincinnati Police Athletic League. The rich heritage of boxing in Cincinnati was underscored by the celebration at the CAC since the club has sponsored a variety of sports and physical fitness activities since its founding in 1853. Drawing its membership throughout its history from the ranks of Cincinnati's professional men, the club first offered regular boxing instruction in 1891. Under the leadership of Bart Do Ran, the CAC provided 12 group lessons for $12 or $18 for 12 private lessons in the gentlemanly art of "sparring."

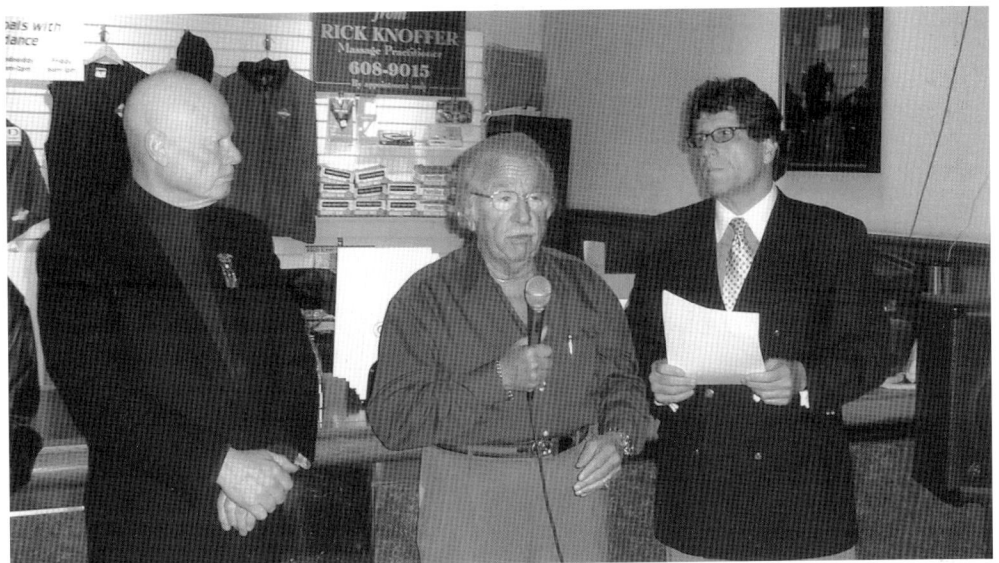

At the opening ceremony, Cincinnati vice mayor Jim Tarbell (left) cut the ribbon with organizers Buddy LaRosa (center) and Martin J. Horwitz as they dedicated the founding of the museum. Along with Horwitz, a local attorney and a prime mover to establish the museum who acted as master of ceremonies for the evening, the CAC social director, Ron Severe, and the general manager, Dan Hayes, ushered in a renewed appreciation for Cincinnati's deep love of sports.

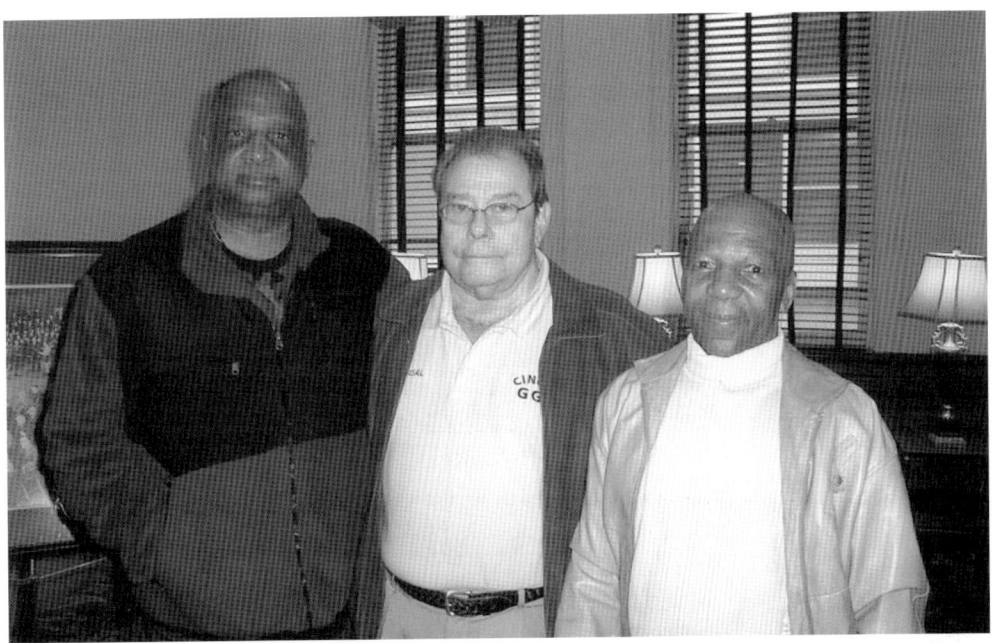

As part of the evening's activities at the historic building on Shillito Place, many of the prominent figures in Cincinnati boxing were invited, including the two Joiner brothers, Billy (left) and Johnny (right). The Joiners represent a seven-decade involvement in local boxing by their family. Standing with Billy and Johnny is longtime boxing trainer and official Arthur Neuman.

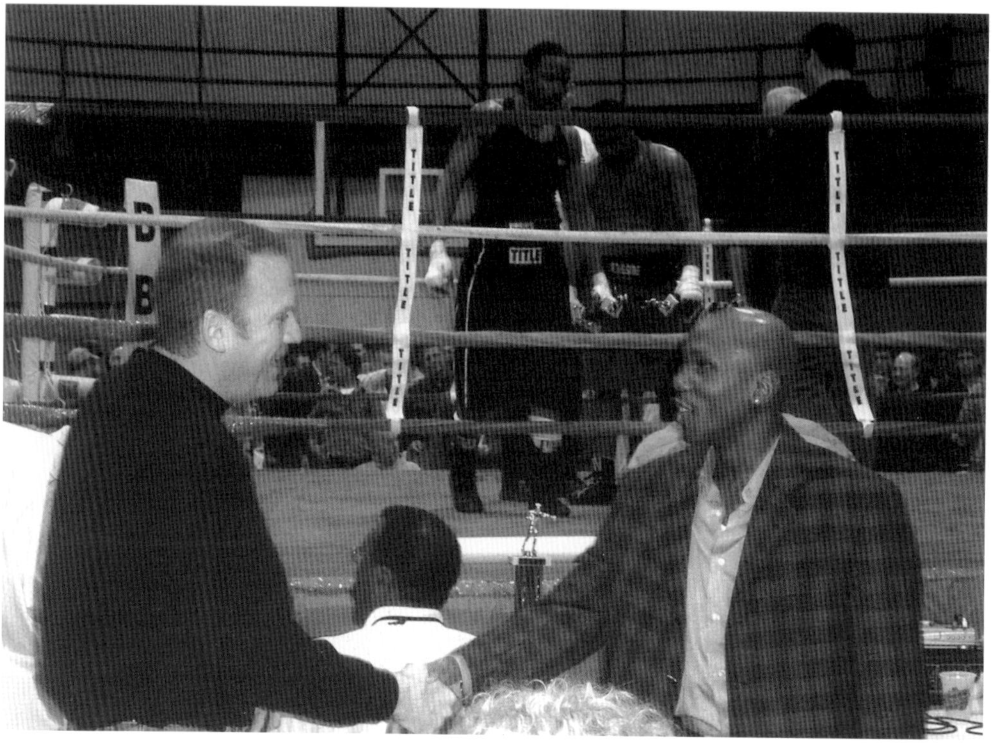

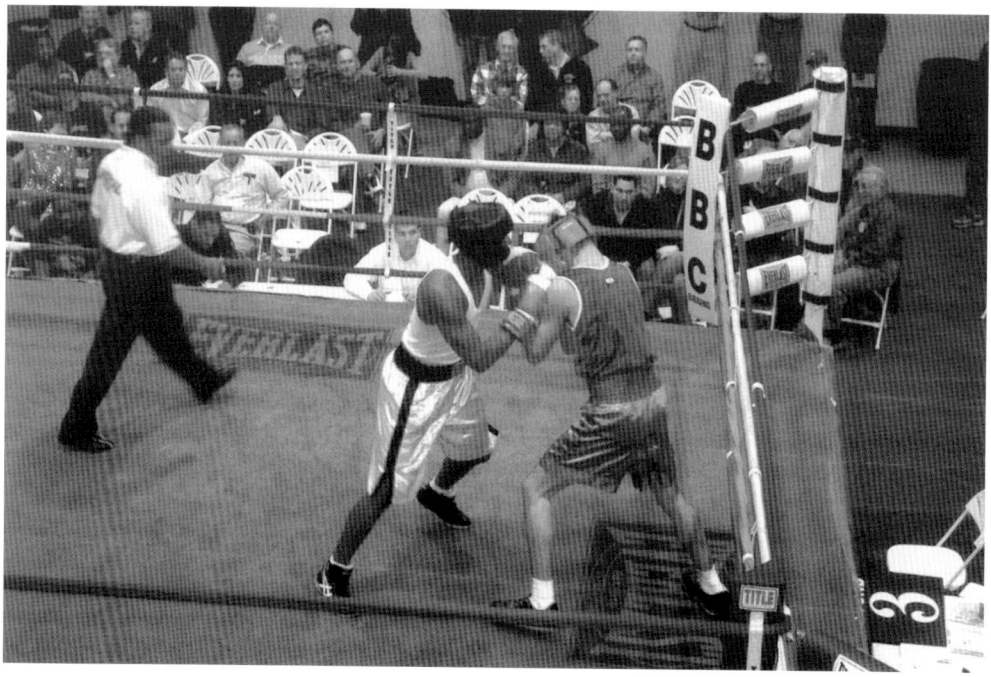

The Friday Night Fights attracted a number of former boxers as well as one making a comeback. The most recent Cincinnati Kid, Tim Austin, is greeted by a well-wisher at ringside, as the action continued throughout the evening inside the ring. (Photographs by Sean Grace.)

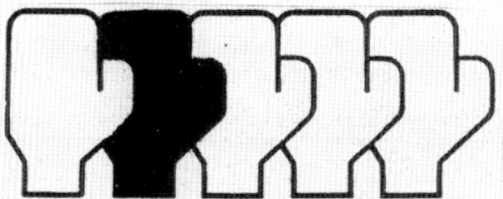

2006 CINCINNATI GOLDEN GLOVES TOURNAMENT
AT THE
MT. AUBURN POLICE ATHLETIC LEAUGE, 270 SOUTHERN AVE.
MARCH 18th, 2006 7:00p.m.

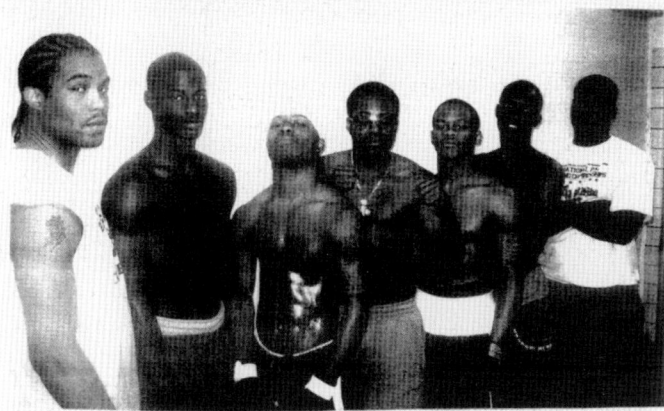

CINCINNATI
-VS-
KENTUCKY

FOR TICKET INFO CALL
(513)381-1760 OR (513) 470-0063

ADDMISSION
$8: ADULTS $3: 12-UNDER

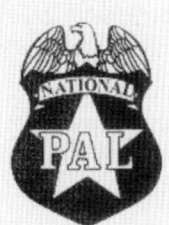
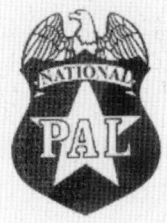

The Police Athletic League (PAL) sponsors regular amateur bouts in Cincinnati to help prepare the fighters in Golden Gloves competition. One of the strongest local amateur clubs is located at the Mount Auburn Community Center above the city's basin. For a 2006 bout, it was Cincinnati fighters against those from Kentucky clubs. Pictured from left to right are Joey Isaacs, William Jackson, Rau'Shee Warren, Mike Adams, Brandon Bennett, Ronnie Howell, and Eron Neal. Warren will be Cincinnati's next Olympic medal contender in 2008.

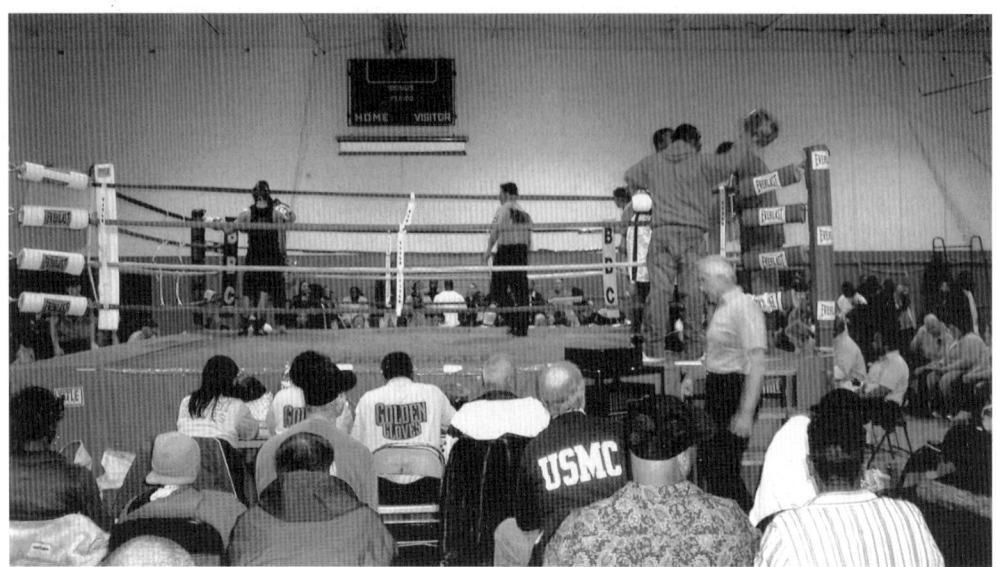

Millvale, Northside, Price Hill, and Mount Auburn are just a few of the Cincinnati gyms turning out top-notch amateurs. From a 2006 fight night in Mount Auburn, the fighters go at it in a PAL evening of bouts. The national PAL had its beginnings in New York City in 1914 as part of a social program to provide havens for urban kids from the city streets. Since then, the PAL has spread around the country to sponsor youth sports.

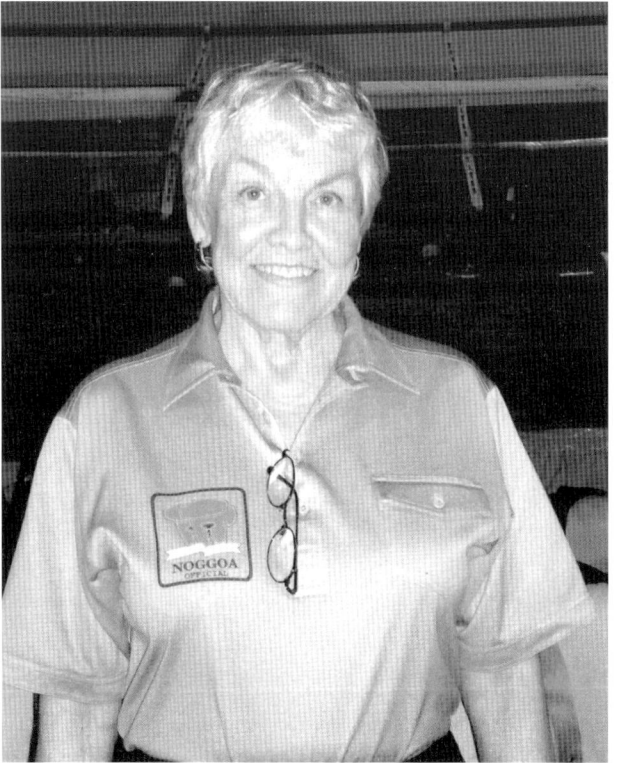

A member of the Golden Gloves Hall of Fame, Marty Smith has been involved with local amateur boxing for more than 40 years. Smith is a licensed boxing judge, getting her start in the sport by working with her late husband, Phil Smith, in their Norwood Boxing Club. Phil Smith was a notable presence in national amateur coaching and, along with Rollie Schwartz and Buddy LaRosa, helped revive the Cincinnati Golden Gloves. Smith is best known simply as "Miss Marty" in local boxing venues.

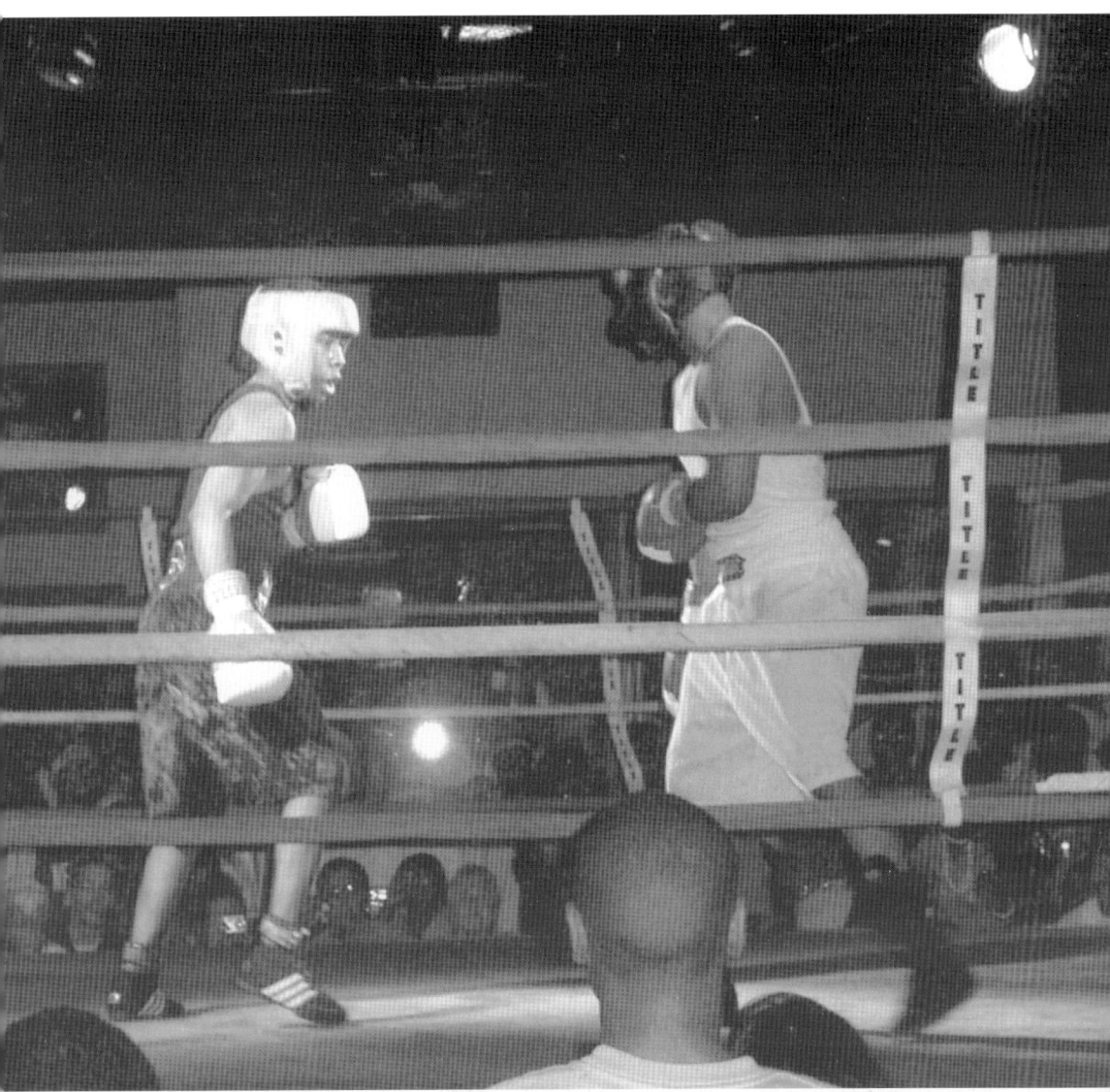

Rau'Shee Warren (left) went into the 2004 Athens Olympics, along with fellow Cincinnatian Ron Siler Jr., as the youngest member of the United States boxing team. After failing to win a medal, Warren delayed turning pro in order to set his sights on another Olympic trip in 2008. As the first United States boxer to return to the amateurs since 1992, Warren has racked up victories and championships while honing his craft. This image is of Warren fighting in April 2006 at an amateur night held in Bond Hill.

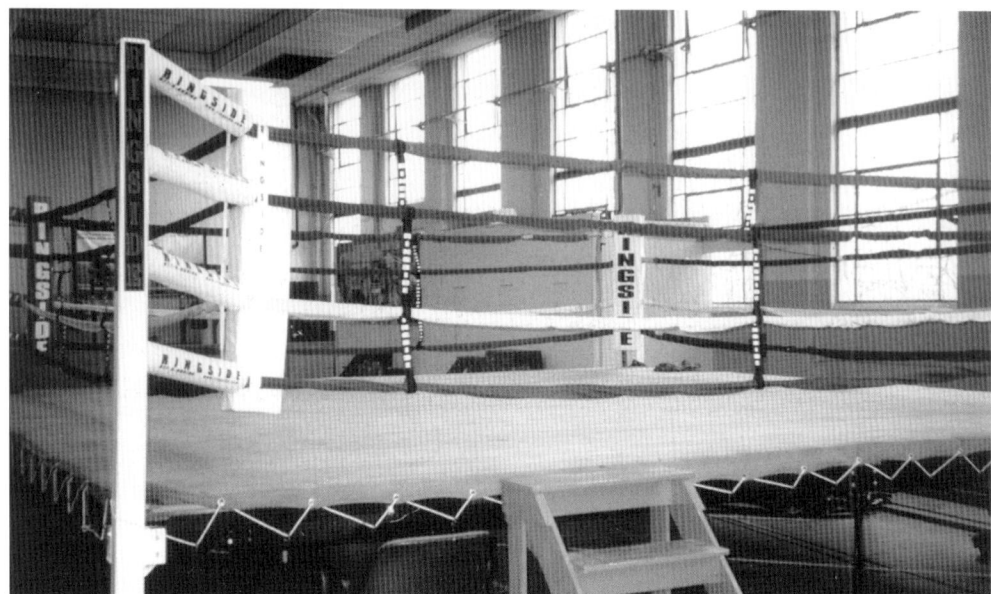

Xavier University continues its boxing tradition with its current coed boxing club. Students participate in training at Xavier's Armory Fieldhouse, where they practice the fundamentals of the sport as they prepare to enter the ring in competition. Local boxing coach Neil Patrick fought under the tutelage of Olympic coach Rollie Schwartz at Xavier, and he still helps out with the coaching at Xavier as well as at Northern Kentucky University. In 1996, he started a boxing program at Moeller High School, taking the school's boxers to matches around the Midwest. Patrick is shown with one of his Moeller Crusader boxers, Zack Kaylor. (Below, photograph courtesy of Neil Patrick.)

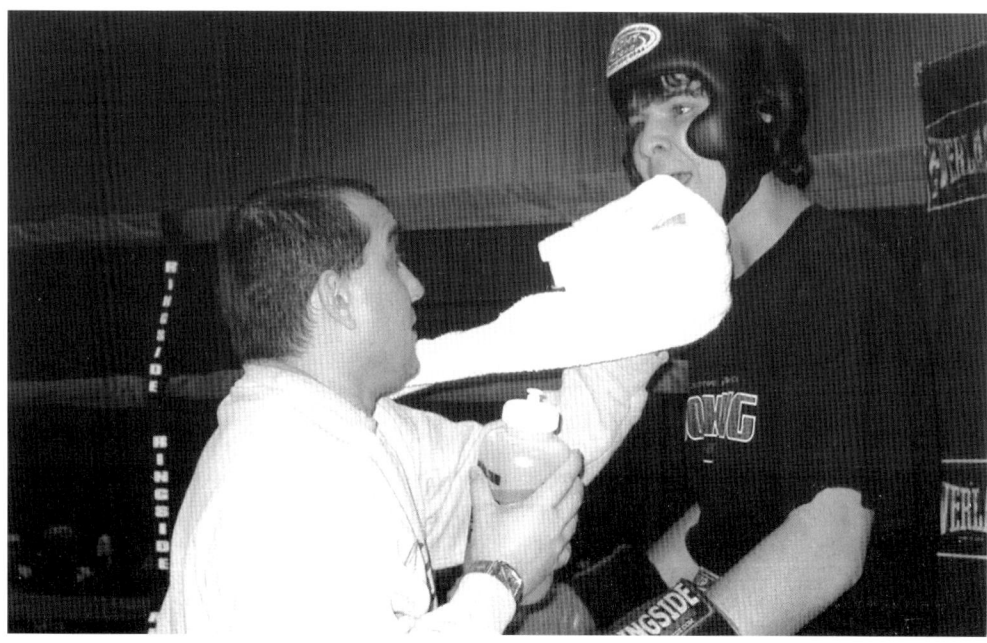

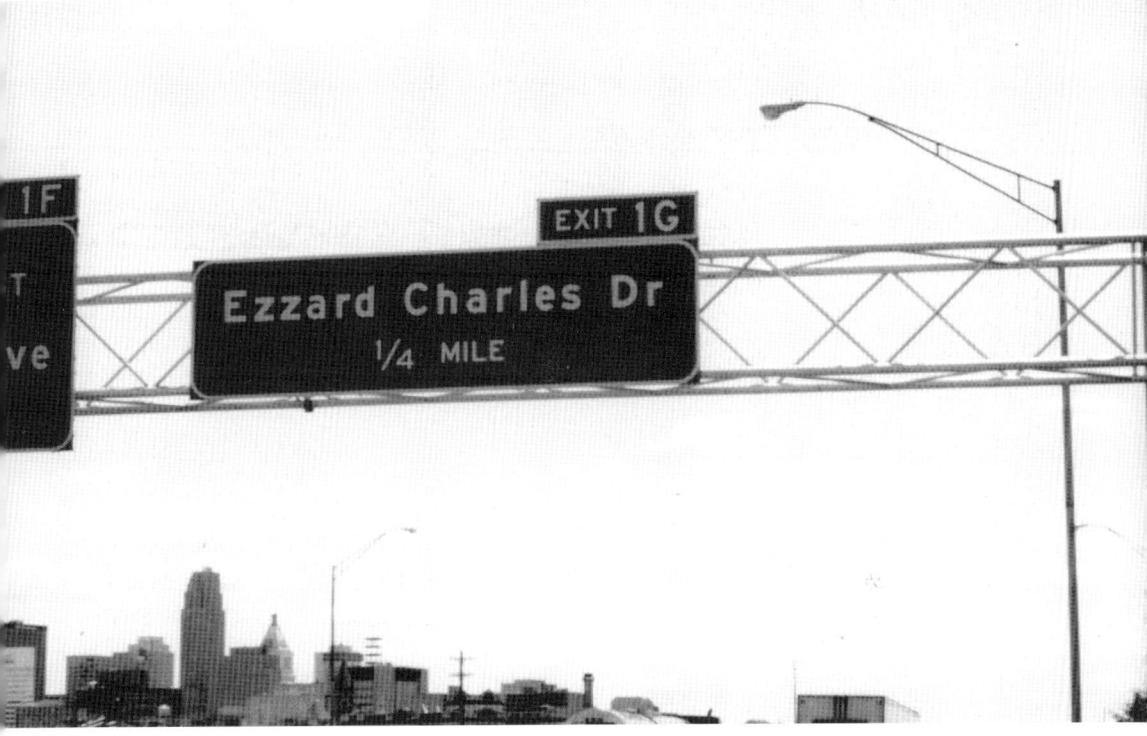

At the time of his championship victory over Jersey Joe Walcott in 1949, Ezzard Charles lived on Lincoln Park Drive in Cincinnati. In 1976, the year after he died, Cincinnati's city council renamed the street Ezzard Charles Drive to honor the late champion and to recognize the beloved hold his memory has on the city to this day. Down in his birthplace of Lawrenceville, Georgia, the Gwinnett County Commission also recognized him. A monument with a boxer in punching stance and details of Charles's career stands in front of the courthouse in downtown Lawrenceville.

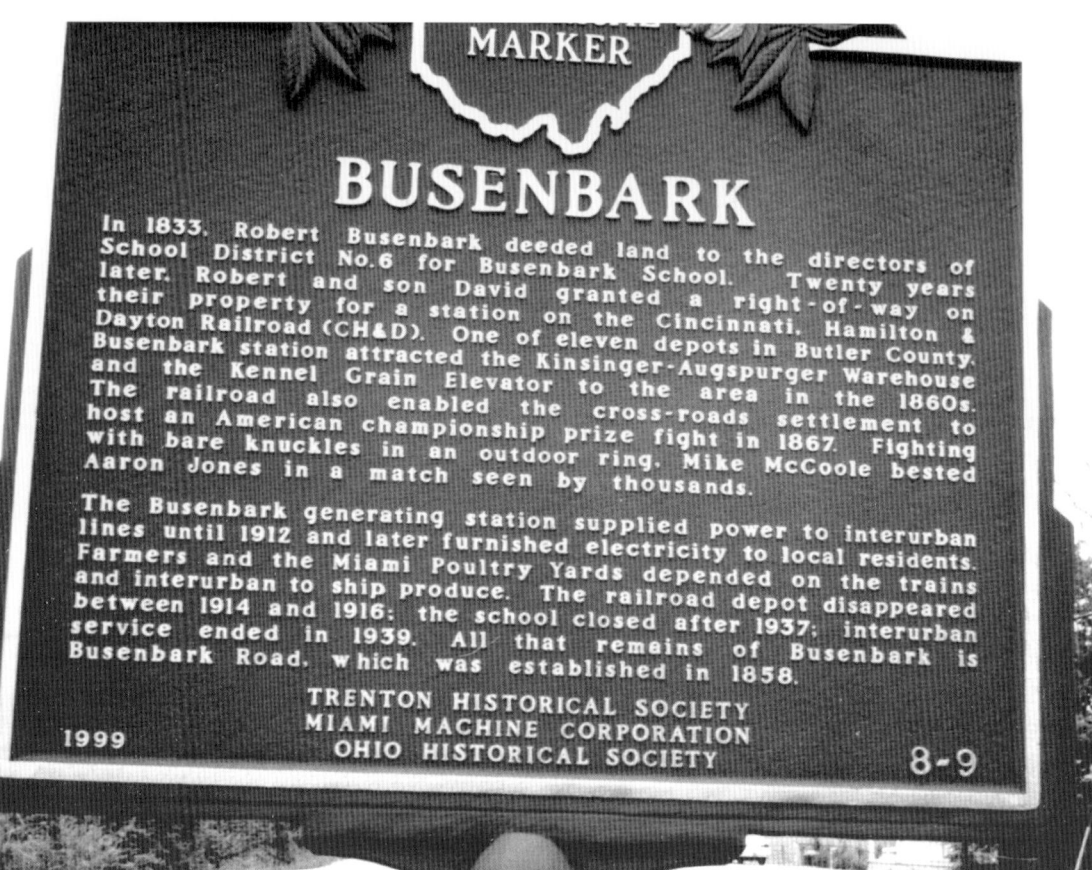

And so it comes around to the beginning. On a remote Butler County road several miles north of Cincinnati, there is an historical marker that notes the first championship prizefight in Cincinnati in 1867. It was that fighting riverman again, Mike McCoole taking on Aaron Jones. The cantankerous McCoole claimed the heavyweight championship at various times from 1863 to 1873 and was about to claim it one more time. To escape a threatened arrest in Hamilton County for prizefighting, McCoole and Jones took a train to Busenbark station on August 31, 1867. The station was a railroad depot where farmers shipped their grain down to the Ohio River. Reportedly over 3,000 people followed the fighters to the rural crossroads, including sporting reporters from several cities. According to one newspaper account, it was "the largest crowd of decent people that ever gathered around a prize ring." The bare-knuckle match went 34 rounds before McCoole knocked his opponent through the ropes. Unable to continue because of his injuries, Jones saw the match awarded to McCoole. In 1999, the Ohio Historical Society placed a marker on the site commemorating, in a fashion, Cincinnati's place in the heritage of the squared circle.

SELECTED BIBLIOGRAPHY

Castor, Dennis. *Freddie Miller, World's Featherweight Champion, 1933–1936.* Video documentary.
Cincinnati Commercial Tribune, 1860–1930.
Cincinnati Enquirer, 1860–2006.
Cincinnati Post, 1940–2006.
Cincinnati Times-Star, 1860–1958.
Erenberg, Lewis A. *The Greatest Fight of Our Generation: Louis vs. Schmeling.* New York: Oxford University Press, 2005.
Fried, Ronald K. *Corner Men: Great Boxing Trainers.* New York: Four Walls, Eight Windows, 1991.
Gorn, Elliot J. *The Manly Art: Bare-Knuckle Prize Fighting in America.* Ithaca, NY: Cornell University Press, 1986.
Kahn, Roger. *A Flame of Pure Fire: Jack Dempsey and the Roaring '20s.* New York: Harcourt, 1999.
Roberts, James B., and Alexander G. Skutt. *The Boxing Register: International Boxing Hall of Fame Official Record Book.* Ithaca, NY: McBooks Press, 1996.
Sammons, Jeffrey T. *Beyond the Ring: Boxing in American Society.* Urbana: University of Illinois Press, 1988.
Sugar, Bert Randolph. *Bert Sugar on Boxing: The Best of the Sport's Most Notable Writer.* New York: The Lyons Press, 2003.
Sullivan, Russell. *Rocky Marciano: The Rock of His Times.* Urbana: University of Illinois Press, 2002.
Terrill, Marshall. *The Flight of the Hawk: The Aaron Pryor Story.* Sun Lakes, AZ: Book World/Blue Star, 1996.
www.boxrec.com.

Across America, People are Discovering Something Wonderful. Their Heritage.

Arcadia Publishing is the leading local history publisher in the United States. With more than 3,000 titles in print and hundreds of new titles released every year, Arcadia has extensive specialized experience chronicling the history of communities and celebrating America's hidden stories, bringing to life the people, places, and events from the past. To discover the history of other communities across the nation, please visit:

www.arcadiapublishing.com

Customized search tools allow you to find regional history books about the town where you grew up, the cities where your friends and family live, the town where your parents met, or even that retirement spot you've been dreaming about.

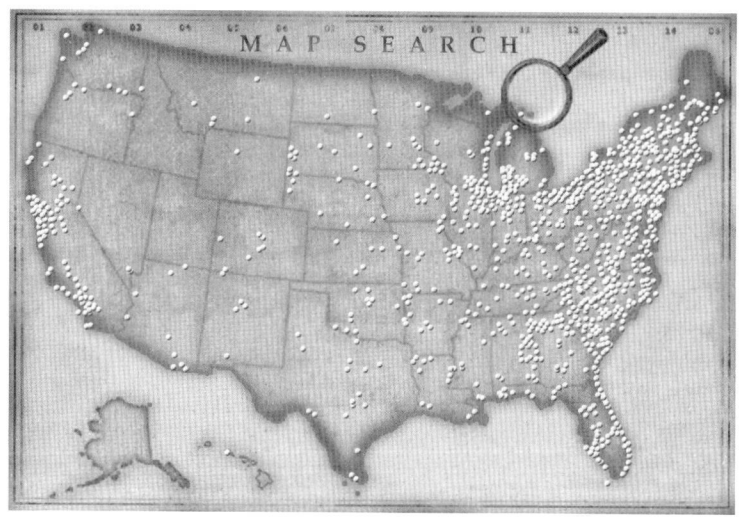